RE-ENERGISING INDIAN INTELLIGENCE

RE-ENERGISING INDIAN INTELLIGENCE

Manoj Shrivastava

Centre for Land Warfare Studies   Vij Books India Pvt Ltd

Published by

Vij Books India Pvt Ltd
(Publishers, Distributors & Importers)
2/19, Ansari Road, Darya Ganj
New Delhi - 110002
Phones: 91-11-43596460, 91-11- 47340674
Fax: 91-11-47340674
e-mail : vijbooks@rediffmail.com
web: www.vijbooks.com

The Centre for Land Warfare Studies (CLAWS), New Delhi, is an autonomous think tank dealing with contemporary issues of national security and conceptual aspects of land warfare, including conventional and sub-conventional conflicts and terrorism. CLAWS conducts research that is futuristic in outlook and policy-oriented in approach.

Centre for Land Warfare Studies
RPSO Complex, Parade Road, Delhi Cantt, New Delhi-110010
Phone: 011-25691308; Fax: 011-25692347
email: landwarfare@gmail.com ; website: www.claws.in

Contents

Foreword

Intelligence is reputed to be the second oldest profession of the world and yet, inexplicably, there is a dearth of professional books on this critical craft both abroad and especially in India. I would perhaps be emphasizing the obvious when I state that government, armed forces and other organs and institutions of the state, when surprised or struck by unforeseen security calamities, conveniently ascribe these systemic and leadership failures to lack of hard and timely intelligence. That there can be never foolproof and the desired levels of intelligence required, always available, makes the task of intelligence agencies all the more arduous—— thus the significance of timely intelligence acquisition, interpretation and analysis and more importantly, the seamless and unselfish flow of intelligence inputs to sister intelligence agencies, as required, is sine-qua-non.

As the threats to a nation ascend on the criticality or the escalation ladder, intelligence sharing between various security organs of the nation and its speedy analysis for the nation's decision makers makes intelligence a more than vital tool in the overall security management of the nation. Notwithstanding its indispensability and despite India having been surprised on many occasions notably in 1962, preceding the Indo-Chinese conflict, Pakistan's perfidy in Kargil in 1999, the attack on the Indian Parliament in 2001 which nearly led to another Indo Pak War, the tragic and avoidable assassinations of Prime Ministers Indira Gandhi in 1984 and then Rajiv Gandhi in 1991 point to a question whether India has given sufficient importance to this specialized discipline which is a force multiplier by any standards. Have we adequately endeavoured to inject some energy and resources into this critical capability and skill or do we have to wait for being harshly surprised over and over again? After the Kargil War and especially since the Pakistani ISI engineered terror attacks in Mumbai in

Nov 2008, there have been some welcome accretions to and streamlining of our intelligence set-ups. Perhaps, like the 10 yearly Pay Commissions, India will do well to have institutionalized reviews of its intelligence agencies and their functioning in totality and carry out corrections and improvements as felt.

To the not so liberal availability of books on intelligence in India, the publication of Manoj Shrivastava's comprehensive work 'Re-energising Indian intelligence' is more than a timely and apt addition. This book indeed covers a vast canvas historically as regards Indian Intelligence, as also gives an adequate insight into the functioning of the important intelligence agencies of the world. Manoj has analysed the current functioning of Indian Intelligence in great detail and has come out with some useful suggestions. I am sanguine that the suggestions he has proffered to galvanise our intelligence set-up will be of particular interest to not only members of the growing Indian Intelligence community but also to the Government of India to ponder over and implement as necessary.

My congratulations to Col Shrivastava on his debut and I wish him many more books in the future to be penned by him in the research of and for the benefit of national security.

Himachal Pradesh   Lt Gen Kamal Davar (retired)
Founder Director General Defence Intelligence Agency
and Deputy Chief of the Integrated Defence Staff

Acknowledgements

I wish to place on record my heartfelt gratitude to members of strategic and intelligence community whom I have interviewed during the course of my research. I am indebted to a large number of serving officers of civil and military intelligence agencies who expressed a desire to remain anonymous. Their names have deliberately not been included in this book.

During the course of this project, I have drawn a lot of inspiration and ideas from the report of IDSA task force on 'Intelligence Reforms' since I have been attending their deliberations and we were working simultaneously on similar project. I also wish to convey my gratitude to large number of seminars, workshops, books and publications from where I have drawn inputs for my book.

This book could not have been possible without the institutional support from Centre for Land Warfare Studies (CLAWS). For this I would like to convey my sincere gratitude to Brig Gurmeet Kanwal (Retd), former Director, CLAWS for his highly valued guidance which proved to be the springboard for further ideas and launch pad for this analysis. My special gratitude goes to Maj Gen Dhruv C Katoch, SM, VSM (Retd), Director, CLAWS for reposing faith in my abilities and for his unflinching support for this research. I am indebted to Colonel Ashwani Gupta and Colonel Vivek Verma, former and present Deputy Director, CLAWS for their candid views and providing enabling environment for this research. I gratefully acknowledge the support extended by Ms Pallavi Ade, Publications Manager, CLAWS and Miss Aditi Malhotra in editing my book with great zeal and enthusiasm. I also wish to thank Lt Gen Kamal Davar, founder Director General, Defence Intelligence Agency (DIA) for providing detailed comments on my book and contributing the 'foreword '.

In the end, I profusely thank my wife Sudha and son Prakhar for their support, empathy and good wishes during the course of this study. I sincerely acknowledge their contribution for bearing with my confused and preoccupied state of mind while penning my thoughts.

New Delhi   Manoj Shrivastava

Jan 2013

ACRONYMS AND ABBREVIATIONS

(As they appear in the book in sequential order)

Open Source Intelligence	-	OSINT
Internal Security	-	IS
Left Wing Extremism	-	LWE
Intelligence Bureau	-	IB
Research and Analysis Wing	-	R&AW
Military intelligence	-	MI
Defence Intelligence Agency	-	DIA
Centre for Land Warfare Studies	-	CLAWS
Joint Intelligence Committee	-	JIC
Institute of Defence Studies and Analysis-		IDSA
Central Intelligence Agency	-	CIA
National Intelligence Assessment and Coordination Council	-	NIACC
Director of Intelligence Bureau	-	DIB
Criminal Investigation Departments	-	CIDs
Central Intelligence Officer	-	CIO
Subsidiary Intelligence Bureau's	-	SIB
Chief of Staff Committee	-	OSC
Joint Planning Committee	-	JPC

Ministry of External Affairs   -   MEA

Electronic intelligence   -   ELINT

Aviation Research Centre   -   ARC

Directorate General of Security   -   DGS

Prime Minister Office   -   PMO

Ministry of Defence   -   MoD

Central Bureau of investigation   -   CBI

National Security Council   -   NSC

United Progressive Alliance   -   UPA

National Security Council Secretariat   -   NSCS

National Security Advisor   -   NSA

Strategic Policy Group   -   SPG

National Security Advisory Board   -   NSAB

Kargil Review Committee   -   KRC

Group of Ministers   -   GoM

National Institute of Advanced Studies   -   NIAS

Human Intelligence   -   HUMINT

Joint Task Force on Intelligence   -   JTFI

Multi-Agency Centre   -   MAC

National Technical Research Organisation-   NTRO

Intelligence Coordination Group   -   ICG

Technical Coordination Group   -   TCG

National Information Board   -   NIB

Technical intelligence   -   TECHINT

National Technical Facilities Organisation	-	NTFO
Subsidiary Multi Agency Centers	-	SMACs
National Counter Terrorism Centre	-	NCTC
National Intelligence Grid	-	NATGRID
Cabinet Committee on Security	-	CCS
Unique Identification	-	UID
Crime and Criminal Tracking Network System	-	CCTNS
The National Investigation Agency	-	NIA
Lashkar-e-Tayyiba	-	LeT
Indian Police Services	-	IPS
Narcotics Control Bureau	-	NCB
Directorate of Revenue Intelligence	-	DRI
Economic Offences Wing	-	EOW
Ministry of Home Affairs	-	MHA
Directorate General of Military Intelligence	-	DGMI
Chief of Defence Staff	-	CDS
Armed Forces Special Powers Act	-	AFSPA
Defence Image Processing and Analysis Centre	-	DIPAC
National Institute of Cryptology Research and Development	-	NICRD
Defence Research and Development Organisation	-	DRDO

Central Economic Intelligence Bureau	-	CEIB
Border Security Force	-	BSF
Indo Tibetan Border Police	-	ITBP
Central Reserve Police Force	-	CRPF
Psychological operations	-	Psy ops
Non-government organizations	-	NGO
Information Warfare	-	IW
Chief of the General Staff	-	CGS
Chief of the Army Staff	-	COAS
Force Commander Northern Area	-	FCNA
Central Monitoring System	-	CMS
Unique Identification Authority of India	-	UIDAI
Inter Service Intelligence	-	ISI
Ministry of State Security	-	MSS
Ministry of Public Security	-	MPS
People's Liberation Army	-	PLA
Department of Military Intelligence	-	DMI
Financial Information Unit	-	FIU
Directorate General of Forces Intelligence	-	DGFI
Director of National Intelligence	-	DNI
Federal Bureau of Investigation	-	FBI
Department of Defence	-	DoD
National Security Agency	-	NSA
National Geospatial Intelligence Agency	-	NGA

National Reconnaissance Office	-	NRO
Department of Energy	-	DOE
The Drug Enforcement Administration	-	DEA
National Security Council Staff	-	NSCS
Joint Terrorism Task Force	-	JTTF
Department of Homeland Security	-	DHS
National Joint Terrorism Task Force	-	NJTTF
National Operations Center	-	NOC
Secret Intelligence Service	-	SIS
Government Communications Headquarters	-	GCHQ
The Defence Intelligence Staff	-	DIS
Defence Geographic and Imagery Intelligence Agency	-	DGIA
Defence Intelligence and Security Centre	-	DISC
Chief of Defence Intelligence	-	CDI
The Intelligence and Security Committee	-	ISC
Joint Terrorism Analysis Centre	-	JTAC
Australian Security Intelligence Organisation	-	ASIO
Australian Protective Service	-	APS
Australian Secret Intelligence Service	-	ASIS
Defence Signals Directorate	-	DSD
Royal Canadian Mountain Police	-	RCMP
Office of National Assessment	-	ONA

National Intelligence Group	-	NIG
Secretaries' Committee on National Security	-	SCoNS
Israeli Security Agency	-	ISA
Israel Defence forces	-	IDF
The Scarecrow Professional Intelligence Education Series	-	SPIES
Geospatial Intelligence	-	GEOINT
Measurement and Signature Intelligence	-	MASINT
Signals Intelligence	-	SIGINT
Communications Intelligence	-	COMINT
Foreign Instrumentation Signals Intelligence	-	FISINT
Counter Intelligence	-	CI
Cyber Counter Intelligence	-	CCI
Order of Battle	-	ORBAT
Intelligence and Field Surveillance Unit	-	I&FS
Brigade Intelligence Team	-	BIT
Shanti Suraksha Bal	-	SSB
Counter-Terrorism Centre	-	CTC
Unmanned Aerial Vehicles	-	UAVs
Synthetic Aperture Radar	-	SAR
Intelligence Reform and Prevention of Terrorism Act	-	IRPTA
Liberation Tigers of Tamil Eelam	-	LTTE

Special Police Establishment	-	SPE
General Offences Wing	-	GOW
Conservation of Foreign Exchange & Prevention of Smuggling Activities Act	-	COFEPOSA
Joint Cipher Bureau	-	JCB
All India Radio Monitoring Service	-	AIRMS
Special Frontier Force	-	SFF
President's Daily Brief	-	PDB
Federal Aviation Administration	-	FAA
Carrier Strike Group	-	CSG
Foreign Emergency Support Team	-	FESTs
Line of Control	-	LOC
Naval Special Warfare Development Group	-	DEVGRU

ENHANCING INTELLIGENCE ASSESSMENT AND COORDINATION AT NATIONAL LEVEL

"When you can measure what you are speaking about and express it in numbers, you know something about it; but when you cannot measure it, when you can't express it in numbers your knowledge is of meager and unsatisfactory kind; it may be the beginning of knowledge; but you have scarcely advanced to the stage of science."

Lord Kelvin

"You cannot convert the absence of information into a conclusion."
Sum of all fears, p. 935.

Intelligence capabilities are critical components of national power and are integral to the implementation of national security strategy. Intelligence is that information which is made available to national security decision makers to protect the unity and integrity of the nation. This information is then processed and analysed. This processed information is made available to the policy makers by intelligence agencies in the form of an advice to help them take a decision. Like any advice, the decision makers are not bound to adhere to the proposed advice. However, history tells us that the results have been catastrophic when such advice (assessment/warning) of intelligence agencies is ignored. Intelligence vulnerability and inadequacy has been common even with developed nations. Japanese attack on the US naval fleet at Pearl Harbour in 1941, the Arnehm Bridge massacre of British troops by German Resistance forces in World War II and 9/11 attack on Twin Towers are apt example to support the above statement. The point to drive home is that intelligence coverage is required 24x7 and being surprised is always on the cards and thus systemic failures must not be clubbed as intelligence failures.

'The information is power' couldn't have been more applicable than in today's turbulent world. This has, however, compounded the problem of information management for intelligence agencies. The information explosion in the last few decades has catapulted the intelligence as the first line of defence. The intelligence agencies are busy most of the time in managing the information overload which adversely affects their performance. Too much of information makes the task of intelligence assessment even more daunting.

The capability of an agency to make comprehensive intelligence estimates for the policy makers depends largely on its assessment and analytical capabilities. Coherent intelligence appraisal greatly assists in arriving at long-term strategic assessments on issues of ongoing interest. The task of assessment making is not easy. The availability of Open Source Intelligence (OSINT) has added to the enormous data which is to be processed before making an assessment for the decision makers. No agency can provide 100 percent coverage. There are bound to be some gaps both qualitative and quantitative. In such cases comes the requirement of good analysis and assessment. A good analyst with previous knowledge and experience can make near accurate intelligence assessments.[1] A realistic assessment can only be made if information from all sources is made available to an analyst. However, higher the number of sources of intelligence inputs, higher is the degree of coordination needed to have 'intelligence fusion' in the real sense.

India today faces a myriad of Internal Security (IS) challenges besides external threats and new challenges that are emerging on the horizon. The present internal security scenario is dominated by ever expanding arc of urban terrorism, Left Wing Extremism (LWE), narco terrorism and proliferation of small arms. In such environment, the vitality of intelligence has increased manifolds. The traditional intelligence requirements in the unresolved territorial disputes with China and Pakistan continue to overstretch our intelligence agencies. In that scenario, they are as much involved in internal dynamics as they are in assessing external threats. The added dynamics of economic and cyber intelligence, to name a few, have made the task of intelligence agencies more complex. Economic and cyber intelligence is fast growing into the prime requirement and is likely to draw maximum resources of intelligence agencies. As a result, the role of intelligence in ensuring Indian National Security can no longer be ignored by decision makers.

The Indian intelligence agencies have been lately under severe criticism for their performance. They are mostly blamed for not being able to issue warnings of impending terrorist strikes. It is a common fallacy that incidents like Kargil or 26/11 Mumbai terrorist strike couldn't be prevented due to lack of information (intelligence). The cynicism towards them has been further reinforced in the public mind mainly because of the media outburst against intelligence community in recent terrorist strikes in the hinterland. The intelligence agencies can predict a broad shift in terrorist strategy at the national level; they cannot provide specific details of terrorist plan.[2] The post incident analysis of most of such incidents has revealed that sufficient information/indicator was available with the intelligence agencies albeit in an unprocessed state. They, however, couldn't convert these strands of information into a well assessed input. The same inputs once analysed carefully in light of previous trends could have been converted into a warning for the security forces. It has also been noted that in some cases the agencies were able to make near accurate assessment but failed to share it with fellow agencies. In such cases, they faltered in coordinating intelligence efforts leading to catastrophic results.

The prime argument of this book is that there has been no dearth of information/ indicators available to the Indian intelligence agencies. It is true even in the cases of so called 'intelligence failure'. However, they have been found wanting in their assessment making capabilities. Post incident analysis of major security lapses analysed in this book, as revealed from the case studies is that the information indicating an imminent threat was misunderstood, lost, or ignored by the analysts. The lack of cogent intelligence assessment led to incoherent intelligence warnings which only worsened the image of the intelligence agencies.

Post independence, some exercises have been undertaken to bring about significant re-structuring in India's intelligence community. These review committees recommended the creation of additional intelligence agencies to handle information overload. However, the committees in the same breath also recommended shedding out of outdated agencies. Over a period, new agencies were created but redundant organisations were never disbanded for obvious reasons. The result was 'plethora of intelligence agencies working in 'watertight compartments'. The addition of new agencies kept previous agencies busy in protecting their 'turfs' thereby degrading the quality of intelligence that emanated from them.

The agencies are reluctant to share actionable intelligence with each other for obvious reasons of 'turf wars'. In the bargain, all available data is not brought together for evaluation and assessment. This generates knowledge gap which if left unidentified and unfilled can adversely affect the intelligence assessment. The lack of coordination in information sharing mechanism can also adversely affect the quality of assessment. For instance, in the border areas there are number of intelligence agencies involved in intelligence collection namely Intelligence Bureau (IB), Research and Analysis Wing (R&AW), Military intelligence (MI), intelligence wings of Para Military Forces and the local police. In most cases, their 'sources' are also common, passing the same information to these agencies. The agencies tend to share this information without processing and at irregular intervals. As a result, this information is deemed to be corroborated and leads to faulty intelligence assessment. The adverse impact of this gets proportionally large at the national level. This duplication can be avoided if these agencies share this information in a coordinated manner both horizontally and vertically. Hence, the second argument in this book rallies around the point that inadequate intelligence assessment stems from the lack of adequate information sharing mechanism (coordination) amongst them. The need for enhancing intelligence assessment and coordination at the national level has been pointed out by many strategic thinkers and intelligence experts. Some of these are reproduced below.

Vikram Sood, former Director (R&AW) comments that "Mumbai was more than just intelligence failure. Like Kargil, it was also a systemic failure but the starting point is inadequate intelligence, the failure to connect the dots within the system and then the rest just happened as the world saw on TV".

Lt Gen Kamal Davar, former Director General Defence Intelligence Agency(DIA), comments that "Whenever strategic surprise or security lapses occur, accusations of intelligence failures are the most convenient fallout, at times rightly, more often than not, wrongly as a cover up for other failings. Both Kargil and the recent Mumbai mayhem were essentially systemic shortcomings and it is grossly unfair to brand them exclusively as intelligence failures."

Brig Gurmeet Kanwal (Retired), former Director, Centre for Land Warfare Studies (CLAWS) notes that "Intelligence coordination at the national level has a lot of scope for improvement. The day today functioning of intelligence agencies is satisfactory but most of the information shared by intelligence agencies is vague, lacks specificity and time frames and does not lead to any relevant assessment".[3] The Kargil Review Committee remarked, "There is a general lack of awareness of the critical importance and the need for assessment at all levels. Joint Intelligence Committee (JIC) report doesn't receive the attention they deserve at the political and bureaucratic levels. The assessment process has been downgraded in importance."

Rana Banerji, former Special Secretary, R&AW and head of Task Force on Intelligence Reforms at Institute of Defence Studies and Analysis (IDSA) acknowledges that turf wars have proved to be a major impediment. The unpublished report notes that they have "taken a toll by slowing down or even completely blocking reform". It has led to lack of national intelligence coordination.

Maloy Krishna Dhar observes that "Serious gaps of communication between the IB and the State Police on one hand and the IB and the R&AW and CBI on the other hand became apparent during the security operations in Punjab, Kashmir, Assam and against the Pakistan sponsored jihadist elements. The most glaring example of total intelligence failure was the Kargil adventure by Pakistan Army. The R&AW, the MI and, to a lesser extent the IB had miserably failed to unearth the Pakistani design and warn the policy planners. Whatever intelligence was available was not coordinated to cull out a coherent collage. The rest is history".[4]

"The function of the intelligence agencies is not merely to inform, but to assess. But the evidence gathered by Kargil Review Committee shows that intelligence was available, what was missing were the assessment", comments Dr Bhashyam Kasturi.[5]

Michael Turner in his book 'Why Secret Intelligence Fails' points out that the intelligence officials across the world are reluctant to talk about intelligence success, claiming that secrecy of their success is the secret of their success. He further adds that they are reluctant to talk about failures as well since it would expose their shortcoming and make policy makers more reluctant to accept and act on the intelligence they receive.[6] A large section of the strategic community may agree with Michael A Turner. However, such criticism of intelligence agencies is nothing new. Even, Central Intelligence Agency (CIA) came under severe criticism post 9/11 or when they failed to predict/detect India's nuclear explosion in 1974 and again in 1998. The intelligence agencies must take this criticism in a positive manner and thrive for self improvement in the national interest.

US Secretary of State and the National Security Advisor, Henry Kissinger comments "Reform of intelligence should focus on sharpening assessment and not stop with improving collection and coordination. Intelligence agencies should be judged by their ability to collect information, to interpret it, to keep assumptions from determining conclusions and to understand underlying trends.[7] In view of the aforesaid, a pragmatic and empirical analysis has been carried out in this book to ascertain the challenges to coherent intelligence assessment and desired coordination at the national level. The lack of information about our intelligence agencies in the open domain is no secret. The analysis has attempted to cut across these barriers to the extent possible. The aim of analysis is not to point fingers at intelligence agencies. The analysis has aimed to recommend concrete measures to improve intelligence assessment and coordination at the national level. The issues which would allow information sharing, and ensure effective oversight and accountability of intelligence activities have also been examined.

Effective response to any unforeseen security challenge necessitates three prongs namely, intelligence agencies, decision makers and reaction elements who respond to the produced intelligence. It is important for them to remain in the same grid and work as a team in order to read the situation continuously and react within shortest possible time. Unfortunately, in India all three prongs have not been meshed to the desired extent. More often than not, they have been engaged in blame game after a crisis. The intelligence gathering and assessment making infrastructure, decision makers and reaction element are recommended to be meshed into one single point contact, which could have reduced the reaction time of our response to any such attack. The prime aim of this exercise is to recommend a system that allows for coherent intelligence assessment and its sharing amongst intelligence agencies in all dimensions which can finally be tendered to decision makers in the form of an advice. The 'Operation Neptune Spear' is the ultimate example of synergy and intermeshing of all three organs of the state craft.

This book suggests one such model of a single point contact at the national level as its prime recommendation. The book recommends setting up of National Intelligence Assessment and Coordination Council (NIACC) as the nodal point for intelligence fusion thereby reducing the number of intelligence agencies. The NIACC as recommended will bring analysts from the respective intelligence agencies under one umbrella to facilitate the sharing of intelligence and breaking down of cross agency barriers. The details of structure, duties, and powers of NIACC and action plans to integrate it in the national security mechanism have been elaborated in the last chapter.

A study of this kind can't be complete without examining the evolution of intelligence services in India. Most of the factors contributing to the lack of intelligence assessment and coordination have their roots in the British era which have continued till today. The present intelligence set up in India has been modeled on the British or American lines without giving adequate thought to different ground realities of the country. It is in this endeavour that intelligence systems across the world have been examined in this book besides providing an overview of the current intelligence set up in the country. The instances wherein intelligence agencies couldn't convert the available inputs into logical assessment have been covered as case studies to support the central theme of the book. The case studies investigate whether we lacked information or assessment. The book concludes that we had adequate indicators but didn't apply ourselves to draw relevant assessment from it.

If we have to be fair to the intelligence agencies then their successes and failures, both have to be taken into account while evaluating their performance. This adds requisite balance to the analysis. Hence, few case studies both of success and failures have been compiled in the book. This empirical analysis led to the identification of challenges to coherent intelligence assessment and coordination which our intelligence agencies have to face. The book takes into account these challenges and recommends some concrete measures to overcome these challenges culminating into a workable model of intelligence set up at the national level. Besides improving intelligence assessment and coordination at the national level, the state intelligence mechanism also needs to be transformed and networked into the national grid simultaneously. The book, however, covers the recommendations at the national level only.

This book is no memoirs; therefore, it deliberately avoids the names of intelligence officials or political leaders to the extent possible. The book also caters for readers who may not have requisite background knowledge to assimilate the nuances of the intelligence process and its direct linkages with multifarious dynamics of national security. Before embarking on a journey to analyse issues related to intelligence, it is prudent that ground rules are set. It is essential that the readers are brought up to date with terminologies used frequently by the intelligence community. A note on key terminologies used frequently in this book and in the intelligence process as a whole has been included in Appendix A. The requisite background of relevant topics has also been included in the form of appendices for readers with inadequate background knowledge.

It is reiterated that the aim of this book, by no means, is to find faults with the intelligence agencies or the government or security forces. The prime motive of this analysis is to recommend some concrete measures to ensure a high degree of intelligence fusion at the national level by enhancing intelligence assessment and coordination. It is pertinent to quote the founder of Defence Intelligence Agency (DIA), Lt Gen Kamal Davar who wrote that "The practitioners of the art of intelligence have to be silent warriors for there is no place for drum-beating in the business of Intelligence."[8]

Notes

[1] B. Raman, Intelligence: Past, Present, and Future (New Delhi, India: Lancer Publishers & Distributors, 2002), p.71

[2] The Politics of Counter-Terrorism in India — Strategic Intelligence and National Security in South Asia, Prem Mahadevan; I.B. Tauris & Co, London,2012 p.2

[3] Brig Gurmeet Kanwal (Retd), former Director, Centre for Land Warfare Studies (CLAWS) during Seminar on Intelligence assessment and coordination at National level at CLAWS on 24 Nov 10

[4] Maloy Krishna Dhar, Open Secrets: India's Intelligence Unveiled, New Delhi, Manas Publications, 2005,p.15

[5] Bhashyam Kasturi "Intelligence Process and Kargil" accessed online via http://www.ipcs.org/article/india/intelligence-process-and-kargil-359.html on 05 Jan 2012

[6] Michael A Turner, 'Why Secret Intelligence Fails', (Potomac Books Inc, 31 January, 2005), p.112

[7] Dr Henry Kissinger, *The Washington Post* , 2004

[8] Lt Gen Kamal Davar, former Director General   Defence Intelligence Agency (DIA), "Drum-beating has no place in the business of intelligence" Rediff mail, April 15, 2003

1

INTELLIGENCE STRUCTURE IN INDIA - A HISTORICAL PERSPECTIVE

Unless someone has the wisdom of a sage, he cannot use spies; unless he is benevolent and righteous, he cannot employ spies; unless he is subtle and perspicacious, he cannot perceive the substance in intelligence reports. It is subtle, subtle, subtle.

– Sun Tzu, The Art of War

Most of the current issues have their root causes embedded in the history. The lack of coherent intelligence assessment and coordination at the national level can also be traced in the history of intelligence agencies in India. AS Dulat, former Director, R&AW links the lack of coordination and over secretive nature of Indian intelligence agencies to the history. He comments, "I think the problem was the product of history".[1] The secrecy, the mystery, the turf wars and lack of coordination are quite evident once we glance through the history of intelligence services in our country. The inter agency rivalry, lack of trust and low priority to intelligence by our defensive national security strategy has been inherited by our intelligence agencies from history. Writers on counter insurgency have suggested that the answers to today's intelligence challenges can be found by studying the colonial period.[2] The basis of this argument would be covered at the end of this chapter. Let us first get acquainted with the history of intelligence in India.

The intelligence function has been carried on for centuries in India. It was the existence of an extensive espionage network that kept kings informed of the happenings of the state. This was true for the large empires like the Mauryas, the Guptas as well as of regional ones like the Pratiharas, the Rashrakutas or the Andhras.[3] Even though intelligence agencies have been active in India as early as in the period of Emperor Ashoka to Akbar, however, this chapter restricts itself to the British era. The analysis of events is undertaken from the British era as our intelligence set up has evolved mainly after this period.

Pre Independence

In 1885, Major General Sir Charles Metcalfe Macgregor was appointed Quartermaster General and head of the Intelligence Department of the British Indian Army at Shimla. The objective then was to monitor Russian troop deployments in Afghanistan, fearing a Russian invasion of British India through the North-West during the late 19th century. Russia had strong imperial ambitions and a special interest in South Asia.

Before General Macgregor's appointment, an organisation called the Survey of India, located in Dehradun, performed the basic intelligence functions. It gathered the topographical information and made maps based on the information gathered by its agents on the borders. The empire was interested in limited areas of activities of the Indian nationalists, the communal situation, communist infiltration and activities of groups and individuals that threatened the stability of their colony.[4]

In 1920, the Department of Criminal Intelligence made exclusively for political surveillance, was renamed Intelligence Bureau (IB).[5] In 1921, a new state run surveillance and monitoring agency, Indian Political Intelligence (IPI) was established. The IPI was run jointly by the India Office and the Government of India. It reported jointly to the Secretary of Public and Judicial Department of the India office, and the Director of Intelligence Bureau (DIB) in India, and maintained close contact with Scotland Yard and MI5. In 1935, IB created its own organisation going down to the grass root level. In order to supplement the information coming from the provincial Criminal Investigation Departments (CIDs) and special branches, IB set up field units in different parts of the country, under a Central Intelligence Officer (CIO). In 1947, it was recognised as the Central Intelligence Bureau under the Ministry of Home Affairs.[6] Prior to independence, the British were having intelligence system in which external predominance was prevailing. Unfortunately, the mindset is still being carried on with the same staffing norms. Any structure is as good as its staffing; therefore, there is a need to improve our staffing pattern.

Post Independence

The issue that immediately confronted India soon after independence was the reorganisation of Central Intelligence Bureau to suit India's national security. Other issues included restructuring of military intelligence and setting up of a nodal agency for tackling internal and external security threats.[7] Consequently, IB (Intelligence Bureau) was set up. From 1947 to 1951, IB was in charge of internal intelligence. In 1951, the Himmat Singhji Committee recommended that IB should also look after external intelligence. In 1949, Sanjeevi Pillai, then DIB, had set up a foreign intelligence cell. From 1951 to 1968, the IB was looking after external as well as internal intelligence. In the fifties, the insurgency in the North East compelled IB to set up Subsidiary Intelligence Bureau's (SIB) to handle the diverse problems of the region. IB also had to coordinate with the state and the army intelligence during counter insurgency operations in Nagaland and Manipur.[8]

At this time, apart from IB and its provincial setup, each state police had its own intelligence wing. At the level of the cabinet was the Defence Committee of the Cabinet which in turn was supplemented by other committees, including the Defence Minister's Committee, the Chief of Staff Committee (COSC), Joint Intelligence Committee (JIC) and Joint Planning Committee (JPC). The JIC was created as a subordinate wing of the COSC.[9]

The JIC was presided over by a Joint Secretary in the Ministry of External Affairs (MEA) and was constituted by the Directors' of Intelligence of the three services, representatives of the Home and Defence Ministries and the IB. The JIC was given the task of reviewing all the information available on the threat perceptions to India and providing the same to the COSC. With this information and the help of the JPC, the COSC was to advice the government on the course of action needed to be taken.[10]

This arrangement of IB responsible for both internal and external intelligence continued even during the 1962 conflict with China. Post 1962 debacle, the decision to bifurcate external intelligence from internal was taken. After the 1962 War, the need was also felt to create new capability for collecting electronic intelligence (ELINT) and imagery from aerial based platform over our territory in the air space. Hence, Aviation Research Centre (ARC) was created under the Directorate General of Security (DGS) and placed under the overall control of Director Intelligence Bureau (DIB).[11]

The new organisation, known as Research and Analysis Wing (R&AW) of Cabinet Secretariat was established on September 21, 1968. The DGS along with the ARC were shifted to R&AW. The R&AW was modeled on the lines of the American and British intelligence agencies. However, R&AW was kept directly under the control of the Prime Minister Office (PMO) instead of the Ministry of Defence (MoD) unlike CIA and MI 6.[12] The JIC was bifurcated into foreign and domestic intelligence wings in 1983 .The split was later reversed on the grounds that Indian terrorist movements drew sustenance from overseas and owing to the reasons could not be assessed in isolation.[13]

Reforms in India's Intelligence Structures

Post independence, three major exercises had been undertaken to bring about significant re-structuring in India's intelligence community. A brief analysis of these exercises makes an interesting history of the Indian intelligence mechanism. It is amply clear that much needs to be done to make the best use of these attempted reforms. The attempted reforms in the Indian intelligence and security mechanism are enumerated in the succeeding paragraphs.

The LP Singh Committee

The LP Singh Committee was instituted after the Emergency was lifted in 1977 to look into the affairs of the IB and the Central Bureau of investigation (CBI).The Committee was to investigate the misuse of intelligence agencies and the CBI during the Emergency between 1975 and 1977.[14] The Committee worked in 1977-78 to process the recommendations of the Commission on Emergency Excesses headed by former Supreme Court Chief, Justice JC Shah. The 'Shah Commission' gave its third and final report in August 1978. For taking action on the findings of the Shah Commission, the Morarji Desai

Government appointed LP Singh Committee.[15]

The Committee was headed by LP Singh, former Union Home Secretary. The Committee included, D P Kohli, the founder Director of the CBI and MLM Hooja, the Director, IB. BS Raghavan, IAS was the Member-Secretary of this Committee. The L P Singh Committee in its recommendations had asked for a separate parliamentary enactment which would put the CBI out of the clutches of the political party or combine running the government of the day and place it under an independent oversight body of eminent persons.[16]

"The LP Singh Committee carved a legal framework and a charter of duties for the IB, which was still functioning as it did before the departure of the British. The Committee also prepared for the consideration of the Government, detailed model charters for adoption."[17] Indira Gandhi, on returning to power in 1980, buried the recommendations of the LP Singh Committee since she felt that the Committee had been set up to target her politically.[18] The scope of the committee was limited as seen above since R&AW was excluded from the review.[19]

Prime Minister VP Singh announced the establishment of a National Security Council (NSC) to "take a holistic view of national security issues in the light of the external, economic, political and military situations and their linkages with our domestic concerns and objectives."[20] However, political turmoil which also saw Chandra Shekhar and PV Narasimha Rao as the Prime Ministers couldn't sustain the idea of NSC and the idea was almost shelved. The political leadership was so involved in political turbulence that none of the Prime Ministers of the time were keen to devote any time to NSC or any such matter of national security.[21]

KC Pant Task Force

On 10th of April 1998, a task force was constituted by the Prime Minister Atal Bihari Vajpayee to review security related issues. The Task Force was chaired by Mr KC Pant, Deputy Chairman, Planning Commission. The other members were Jaswant Singh, Foreign Minister, and Air Commodore (retd) Jasjit Singh, the then Director, Institute of Defense Studies and Analysis (IDSA). Working on the recommendations of the 'Task Force', the

Government constituted a National Security Council (NSC) on 18th November, 1998.[22] The Task Force introduced the concept of National Security Council armed with a full-fledged secretariat that merged the Joint Intelligence Committee (JIC) with the newly-created NSC. The Gazette of India provided formal sanction to the NSC in April 1999.[23]

NSC was a three tier set up under the Prime Minister. The members included Home Minister, Defence Minister, External Affairs Minister, Finance Minister and Deputy Chairman, Planning Commission. Under the United Progressive Alliance (UPA) government, the Deputy Chairman of Planning Commission was omitted from the reconstituted NSC. It was responsible for co-ordination in intelligence collection and tasking of intelligence agencies so as to ensure the intelligence is focused on areas of concern for the nation.

The second tier comprised of the National Security Council Secretariat (NSCS), the National Security Advisor (NSA), the JIC and the Strategic Policy Group (SPG). The SPG was to consist of the Cabinet Secretary, the three Service Chiefs, Foreign Secretary, Home Secretary, Defence Secretary, Secretary (Defense Production), Finance Secretary, Secretary (Revenue), RBI Governor, Director (IB), Secretary 'R', Cabinet Secretariat, Scientific Advisor to Raksha Mantri, Secretary (Space) and the Chairman, JIC. One of the key tasks of the Strategic Policy Group was to take a strategic defence review.

National Security Advisory Board (NSAB) was to form the third tier. The NSAB was to consist of 'persons of eminence' from outside the Government covering expertise in external security, strategic analysis, foreign affairs, defence, the armed forces, internal security, science & technology, and economics.[24]

Kargil Review Committee (KRC)

On 29th July 1999, the Government of India formally instituted the Kargil Review committee to review the events leading to the Pakistani aggression in Kargil sector of Jammu and Kashmir in May 1998.[25] A further brief was to recommend necessary measures to safeguard national security against such armed intrusions. It was also called the Subrahmanyam Committee, as it was chaired by late Mr K Subrahmanyam, leading defence analyst. The Committee comprised four members namely, K. Subrahmanyam (Chairman), Lieutenant General (Retd) KK Hazari, BG Verghese and Satish Chandra, Secretary, National Security Council Secretariat (NSCS) who was also designated as Member-Secretary. [26]The committee submitted a 228 page report to the Prime Minister on 7th January, 2000.[27]

The KRC report is remarkable in India for being an inquiry commission that analysed causes of the events rather than fixing blame for them. In addition, it is a mini strategic review, which flowed from its second charter. It is detailed, and addresses many popular myths propagated at the time of the crises. It has commented on a wide range of matters, from inadequacy of intelligence to lacuna in the national security apparatus. It also represents a first for India as it has been published and commented on by various experts. In view of aforesaid a brief on KRC report has been included as Appendix B for readers who may be interested in the detailed findings of KRC. [28]

Group of Ministers (GoM)

In the wake of KRC report, on 17th April 2000, the then Prime Minister Vajpayee approved the formation of the GoM under the Chairmanship of Home Minister, LK Advani. The other members included Defence Minister, George Fernandes, the External Affairs Minister, Jaswant Singh, Finance Minister, Yashwant Sinha and Brijesh Mishra, who besides being Principal Secretary to the Prime Minister, was the National Security Advisor. The GoM was to submit its report in six months from the date of its constitution.[29]

On 10th May 2000, the GoM created four 'task forces' to examine the recommendations of the KRC in detail'.[30]The 'task forces' were to probe the issues concerning 'the intelligence apparatus, internal security, border management and management of defence'. The GoM asked the 'Task Forces' to evaluate aspects of national security above and beyond the recommendations of the KRC.[31]

GC Saxena Task Force Report on Intelligence Apparatus

The 'Task Force' on intelligence apparatus was chaired by Girish Chander Saxena, a 1950 batch IPS officer, who was the then Governor of Jammu and Kashmir and former R&AW Chief. The task force included M.K. Narayanan, National Security Advisor and former Director IB, K. Raghunath, former Foreign Secretary, P.P. Srivastav, the then Home Affairs Special Secretary, B. Raman, the then R&AW Additional Secretary; R. Narasimha from the National Institute of Advanced Studies (NIAS) and Maj Gen (retired) Chandan. S. Nugyal. [32]

This classified report pointed out several major flaws in the existing intelligence set up. The recommendations of this task force have not been declassified on ground of security.[33] It reportedly noticed a glaring absence of a body at the highest level for tasking and evaluation of intelligence agencies. It pointed out lack of coordination, cooperation and sharing of intelligence between different agencies. The committee observed that the consumer of intelligence is not involved in tasking of intelligence agencies. It pointed out with concern a general degradation of Human Intelligence (HUMINT) capabilities of our intelligence agencies.[34]

The task force recommended institutionalising the procedures for intelligence agencies to brief the political leadership. It also suggested streamlining and rationalising of agencies' fixed assets for cost cutting. The committee advised, ironing out of glitches in sharing technical intelligence outputs.[35] It provided the texts of formal charters for the R&AW, IB and the newly set-up Defence Intelligence Agency (DIA).[36] The Saxena Committee called for a Multi-Agency Centre (MAC) and a Joint Task Force on Intelligence (JTFI) to be set up under the IB. The MAC was to collect and coordinate terrorism-related information and the JTFI was to share the information with state governments.[37]

The report of this task force is regarded as a defining moment in the history of Intelligence reforms in India. Accordingly, a brief on the report has been included in this book as Appendix C to give the readers a better insight into the recommendations of the Committee.

Intelligence Reforms: Follow up of GoM Report

On 5th January 2001, all the 'Task Forces' had submitted their reports to the GoM. The recommendations made by the GoM were approved by the Government on 11th May, 2001.[38] It led to the creation of National Technical

Research Organisation (NTRO) and mechanisms like the Intelligence Coordination Group (ICG), Technical Coordination Group (TCG), and National Information Board (NIB). The idea of setting up an apex technical intelligence (TECHINT) organisation, like the NTRO, emanated, ab initio, from the KRC Report which recommended that the possibility of establishing such a body patterned on the US National Security Agency which should be examined, as it was "neither healthy nor prudent" to endow one agency alone, notably R&AW, with "multifarious capabilities" for both HUMINT and TECHINT capabilities.[39]

The GoM duly examined this idea and after endorsing it, proposed the creation of the National Technical Facilities Organisation (NTFO), subsequently renamed as the National Technical Research Organisation (NTRO), as an apex TECHINT organisation, which would do the following:-

(a) Plan, design, set up and operate any major new strategic and expensive TECHINT facilities as approved by the TCG keeping in view the rapid convergence now taking place among hitherto different technologies.

(b) Examine and process plans of the intelligence agencies for the acquisition of all new facilities/equipment costing more than Rs 3 crores, for consideration by TCG.

(c) Plan and establish modern, secure digital networks connecting the intelligence agencies in Delhi as well as (where required) outside Delhi.

(d) Create, support and maintain a common data base of requisite information as approved by the TCG so that intelligence can be rapidly disseminated among all concerned agencies according to authorised guidelines and protocols.

(e) Explore and establish facilities required for monitoring missile launches, or preparations therefore, in any country of interest.

(f) Develop capabilities for defensive and offensive cyber operations.

(g) Carry out such other projects or programmes as TCG may direct.[40]

The **Technical Coordination Group (TCG)** was constituted in June 2003 soon after the appointment of the Chairman NTRO. Its main function is to coordinate and regulate plans for acquisition of all new, costly, major strategic facilities/equipment by the intelligence agencies, provide oversight to the TECHINT capabilities of the intelligence agencies and to examine issues relating to the allocation of funds for this purpose.[41]

The **Intelligence Coordination Group (ICG)** became operational as early as June 2001. It is presided over by the NSA and includes the Cabinet Secretary and Secretary, NSCS, as member secretary. Other secretaries, Secretary (R), DIB, DG DIA, the NTRO head, Chairman COSC, Service Chiefs etc are called for meetings as and when required. The main aim of setting up an intelligence coordination group was to coordinate and task intelligence and annual evaluation exercises. The main purpose of ICG was to provide systematic intelligence oversight at the apex level. It addresses the following issues:

- Allocation of resources to the intelligence agencies.

- Consideration of annual reviews on the quality of inputs.

- Approve the annual tasking of intelligence collection.

- Oversee the functions of intelligence agencies.

- Examine national estimates and forecasts.[42]

In 2005, this entity fell out.[43] Initially, NSCS and the Joint Intelligence Committee (JIC) was merged and then recreated in 2005 from within NSCS thereby putting ICG in disuse.[44]

The National Information Board **(NIB)** was constituted in August 2002 for national level policy formulation on Information Warfare and Information Security as well as for the creation of the required institutions and structures for implementation of the policies developed. The NIB was also mandated to task and monitor the institutions and structures created by it. Chaired by the NSA, the NIB is serviced by the NSCS.[45] The NIB which was instituted for national policy formulations on information warfare and cyber security also fell into disuse.[46]

INTELLIGENCE REFORMS POST 26/11 MUMBAI TERRORIST ATTACK

The Ram Pradhan Committee was instituted by the Government of Maharashtra to probe the police's and government's response to the 26/11 Mumbai attacks. This was a two-member committee comprising former Home Secretary, Ram Pradhan and Special Secretary (retd), Cabinet Secretariat, V Balachandran. The Committee evaluated lapses in the law enforcement agencies and suggested measures to prevent events like 26/11 Mumbai attacks. On December 21, 2009 the Committee report was presented to the then Chief Minister. It described the Mumbai attacks as "war-like" and also found that it was beyond the capacity of the Mumbai Police. The report was later rejected by the Maharashtra Government and no worthwhile lessons were drawn by authorities from this report. Ironically, against the popular demand, no national level committee was constituted to look into the intelligence lapses in the tragic episode.[47] However, numerous steps were announced by the Central Government which is enumerated in the succeeding paragraphs.

After the Mumbai attack in November, 2008 question marks arose once again about the effectiveness of the intelligence co-ordination mechanisms. The role of the NSCS and the JIC was redefined. The JIC now focuses more on the immediate or short-term intelligence inputs predominantly related to terrorism. The NSCS has reverted to more in-depth, policy oriented analysis relating to intelligence and national security priorities.[48]

Refurbishing the terror combat infrastructure after the Mumbai terrorist attacks, the government made the Multi-Agency Centre (MAC), the nodal agency for intelligence related to terrorism. The MAC was also designated as the nodal agency for intelligence sharing and to formulate responses to terrorism related incidents. The Subsidiary Multi Agency Centers (SMACs) were also established at the state level.[49]

National Counter Terrorism Centre (NCTC)

National Counter Terrorism Centre (NCTC), which is modeled on a variant of the US Homeland Security Department, was proposed to be set up post

26/11. The idea behind NCTC was outlined by the Union Home Minister while delivering the 22nd Intelligence Bureau Centenary Endowment Lecture on 23 Dec 2009 extract of which is reproduced below:-

> Another major idea is the proposal to set up the National Counter Terrorism Centre (NCTC). As the name suggests, the goal is to *counter* terrorism. Obviously, this will include *preventing* a terrorist attack, *containing* a terrorist attack should one take place, and *responding* to a terrorist attack by inflicting pain upon the perpetrators. Such an organisation does not exist today. It has to be created from scratch. I am told that the United States was able to do it within 36 months of September 11, 2001. India cannot afford to wait for 36 months. India must decide now to go forward and India must succeed in setting up the NCTC by the end of 2010.[50]

The NCTC has not become operational till today. While reviewing our national intelligence set up, there is no harm in learning from the best practices abroad and incorporating them into Indian policies. But, there is no need to blindly ape any country. The NCTC is a glaring example of adopting good model with incorrect procedure of adoption. The delay in NCTC being operational ever since its proposal in 2009 is a case study in itself. An in depth analysis of the controversy related to NCTC was done by Chandigarh *Tribune* through "The Tribune Debate on NCTC" in Jan 2012. The views of noted security analysts appeared in it highlighting the Centre State relations. It can be a useful aid for scholars in understanding the NCTC and issues related to it. Accordingly, various views on NCTC are attached as Apendix D.

National Intelligence Grid (NATGRID)

A project to centralise data from multiple sources for better intelligence analysis was announced after 26/11.NATGRID was expected to be the mechanism for synergy for intelligence and a trigger for precision operations. NATGRID when fully established will link 21 data bases accessible to 11 agencies thereby facilitating real time tracking of inputs to include personal transactions such as travel, banking and insurance. The data is available even today but it is difficult to be retrieved even by the intelligence agencies due to its dispersed location in separate and disjointed databases of banks, airlines or insurance companies. The basic purpose of NATGRID will be to track suspicious transactions thereby assisting in identification of suspicious activities by individuals or groups. Timely availability of sensitive information can help the intelligence agencies place suspicious people under surveillance or arrest them.[51] The NATGRID was expected to provide focused information and assist in intelligence fusion.

Setting up of NATGRID was approved by the Cabinet Committee on Security (CCS) in November 2010 but it is yet to become fully functional. It is learnt through media reports that the project is facing severe resistance from various corners. Not surprisingly, the project has not taken off till today. The banks are reportedly opposed to the idea of sharing details of personal transactions. A major section of opposition to NATGRID is the privacy of individual details which are liable to be misused.

The Central Government also announced a project "Aadhaar" - to give Unique Identification (UID) - number to all its citizens and it was to be linked ultimately to NATGRID. Even this pilot project of Central Government could not make satisfactory progress since a major section of users thought that it would infringe on their privacy.[52]

The Central Government also announced an ambitious scheme called "Crime and Criminal Tracking Network System (CCTNS)." The goals of the system were to facilitate collection, storage, retrieval, analysis, transfer and sharing of data and information at the police station and between the police station and the State Headquarters and the Central Police Organisations.[53] The progress on this project is not available in open forum.

The National Investigation Agency (NIA). The National Investigation Agency (NIA) was set up by the Central Government in the weeks after the November 2008 assault by Lashkar-e-Tayyiba (LeT) on Mumbai with the aim of enhancing its intelligence and investigative apparatus. The NIA is now the only federal agency able to supersede the state police in the investigation and prosecute people for particular offences.

Naresh Chandra Task Force

The government constituted a task force in June 2011 to carry out a holistic review of national security and the country's preparedness to face the myriad challenges. The Task Force was headed by former cabinet secretary, Naresh Chandra. The Task Force had a few sub-committees that dealt with internal security, defence and intelligence related issues. The Naresh Chandra committee had intelligence experts like PC Haldar, former chief of Intelligence Bureau, KC Verma, former chief of Research and Analysis Wing, and former National Investigation Agency Chief Radha Vinod Raju.

It also had former defence officers like Admiral Arun Prakash, Air Chief Marshal S Krishnaswamy, and former Director General of Military Operations Lt Gen VR Raghavan, apart from bureaucrats like Brajeshwar Singh and Vinod K Duggal.

Suman K Berry, director, National Council of Applied Economic Research, senior journalist, Manoj Joshi, former Mumbai police commissioner D Sivanandan, former diplomat G Parthasarathy, former chief of Atomic Energy Commission Anil Kakodkar were also part of the Task Force. B Raman, strategic expert and former intelligence officer with R&AW, was advisor to the task force. [54]

This task force was constituted a decade after the Kargil Review Committee carried out a similar assessment in the wake of the Kargil conflict of 1999. The review has been completed and the task force submitted its recommendations in June 2012.[55]

The panel has given a set of recommendations for reforming the national security architecture, covering both intelligence and military apparatus, as part of its mandate to review it. [56] The committee has recommended that ARC be merged with R&AW, the external intelligence agency, to avoid unnecessary turf battles among various intelligence agencies.[57]

Naresh Chandra Committee has recommended creation of a new post of Intelligence Advisor to assist the NSA and the National Intelligence Board on matters relating to coordination in the functioning of the intelligence community as a whole. It also recommended expediting the creation of new instruments for counter-terrorism such as NCTC and NATGRID. The Task

Force recommended deputation of officers from services up to director's level in MoD. It also focused on measures to augment the flow of foreign language experts into the intelligence and security agencies, which face a severe shortage of trained linguists.[58] It has also recommended that India set up a dedicated new agency or department to generate intelligence based on information available from open source.[59]

Conclusive Analysis

Let us now examine how the practices / attitude embedded in history of intelligence services are responsible for the current problem of lack of requisite intelligence assessment and coordination.

Intelligence at the time of independence symbolised ultimate and secret imperial power that helped its masters hunt Indian nationalists or kept a watch on Indian dissidents. It was a government agency that had been run by the British with Indian employees to serve imperial interests. Intelligence agencies at that time were meant to provide a curtain on the activities of colonial masters. Soon after independence and for many years after that, there was suspicion, fear or contempt about intelligence activities. The legacy continues even today wherein general public views intelligence operatives with suspicion and doesn't interact with them freely. The British legacy of 'secrecy' was inherited by the IB after independence and was later passed on to R&AW since it derived its personnel from IB in 1968. The same was bound to be inherited by defence intelligence agencies since defence forces also carry on with British legacy. We know more about the CIA than about the R&AW, because everything about the former is on their official website.[60] Intelligence agencies practice near opaqueness, particularly with regard to covert operations, thereby making it difficult for academics to access basic data.[61]

Intelligence services in India have their origin in the British Raj with its roots in the policing systems created to sustain the British colonial rule. As a result, Indian intelligence services till date derive their officers mainly from Indian Police Services (IPS). Experts from other walks of life are still excluded from this elite service. In the bargain, the mindset of intelligence operatives still remains fixated with investigation and law enforcement. Over a long period, it has fueled analytical vacuum in the intelligence agencies.

Similar sentiments are echoed by Maloy Krishna Dhar, former Joint Director, IB when he writes "The perennial philosophers of the organisation, vested interests of the IPS cadre and the political breed have scrupulously maintained the essential 'police culture' of the IB, almost as it were during Imperial days.[62]

As is evident from the history of intelligence and security mechanism in our country that attempts have been made to take stock of the adverse situation. The review committees have carried out introspection for improvement. However, the will to implement the recommendations of review committees discussed in this chapter has been lacking. As brought out earlier, the new organisations have been mindlessly added to give semblance of seriousness on the part of the government but the action plan to implement these recommendations has been missing. With every new setback to national security, the previous recommendations have been put on the back burner, and a new set of committees and recommendations are announced to fire fight the new situation. The results of our fallacies in the past are staring at us today.

An overview of the present intelligence mechanism as has evolved over a period of time, is critical to any analysis attempting to improve the present set up. With this in mind, we will analyse the existing intelligence mechanism in our country in the next chapter.

Notes

[1] Praveen Swami, " New intelligence technology feeding surge in political espionage", accessed online at http://www.thehindu.com/news/national/article2687373.ece on 06 Dec2011

[2] Nicola Perugini, 'Anthropologists at War: Ethnographic Intelligence and Counter-Insurgency in Iraq and Afghanistan', International Political Anthropology, Vol.1, No. 2 (2008), p. 221

[3] Intelligence Services, Bhashyam Kasturi, (Lancer Publications,1995), p.17

[4] Maloy Krishna Dhar, Open Secrets: India's Intelligence Unveiled, New Delhi, Manas Publications, 2005,p.8

[5] The Politics of Counter-Terrorism In India — Strategic Intelligence and National Security in South Asia, Prem Mahadevan; I.B. Tauris & Co, London,2012 p. XV

[6] SS Trivedi, Secret Services in Ancient India , Allied Publication, 1984, p.16

[7] Intelligence Services, Bhashyam Kasturi ,Lancer Publications,1995,p.25

[8] Intelligence Services, Bhashyam Kasturi ,Lancer Publications,1995,p.39

[9] ibid.

[10] PVR Rao, Defence without drift (Bombay 1970) pp307-08

[11] B. Raman, Intelligence: Past, Present, and Future (New Delhi, India: Lancer Publishers & Distributors, 2002), p.58-59

[12] India's External Intelligence –Secrets of Research and Analysis Wing (RAW), Maj Gen VK Singh, Manas Publications ,2007

[13] The Politics of Counter-Terrorism In India — Strategic Intelligence and National Security in South Asia, Prem Mahadevan; I.B. Tauris & Co, London,2012 p. 34

[14] B Raman, "Why India should declassify historical documents" accessed online through http://news.rediff.com/column/2010/may/10/why-india-should-declassify-historical-documents.htm on 23 Nov 2011

[15] Era Sezhiyan, "Shah Commission Report, Lost and Regained" accessed online through http://blog.lkadvani.in/blog-in-english/a-signal-service-to-history on 16 Mar 2012

[16] B. S. Raghavan, "CBI's anti-graft wing should be under Lokpal" accessed online through http://www.thehindubusinessline.com/opinion/columns/b-s-raghavan/article2656624.ece on 23 Dec 2010

[17] B Raman, "Changing the Indian Intelligence Culture" accessed through http:// www.southasiaanalysis.org/%5Cpapers37%5Cpaper3616.html on 23 Nov 2011

[18] http://www.indiatogether.org/2007/oct/rvw-rawraman.htm accessed online on 24 Nov 2010.

[19] B. Raman, Intelligence: Past, Present, and Future (New Delhi, India: Lancer Publishers & Distributors, 2002), p.62

[20] Government of India, Gazette of India, September 22, 1990 (New Delhi: Rama Publishers, 1990), pp. 652–653.

[21] Shyam Babu, "India's National Security Council: Stuck in the Cradle?" Security Dialogue, Vol. 34, No. 2, 2003, pp. 217-229 accessed online via http://sdi.sagepub.com/content/34/ 2/215.short on 23 Dec 2010

[22] PIB Press Release, National Security Council set up- accessed online via http://pib.nic.in/archieve/lreleng/lyr98/l1198/r191198.html on 23 Dec 2010

[23] Government of India, Gazette of India, April 19, 1999 (New Delhi: Rama Publishers, 1999), p.8

[24] http://www.indiadefence.com/NSAB.htm and the unpublished report of IDSA Task Force on Intelligence Reforms

[25] 'From Surprise To Reckoning, The Kargil Committee Report' Executive Summary accessed online via http://nuclearweaponarchive.org/India/KargilRCA.html 0n 20 Sept 2010

[26] Ibid

[27] From Surprise To Reckoning , The Kargil Review Committee Report, (Sage Publications, Jul 2000) ,Para 6.22, pp. 116

[28] D Ramana , 'Kargil Review Committee: A Commentary', Bharat Rakshak Monitor - Volume 2(6) May-June 2000

[29] Reforming the National Security System- Recommendations of the Group of Ministers, Annexure A accessed online via http://mod.nic.in/newadditions/welcome.html on 14 Dec 2010

[30] Bharat Rakshak Monitor- Volume 3 (4) January- February, 2000, Featured Articles, Intelligence Reforms, Sunil Sainis- http://www.bharat-rakshak.com/MONITOR/ISSUE3-4/sainis.html

[31] Reforming the National Security System: Report of the Group of Ministers on National Security (New Delhi: Government of India, 2001), pp130 -.132.

[32] G C Saxena. J&K Rajbhavan Profile http://jkrajbhawan.nic.in/His%20Excellency/present10.htm

[33] B. Raman, Intelligence: Past, Present, and Future (New Delhi, India: Lancer Publishers & Distributors, 2002), p.69

[34] V. Sudarshan, 'What's Wrong With Our Intelligence? ', 'Outlook' July 2002 accessed online via http://www.outlookindia.com/article.aspx?216296 on 19 Dec 1010

[35] Praveen Swami, "For a paradigm shift' Frontline Volume 18 - Issue 07, Mar. 31 - Apr. 13, 2001

[36] Saikat Datta ," Creating a successful Intelligence and Counter –Terrorism Matrix: Lessons from 26/11" The CLAWS Journal summer 2011 edition,p.102.

[37] Praveen Swami, "Stalled Reforms," Frontline ,Volume 20 - Issue 09, April 26 - May 09,

2003

[38] V. Sudarshan, 'What's Wrong With Our Intelligence? ', 'Outlook' July 2002 accessed online via http://www.outlookindia.com/article.aspx?216296 on 19 Dec 1010

[39] Anit Mukherjee, "Failing to Deliver -Post-Crises Defence Reforms in India, 1998-2010" IDSA Occasional Paper No. 18

[40] Reforming the National Security System- Recommendations of the Group of Ministers, Annexure A accessed online via http://mod.nic.in/newadditions/welcome.html on 14 Dec 2010

[41] Saikat Datta, 'Low on the IQ' accessed online via http://www.outlookindia.com/printarticle.aspx?227823 on 29 Dec 2010

[42] Saikat Datta, 'Low on the IQ' accessed online via http://www.outlookindia.com/printarticle.aspx?227823 on 29 Dec 2010

[43] Amb Satish Chandra, former Depty NSA during CLAWS seminar on 'National Security Reforms: A Decade After The GoM Report' on 12 May 2011

[44] Lt Gen Kamal Davar, PVSM, AVSM (Retd), former DG DIA during CLAWS seminar on 'National Security Reforms: A Decade After The GoM Report' on 12 May 2011

[45] Press release issued following CCS meeting of May 11, 2001. Also drawn in parts from report of IDSA Task Force on Intelligence Reform , 2011

[46] Amb Satish Chandra, former Deputy NSA during CLAWS seminar on 'National Security Reforms: A Decade After The GoM Report' on 12 May 2011

[47] Accessed online at http://news.oneindia.in/2009/06/17/ram-pradhan-committee-report-state-govt-disagrees.html

[48] Interview of Rana Banerji, Special Secretary, R&AW

[49] Saikat Datta ," Creating a successful Intelligence and Counter –Terrorism Matrix: Lessons from 26/11" The CLAWS Journal summer 2011 edition,p.104

[50] http://pib.nic.in/newsite/erelease.aspx?relid=56395 accessed on line on 13 Mar 1012

[51] Col. Rahul K. Bhonsle, NATGRID: Relevance in the Indian Context, accessed online through http://www.claws.in/index.php?action=Articles&start=30&pagesize=30 on 13 Mar 12

[52] Pavan Duggal, Advocate, Supreme Court, " Does the UID project infringe on privacy?", Business Standard, New Delhi, 03 Aug 11

[53] Home Minister, proposed while delivering the 22nd Intelligence Bureau Centenary Endowment Lecture on 23 Dec 2009 accessed online at http://pib.nic.in/newsite/erelease.aspx?relid=56395 accessed on line on 13 Mar 1012

[54] http://www.rediff.com/news/report/naresh-chandra-task-force-to-recommend-permanent-head-chiefs-of-staff-committee/20120 accessed online on 20 Jun 2012

[55] http://articles.timesofindia.indiatimes.com/2012-07-11/india/32631950_1_intelligence-agencies-national-technical-research-organisation-intelligence-front accessed online on 01 July 2012

[56] http://economictimes.indiatimes.com/news/politics/nation/naresh-chandra-panel-recommends-military-preparedness-to-deal-with-assertive-china/articleshow/151358 accessed online on 20 July 2012

[57] http://articles.timesofindia.indiatimes.com/2012-07-11/india/32631950_1_intelligence-agencies-national-technical-research-organisation-intelligence-front accessed online on 11 July 2012

[58] http://millenniumpost.in/NewsContent.aspx?NID=3084 accessed online on 20 July 2012

[59] Josy Joseph, 'Chandra panel bats for open source intel gathering', *Times of India*, 08 July 2012

[60] This section is derived in parts from India's External Intelligence –Secrets of Research and Analysis Wing (RAW), Maj Gen VK Singh, Manas Publications, 2007, pp 13-29

[61] The Politics of Counter-Terrorism In India — Strategic Intelligence and National Security in South Asia, Prem Mahadevan; I.B. Tauris & Co, London,2012 p.9

[62] Maloy Krishna Dhar, Open Secrets: India's Intelligence Unveiled, New Dehli, Manas Publications, 2005, p.11

2

PRESENT INTELLIGENCE SET UP AT THE NATIONAL LEVEL

"For our state which since its creation has been under siege by its enemies, Intelligence constitutes the first line of defence...we must learn well how to recognise what is going on around us."

David Ben Gurion
Prime Minister of Israel, 1951

After having an overview of the historical perspective of intelligence mechanism in our country, let us now examine the present intelligence machinery. Presently, we have number of intelligence agencies functioning in the country. Some of them have investigative roles while others are involved in intelligence collection. The boundaries between them mostly remain blurred and undefined. Over a period, numerous agencies have been added in the set up, attempting to contribute to investigation as well as intelligence collection, but the task of intelligence assessment has been given a lower priority. The lack of suitable supervisory mechanism has also affected the intelligence assessment and coordination at the national level. The presence of such large number of agencies today necessitates a high degree of coordination amongst them. The Home Minister, while delivering the 22nd Intelligence Bureau Centenary Endowment Lecture on 23 Dec 2009 aptly summed the situation as below:

"The intelligence elements are spread over different ministries: there is the Intelligence Bureau which reports to the Home Minister; there is the Research and Analysis Wing which falls under the Cabinet Secretariat and, hence, reports to the Prime Minister; there are organisations such as Joint Intelligence Committee (JIC), National Technical Research Organisation (NTRO) and Aviation Research Centre (ARC) which report to the National Security Advisor; and there is the National Security Council Secretariat under the NSA which serves the National Security Council. The armed forces have their own intelligence agencies, one each under the Army, Navy and Air Force and an umbrella body called the Defence Intelligence Agency. There are other agencies which specialise in financial intelligence. These are the Directorates in the Income Tax, Customs and Central Excise departments, the Financial Intelligence Unit, and the Enforcement Directorate. The enforcement element of this architecture consists of the central para-military forces such as CRPF, BSF, CISF, ITBP, Assam Rifles, SSB and the NSG. What will strike any observer is that there is no single authority to which these organisations report and there is no single or unified command which can issue directions to these agencies and bodies." [1]

JIC/NSCS, R&AW, IB, DIA, MAC, NIA are few agencies involved in the various stages of intelligence process besides Narcotics Control Bureau (NCB), Directorate of Revenue Intelligence (DRI), and Economic Offences Wing (EOW) of Delhi Police. The three wings of armed forces have their dedicated intelligence set up.Today, almost every paramilitary and police force has its own intelligence network. The long list of Indian intelligence agencies has been summarised below as under:

Higher Intelligence Organisation

Prime Minister	
Cabinet Secretariat	
National Security Council (NSC)	Joint Intelligence Committee (JIC)

Indian intelligence agencies

Internal Security	External Intelligence	Defence Intelligence	Economic Intelligence
Intelligence Bureau	Research and Analysis Wing	Defence Intelligence Agency	Directorate of Revenue Intelligence
Central Bureau of Investigation	Aviation Research Centre	Image Processing and Analysis Centre	Economic Intelligence Council
All India Radio Monitoring Service	Radio Research Center	Directorate of Signals Intelligence	Central Economic Intelligence Bureau
National Investigation Agency	Electronics and Technical Services	Directorate of Military Intelligence	Directorate General of Economic Enforcement
	National Technical Research Organisation	Directorate of Naval Intelligence	Directorate General of Income Tax Investigation
		Joint Cipher Bureau	Narcotics Control Bureau

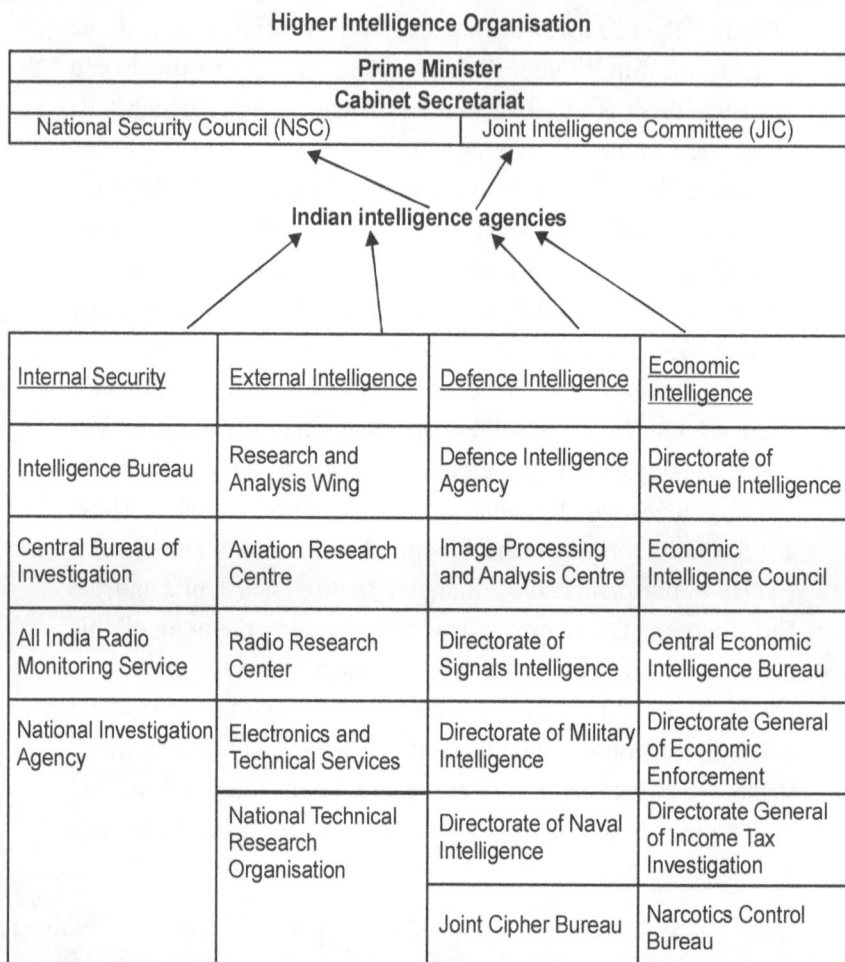

In the above table, the joint intelligence organisations such as MAC, JTFI and NCTC (proposed) have not been included. If we include the intelligence agencies of para military forces such as BSF and CRPF, then the chart would appear more cluttered up. An overview of present intelligence mechanism clearly points towards a plethora of agencies. If we analyse their role and charter (if at all defined), we realise that there is an avoidable duplication in this area. Let us now examine the role of major intelligence agencies with a view to pinpoint the areas which require fine tuning. The role of major intelligence agencies is enumerated in succeeding paragraphs.

The Joint Intelligence Committee (JIC)

The JIC is the highest intelligence assessment body in India comprising of representatives of all the intelligence services. Its job is to review political, economic, and scientific and military intelligence with a bearing on national security.[2] The JIC produces a weekly review, and papers as required. The JIC prepares national intelligence estimates for the Cabinet, the Prime Minister and concerned ministries and departments of the Government of India. The JIC has a permanent secretariat, with people drawn from various disciplines including specialists. The JIC is not a collecting agency but is totally dependent on intelligence inputs from the various agencies like the R&AW, IB, DIA etc.[3] The JIC under the Cabinet Secretariat, is responsible for co-coordinating and analysing intelligence activities between the R&AW, the IB and the DIA whose heads are members of the JIC.

JIC has been mandated to assemble, evaluate and present intelligence from different sources pertaining to internal and external developments, as it may have a bearing on national security. It prepares reports on its own initiative or as required by the Policy Planning Group on National Security or by the Cabinet Committee on Security (CCS). JIC is also mandated to prepare special reports which would help in policy formulation in the Ministry of Home Affairs (MHA) /Ministry of Defence (MOD) / Ministry of External Affairs (MEA). [4]

NSC

NSC was formally established in 1999. NSC is a three tier set up under the Prime Minister. The members include the Home Minister, the Defense Minister, the External Affairs Minister, and the Finance Minister.

In practice, the effectiveness of the JIC has been varied. With the establishment of the National Security Council in 1999, the role of JIC was merged with the NSC. The JIC was revived in 2005. As the system now stands, both the National Security Council Secretariat (NSCS) and the Joint Intelligence Committee (JIC) are responsible for coordinating intelligence assessments. JIC, however, focuses more on the immediate or short-term intelligence inputs, with major focus on terrorism. The NSCS is involved in policy oriented prognoses relating to intelligence and national security priorities.[5]

Intelligence Bureau (IB)

IB functions as India's internal security agency.[6] One of the longest functioning intelligence agencies, its roots can be traced back to the Imperial Intelligence Bureau, which served the British interests in India.[7]

The IB was created on December 23, 1887, originally named the Central Special Branch. At that time, it coordinated the activities of provincial Special Branches across British India. These branches handled the day-to-day task of performing surveillance on Indian political parties and religious movement. Their reports were consolidated into finished assessment by the Central branch, which renamed itself as the Department of Criminal Intelligence in 1903 and finally adopted the name 'Intelligence Bureau' in 1920.[8]

IB is chartered with a wide range of responsibilities spanning from combating terrorists, separatism endorsed by the Naxals to critical infrastructure protection, particularly aviation security.[9] The IB (under Home Ministry) is the prime agency for internal intelligence and security. All matters pertaining to internal security are dealt by Home Ministry. The IB today looks after collection, analysis and dissemination of intelligence pertaining to internal security. It looks after a host of internal problems ranging from insurgency, terrorism and communal rioting, and is the key player in the field of counter intelligence[10].

The IB operates both at the national and state level. At the state level, all IB officers are part of the State Special Bureau. Additionally, at the national level, the IB has several units (in some cases Subsidiary Intelligence Bureaus) to keep track of issues like terrorism, counter-intelligence, VIP security and threat assessment.[11]

The Research and Analysis Wing (R&AW)

The R&AW (under Cabinet Secretariat) is responsible for external intelligence and external origin threats to internal security. R&AW in its present form was instituted in September 1968 and was mandated to oversee external intelligence. It is tasked to collect, analyse and disseminate intelligence on all aspects of the national security concerning external dimensions.[12] The R&AW is accountable to the Cabinet Secretary and the Prime Minister.[13]

The R&AW is primarily involved in the collection of external intelligence, counter-terrorism and covert operations. In addition, it is responsible for obtaining and analysing information about foreign governments, corporations, and persons, in order to advise Indian policy makers.[14] It also has a role to play in assessing trans border threats in the form of insurgencies, terrorism and narco-terrorism. R&AW's objectives are to collect intelligence on all nations adjoining India, who's military and foreign policies affect our national security. It also keeps a close watch on China and its northern neighbour, Russia. R&AW also keeps a close watch on the supply of military hardware to Pakistan. It keeps its links with ethnic Indian communities abroad to build a long term lobby in these nations where Indians are in positions of influence.[15]

R&AW's legal status is unusual. It is not an "Agency" but a "Wing" of the Cabinet Secretariat. Hence, R&AW is not answerable to the Parliament of India on any issue, which keeps it out of reach of the *Right to Information Act*. Working directly under the Prime Minister, the structure, rank, pay and perks of the Research & Analysis Wing are kept secret from Parliament.[16]

Defence Intelligence Agency (DIA)

Based on recommendations of the Group of Ministers's report post Kargil War, DIA was created in March 2002. The DIA was established primarily for "coordinating the functioning of different service intelligence directorates."[17] It was created to ensure better integration of intelligence collected by the three service directorates and to serve as the principal military intelligence agency.[18] The DIA is tasked to collect, interpret and disseminate all defence related information, whosoever may have first generated it, and also coordinates between the directorates of military, air force and naval intelligence.[19] The DIA is also mandated to coordinate the intelligence requirements of the Directorate of Military Intelligence, Directorate of Air Intelligence and the Directorate of Naval Intelligence.

The creation of the DIA significantly reduced the reliance of the Indian Armed Forces on civilian intelligence agencies such as IB and R&AW for operational information. It is no longer dependent on these agencies for enemy troop assessments. The gap in military intelligence availability was reported during the conflicts of 1948 with Pakistan, 1962 with China, 1965 and 1971 with Pakistan and during the Kargil intrusion of 1999. During these operations, intelligence products were not up to the requirements of the defence forces.

The Agency's primary task is to track troop movement in countries neighbouring India. Unlike the Directorate General of Military Intelligence (DGMI), it is also assigned the mission of monitoring terrorist groups operating both within and outside the country. Apart from this, one of its sections is dedicated to gathering intelligence on terrorist groups and monitoring the internal security threat. The Agency's mission is to be accomplished using satellite and high-altitude aerial reconnaissance imagery.

The head of the Agency is the Director General, who reports to the Defence Minister and will report to the Chief of Defence Staff (CDS), should the position be created. The Director General is the principal advisor on intelligence to the Defence Minister and the Chief of Defence Staff as and when created. Presently, he functions through the National Security Advisor (NSA) since the CDS has not yet been appointed by the Government.[20] The DIA is also involved in intelligence support groups with the IB and R&AW to coordinate military related intelligence etc. These groups are run jointly with the IB and R&AW, to provide coordinated information to army corps commanders in areas where the Armed Forces Special Powers Act (AFSPA) is imposed.[21]

DIA, with existing expertise of Signal Intelligence Directorate and Defence Image Processing and Analysis Centre (DIPAC) caters for technical intelligence (TECHINT) requirements of all the three armed services[22]. The DIA armed with these tactical inputs merges these with strategic intelligence it collects from the DIPAC and the Signals Intelligence, HUMINT and thus makes an accurate and comprehensive intelligence mosaic for national security planners and the three services.

Multi Agency Centre (MAC)

Based on the recommendations of the Group of Ministers' report, MAC and Joint Task Force on Intelligence (JTFI) were created from the IB by 2003-2004. It was done with a view to effectively co-ordinate inputs related to terrorism from different field agencies on a day-to-day basis. Subsidiary MACs (SMACs) was also established at the state level. Their main task was to synergise the state police's special or intelligence branches and to bring about operational convergence between them and the central agencies.[23]

While MAC is in charge of collecting terrorism-related information from across the country, the JTFI is responsible for passing on this information to the state governments in real-time. MAC and the JTFI are mandated to ensure that intelligence gathering is aggressive, correct and to-the-point.[24] The effectiveness of these newly created organisations would be dealt subsequently.

National Technical Research Organisation (NTRO)

A new organisation, initially called the National Technical Facilities Organisation (NTFO) and subsequently renamed the NTRO has come up, to focus exclusively on the collection of TECHINT. It also includes National Institute of Cryptology Research and Development (NICRD). It is somewhat but not totally similar to the National Security Agency (NSA) of the USA. The head of the NTRO, called Chairman, is taken on rotation from the Intelligence Bureau (IB), the Research & Analysis Wing (R&AW) and the Defence Research and Development Organisation (DRDO).

Its main task is to plan, design, set up and operate major new strategic and expensive TECHINT facilities as approved by the TCG keeping in view the rapid convergence now taking place among hitherto different technologies. The agency is involved in examining and processing plans of the intelligence agencies for the acquisition of all new facilities/equipment costing more than Rs 3 crores, for consideration by TCG. It was mandated to plan and establish modern, secure digital networks connecting the intelligence agencies in Delhi as well as (where required) outside Delhi. The agency was to assist in creating, supporting and maintaining a common data base of requisite information as approved by the TCG so that intelligence can be rapidly disseminated among all concerned agencies in accordance with the authorised guidelines and protocols. NTRO is tasked to develop capabilities for defensive and offensive cyber operations.[25]

The National Investigation Agency (NIA)

The NIA was set up in the weeks after the November 2008 assault by Lashkar-e-Tayyiba (LeT) on Mumbai. The shock of that event, in which 164 people were killed and at least 30 wounded, prompted the Central Government to enhance its intelligence and investigative apparatus. The NIA is now the only federal agency able to supersede state police in the investigation and prosecute people for particular offences. The agency is empowered to deal with terror related crimes across states without special permission from the states. The National Investigation Agency Bill 2008 to create the agency was moved in the Parliament by Union Home Minister on 16 December 2008. As per the National Investigation Agency (Manner of Constitution) Rules, 2008 the NIA is mandated to provide assistance to, and seek assistance from other intelligence and investigation agencies of the Central Government and State Governments. At present NIA is functioning as the Central Counter Terrorism Law Enforcement Agency in India.[26]

The Economic Intelligence Agencies

Internal intelligence gathering in India relating to taxation and related issues is primarily the responsibility of the Central Economic Intelligence Bureau (CEIB). This organisation is the secretariat of the Economic Intelligence Council, a nodal body which coordinates the response of various government agencies (CBI, IB etc.) to economic offences. The CEIB coordinates the work of the Directorate General of Revenue Intelligence (Customs), the Directorate of Enforcement (Foreign Exchange), the Directorate General of Anti-Evasion (Central Excise), the Directorate General of Income Tax (income tax evasion), and the Narcotics Control Bureau (controlled substances). The task of collecting and collating data about other economies of hostile countries and economic competitors of nationally sensitive business interests is undertaken by the R&AW. It has built up considerable expertise on the functioning of economies in South East Asia.[27]

Directorate General of Military Intelligence (DGMI)

India's Military Intelligence (MI) traces its origins to the appointment of Maj Gen Sir Charles MacGregor as head of the Intelligence Department of the British Indian Army in 1885. Headquartered in Shimla, the Department was primarily tasked to collect and analyse intelligence relating to Russian troop dispositions in Central Asia. The departure of the British in 1947 marked the low point, as the British left behind very little in the way of assets or infrastructure for the Intelligence Corps of the newly independent India.[28]

MI was initially tasked to generate only tactical or field intelligence of all countries bordering India. The agency was set up in 1941 to generate field intelligence for the Indian Army. Its geographical mandate was set to 50 km from the border. MI's mandate includes counter terrorism in the north and Northeast and generating pinpoint intelligence for small team operations. It is also tasked with counter intelligence in the army, which entails detecting spies in military areas.[29] MI has limited acquisition capabilities and largely depends upon R&AW and IB to meet its strategic intelligence requirements.

Besides MI, the Indian Air Force and Indian Navy also have their own intelligence directorate namely Directorate of Naval Intelligence and Air Force Intelligence which collects intelligence and prepares it for dissemination. Among the services, the three military intelligence directorates of the army, navy and air force still act as the principal field or tactical intelligence collection agencies except SIGINT and IMINT (now done by DIA). These intelligence directorates directly report to their respective service chiefs. The inter service coordination and interface with civil intelligence agencies has a scope of improvement with appointment of CDS.

Intelligence Units of Security Forces

The Border Security Force (BSF), which guards the borders with Bangladesh and Pakistan, has BSF (G). BSF (G) processes intelligence inputs emerging from BSF units along the border. In addition to the counter-intelligence operations near the border and in internal security deployments, the BSF (G) also maintains a close watch on enemy forces close to the border, and carries out intelligence operations against narcotics and arms smugglers. The Indo Tibetan Border Police (ITBP), which guards the border with China, coordinates intelligence collection with the IB and with the SSB. The Assam Rifles too has some capability to collect intelligence inputs and works closely with the DGMI. Central Reserve Police Force (CRPF) has been preparing to create its own intelligence units for quite some time and reportedly some specialised CRPF personnel have already been tasked to gather intelligence in the Naxal infested areas.[30]

Note Owing to paucity of space, only major intelligence agencies which are directly involved in national security management have been included in this analysis. A brief on other intelligence agencies has been included in Appendix E.

Analysis

It is amply clear from the critical analysis of present intelligence and security set up at national level that during the last decade, the country's security and intelligence apparatus has been suitably restructured. Post independence, maximum security related initiatives have been witnessed in this decade. The active media has constantly kept security issues in their prime focus thereby ensuring that a large number of recommendations of review committees were taken up for implementations. The NSC took over the functions of the JIC in 1998. After the Kargil conflict, the DIA and NTRO came into being. However, the intelligence fusion is still not at the desired level.

The exact role and boundaries of these agencies are still not clear. Most of the intelligence agencies including the R&AW and IB remain without a legal framework or a charter of duties.[31] The agencies have been created but the agencies recommended to be 'shed off' have managed to survive on some pretext or the other. As a result, the degree of coordination amongst these agencies has grown in requirement but has become equally difficult in execution.

The DIA is now the nodal agency for defence oriented intelligence, with Directorate of Signals Intelligence as well as the Defence Image Processing and Analysis Centre (DIPAC) under its wings. The R&AW being nodal agency for external intelligence is actively involved in border related intelligence which the DIA also considers as its primary role. The redundancy is beneficial to the organisations but duplication adds to confusion and is against the principle of economy of efforts.

The reluctance of the intelligence agencies to transfer their assets based on recommendations of review committees has been widely reported. It has only led to unfavourable working environments in these agencies and worsened the relations amongst them. The controversy between NTRO and R&AW related to the transfer of assets of Aviation Research Centre (ARC) is a case in example. Inspite of clear instructions, the transfer of assets to NTRO got delayed due to reluctance on part of concerned agency.

There has been a sea change in the perception of what constitutes our 'national space'. The definition is much broader now and issues (such as economics, social media, science) that were for some time removed from the realm of intelligence targeting are now indivisible parts of it. The realms of intelligence have expended in the last few decades. They continue to grow as the security issues become increasingly complex. The perception management is one such growing realms of intelligence today which has been analysed in detail in the next chapter.

Notes

[1] http://pib.nic.in/newsite/erelease.aspx?relid=56395 accessed on line on 13 Mar 1012

[2] Dr Bhashyam Kasturi, Intelligence services –Analysis, Organisation and function,(Lancer, 1995, New Delhi) p. 61

[3] Interview of Rana Banerji, former Special Secretary R&AW and head of Task Force on Intelligence Reforms at Institute of Defence Studies and Analysis (IDSA),New Delhi, 10 Nov 2011

[4] Ibid.

[5] Ibid.

[6] Jane's Intelligence Digest, Jane's Sentinel Security Assessment: South Asia - India: Security And Foreign Forces (London: Jane's Information Group, 2006), 29.

[7] Maloy Krishna Dhar, Open Secrets: India's Intelligence Unveiled (New Dehli, India: Manas Publications, 2005), 11.

[8] The Politics of Counter-Terrorism in India — Strategic Intelligence and National Security in South Asia, Prem Mahadevan; I.B. Tauris & Co, London,2012 p.28

[9] Ministry of Home Affairs, Annual Report 2006-07 (Government of India: 2007), 28, 31-32; http://mha.nic.in/Annual-Reports/ar0607_Eng.pdf

[10] Jane's Intelligence Digest, Jane's Sentinel Security Assessment: South Asia - India: Security and Foreign Forces (London: Jane's Information Group, 2006), 29.

[11] http://www.policeinindia.com/cops.htm - intelligence bureau accessed online on 13 Oct 2010

[12] www.globalsecurity.org/intell/world/india/raw.htm accessed online on 13 Oct 2010

[13] http://www.indiatogether.org/2007/oct/rvw-rawraman.htm accessed online on 14 Feb 2011

[14] Gp Capt SM Hali 'R&AW at War-Genesis of Secret Agencies in Ancient India' accessed online via www.defencejournal.com/feb-mar99/raw-at-war.htm 0n 25 Oct 2010

[15] B. Raman, Intelligence: Past, Present, and Future (New Delhi, India: Lancer Publishers & Distributors, 2002), p.60

[16] Right to Information , Department which are excluded ,accessed on line at http://www.helplinelaw.com/docs/main.php3?id=RTON1 on 13 Jan 1011

[17] Group of Ministers Report, Reforming the National Security System, p. 104

[18] India's External Intelligence –Secrets of Research and Analysis Wing (RAW), Maj Gen VK Singh, Manas Publications ,2007,p.36

[19] Praveen Swami, 'A new Intelligence Organisation', Frontline Volume 19 - Issue 06, Mar. 16 - 29, 2002

[20] Accessed on line at http://www.globalsecurity.org/intell/world/india/dia.htm

[21] Praveen Swami, 'A new Intelligence Organisation', Frontline Volume 19 - Issue 06, Mar. 16 - 29, 2002

[22] India's External Intelligence –Secrets of Research and Analysis Wing (RAW), Maj Gen VK Singh, Manas Publications ,2007,p.36

[23] Saikat Datta, "Creating a successful intelligence and counter-terrorism matrix: Lessons from 26/11",CLAWS Journal, Summer 2011,pp.102-103

[24] MAC Executive Order issued by MHA on December 31, 2008

[25] Sandeep Unnithan ,"Spy versus spy", India Today, 7 September 2007 accessed online via http://indiatoday.intoday.in/story/Spy+versus+spy/1/1067.html on 26 Dec 2010

[26] Official website of NIA accessed online at http://nia.gov.in/aboutus.aspx on 13 Mar 2012

[27] Sunil Saini, Intelligence Reforms, Bharat Rakshak Monitor - Volume 3(4) January-February 2001,p.14

[28] India: Foreign Policy & Government Guide, Volume 1 ,Ministry of Defence Intelligence units p.120

[29] How Indian Army's Military Intelligence Directorate works, Sandeep Unnithan | Jan 28, 2012 acessed online through http://indiatoday.intoday.in/story/bangladesh-indian-army-military-intelligence-directorate-sheikh-hasina/1/170880.html|

[30] Bibhu Prasad Routray, "Intel wing for the CRPF: Not the Right Move", CLAWS web article ,17 Jul 2011

[31] http://www.indiatogether.org/2007/oct/rvw-rawraman.htm. accessed online on 14 Feb 2011

PERCEPTION MANAGEMENT: THE GROWING REALMS OF INTELLIGENCE

"Once formed, perceptions persist unless they are replaced by other more powerful perceptions"

Perception Management is an integral element of any conflict management process. Skillful use of information, propaganda and psychological operations (Psy ops) pays rich dividends in shaping the environment to facilitate successful task accomplishment.[1] During the Vietnam War, the image of the Americans as imperial forces was instrumental in shaping the anti-war sentiment in the US public. More recently, in Afghanistan, the burning of some Qurans in the US base at Bagram on 24 Feb 2012, sparked days of protest and led to undermining the US effort in that country.[2] While wars are still fought in battlefields, they can be won or lost in public opinion. This is where intelligence agencies can assist in shaping perceptions.

Informational power is now increasingly being perceived as the fourth instrument of power, besides diplomatic, economic and the military power. The new information age permits precision guided propaganda, much as modern technology permits precision guided munitions. In the defensive mode, we are actually countering enemy's propaganda in a reactive mode. The offensive or proactive mode deals with attacks on enemy's mind before it subverts the minds of 'target audience'[3].

While formulating a perception management plan, information would be required of various facets of the target audience. Audience profiling has been covered in Chapter 1 and would be a function of intelligence. This would also include aspects such as public leanings, literacy levels and economic profiles. This would be useful to plan the psyops campaign. The intelligence effort is also required to determine if any part of the population is being subjected to hostile propaganda. Subsequently, intelligence would be required to give a feedback on the impact of our perception management efforts to enable modulation of effort if required.

Intelligence agencies can thus assist in the perception management process by providing inputs both for policy formulation as well as for policy implementation. As of now, own intelligence agencies are engaged in monitoring groups engaged in anti-India propaganda but have not been utilised in providing inputs to shape perceptions of target populations. A wide canvas exists today wherein intelligence agencies can be co-opted in a perception management strategy for Northeast India, Jammu and Kashmir and in areas affected by Maoist violence.

Covert Operations by Intelligence Agencies

History is replete with examples of intelligence agencies in shaping perceptions. The Secret Service (SIS/MI 6) of the UK was covertly employed in the Second World War to implant propaganda material at inconspicuous locations in Germany. This was targeted against Nazi forces. The CIA and MI6 were used to shape the perceptions of third world countries against the erstwhile USSR during the cold war. Even today, it is believed that western intelligence agencies are funding some non-government organisations (NGO) and using them to influence the thoughts and attitudes of specific target populations. The role of Pakistan's Inter Services Intelligence (ISI) in subverting the minds of target audience in J&K and its complicity in fomenting insurgency in Punjab has been well established. At the time of the military action against Sikh militants holed up in the Golden Temple, ISI agents spread rumours of the destruction of the Golden Temple to incite the local population. It is also believed that ISI has been making attempts to subvert the local populace in LWE affected states by circulating propaganda material through Naxal cadres.

Role in Psy ops

As a defensive measure, intelligence agencies need to be coopted to determine an adversary's psyops strategy against own population. Intelligence operatives are trained to intermingle with the local populace or they could be locals of the area. Through daily interaction they can discern hostile action such as dissemination of inflammatory material being spread through pamphlets, audio cassettes and video cassettes or subversive activities being carried out through speeches being made in mosques, schools, the town square and other such places. They can also determine the impact such hostile propaganda is having on own population. This can facilitate appropriate counter measures to be taken which could also include targeting hostile operatives. As part of this process, the intelligence agencies would need to monitor the activities of some of the NGOs, think tanks, media houses and others who could be involved in spreading hostile propaganda or assisting in its spread. In a best case scenario, they could be effective in checkmating an adversary's strategy before it has taken root or before it has impacted on the target audience.

As part of offensive psyops, the intelligence agencies can play an invaluable role in profiling target populations in insurgency affected areas. This would include getting all relevant information on the population base to facilitate correct identification of the target as also the most appropriate measures to address it. A large part of the data is available from open or government sources such as population spread and densities, religious profiles, caste identities, literacy levels, language or dialects spoken, wage earning capabilities, electricity penetration, terrain characteristics, local businesses etc. which could be accessed by the operatives. Other data such as type and quantity of magazines and newspaper being sold in particular areas, grass root leadership, political inclinations, fundamentalist leaning etc. will have to be assessed through interaction and other means. The leadership must understand that this is a long term process and should therefore not look for quick fix solutions. Once comprehensive data bases have been prepared through intelligence efforts, they would have to be periodically validated.

To determine the efficacy of own psyops campaign in the affected areas, feedback mechanisms would play an important role. Here too, the intelligence effort could determine the effectiveness or otherwise of own psyops campaign as also the impact of enemy psyops against our population. Based on feedback, own campaign could be modified to suit the ground realities.

The intelligence network can also be used to shape the perception of the target audience through grey or black operations. How this can be accomplished is a matter of planning and detail and the modalities are not being discussed here. Both the print medium and radio could be used to good effect. Radio stations can be used to deliver both grey and black messaging but would require very careful and skillful handling to be taken to be the genuine article. Exploiting the print media would be more challenging for black and grey messaging and would require good rapport with various local media houses. Here too, great skill and sophistication is called for to ensure credibility. Own operatives who have merged with the local population or who are parts of the same population base can be an effective medium of spreading the security forces perspective through subtle means taking advantage of their invisibility. In essence, they must draw the attention of the people to the good work being done by the forces such as in health care, education and other activities which has been published or aired. The name of the Army in such cases should never be mentioned. For example, it would be beneficial to state that a six year old girl was saved from a disease by timely treatment in a medical camp. Or state that more children are now going to school which is helping the community, or that the water supply scheme has eased the life of the women folk. Repeated messaging of the indicators of normal life through word of mouth, and by drawing attention to what appears in the print media and in the radio will indirectly build the image of the force. Directly attributing good work to the Army or the government will be viewed with suspicion and would lose its salience. There can however be no fixed methodology in how intelligence operatives should deliver the message. It would best be left to the situation as existing on the ground but must be an indirect approach.

To exploit psyops in a neighbouring hostile country, we need to develop own intelligence capability to mount such campaigns proactively in enemy population bases. Psyops must form an important component of own war fighting strategy and must be part of the overall operational plan. This would take years to develop and would require long term investment in sources. But the payoffs can be tremendous.

Against Pakistan, the scope is endless as the country has fissiparous tendencies and ongoing insurgencies in many areas. Against China, the situation in Tibet and Xinjiang could be exploited. Techniques and modalities to be used are beyond the scope of this paper and are best left to the agencies themselves. However, they would require specialised language skills, great cultural sensitivity and in depth knowledge of the people, their hopes and aspirations, fault lines in society and other such information to enable effective exploitation. Powerful radio transmitters on own side of the border could be effectively used here. The scope is endless, the field being limited only by the imagination of the operatives and the requirements of the operational plan.

The Challenges

The covert intelligence operations demand high degree of coordination to maintain secrecy of the operatives and the overall plan of operations. The intelligence operatives will have to be specially trained to conduct such activities. The intelligence agencies would require unstinted political and military support to discharge their specialised roles as above.

The intelligence agencies can effectively fulfill above mentioned roles only if the necessary infrastructure and cover up action plan is institutionalised on priority. In order to achieve desired results of our psy ops campaign, it is imperative that requisite intelligence capabilities be created and coordinated with the perception management campaign.

Analysis & Recommendations

With the growth of mass media, it is now possible to evolve an asymmetric situation in a confrontation by projecting fault lines of the enemy nation and highlighting positive aspects of own government's strategy[4]. The mass media boom can be effectively exploited by the intelligence agencies to assist security forces in their perception management plan. As of now, perception management does not form an integral part of the commander's operational objective in the areas where insurgency is being combated by the Army. There is therefore no role for intelligence agencies in the process, despite the fact that said agencies are working independently on some of the issues which relate to perception management. This must change.

That intelligence agencies can contribute a great deal in the information war has been recognised by the US and other Western powers. The US is now looking into doctrinal issues to integrate intelligence with psyops as highlighted in Chapter 3. We need to formulate a doctrine for perception management in which issues pertaining to exploiting intelligence capability must be included.

Our organisational structures for perception management already have intelligence linkages. The Directorate General of Military Intelligence (DGMI) has under its ambit the Additional Directorate General of Public Information (ADGPI) dedicated towards dissemination of information. By virtue of it being a part of the DGMI, the ADG PI is in a position to utilise the inputs of DGMI for coordination of perception management efforts. Information Warfare (IW) subunits of ADGPI have been instituted in Command and Corps Headquarters level which are performing well in the Northeast and in J&K. However, ADGPI needs to have an intelligence cell staffed by personnel who have experience and expertise in intelligence operations to better integrate intelligence inputs in to the psyops campaign.

The co-opting of intelligence agencies in the national level perception management mechanism leaves much to be desired. The ministry of Information and Broadcasting and inter-ministerial group that coordinates the tasking of the various agencies in this sector have not utilised the potential of the intelligence agencies in perception management. It is imperative that concerted efforts are made to co-opt intelligence agencies in the perception management mechanism (inter-ministerial group) at the national level for optimal utilisation of their potential in this field[5].

Notes

[1] Maj Gen Dhruv Katoch, SM, VSM (Retd), Director, CLAWS during seminar titled 'Perception Management of Indian Army' on 21 February 2012

[2] http://www.washingtonpost.com/world/asia_pacific/afghans-protest-improper-disposal-of-koran-at-us-base/2012/02/21/gIQAjhBqQR_story.html accessed online on 27 mar 2012

[3] B. Raman, Intelligence: Past, Present, and Future (New Delhi, India: Lancer Publishers & Distributors, 2002),p.295

[4] B. Raman, Intelligence: Past, Present, and Future (New Delhi, India: Lancer Publishers & Distributors, 2002), p.297

[5] Anil Bhat, 'Information and Security, Where Truth lies?' (Manas, 2008), pp.65-92

4

ANALYSIS: PERFORMANCE OF INDIAN INTELLIGENCE AGENCIES SINCE INDEPENDENCE

"In the intelligence community I am told that the threat is now called multi-faceted or multi-directional, which actually means that we are not very sure what it is or where it's coming from."

Field Marshal Peter Inge, Chief of the General Staff, 1994

The success of intelligence agencies remains a secret since numerous threats or incidents have been prevented in the past. However, their inability to prevent some incidents is widely reported. The contribution of the intelligence community to the victory over Pakistan in 1971, successful counter intelligence programme before 1974 and 1998 nuclear tests, restoration of normalcy in Mizoram and Punjab has been scantly attributed to intelligence agencies. However, the 1962 War or Kargil Intrusion or Mumbai Terrorist Strikes have been widely reported as 'intelligence failures'.[1] The documents show that the US intelligence failed to warn its decision makers about India's nuclear tests despite tracking nuclear weapons potential since 1950s.[2] It was a matter of great pride for India's intelligence community that US intelligence could fathom their counter intelligence efforts in this case. The technical intelligence capabilities of R&AW established during Kargil War that General Pervez Musharraf, Pakistan's Chief of the Army Staff (COAS) was in daily telephonic contact with Lt Gen Mohammad Aziz, the Chief of the General Staff (CGS), in Rawalpindi from his hotel room in Beijing during Kargil. We could provide a proof to the international community of what

Pakistan had been denying till then.[3] The media and critics ignored these conversations intercepted by the R&AW, while evaluating their performance after 26/11 'intelligence failure'. It is recommended that few operations or incidents where the intelligence played a role in their successful conduct should always be mentioned by analysts while examining the performance of our intelligence agencies. There is ample information available in the open domain about these operations but the scholars may find it difficult to locate these at one place. With this as a backdrop, few well known historical intelligence lapses both abroad and in India have been included as Appendix F. The cases of successful intelligence operations have been compiled in Appendix G. It now, adds the requisite balance to the analysis.

It is imperative that we should be pulling a leaf out of these successes as well. The common fallacy is to directly link intelligence agencies to prevention of any security lapse in the country. The other organs of state such as political leadership or security forces are mostly understood to have done their bit which may or may not be true. The above correlation is not based on facts but on presumption of the most obvious assessment.

The report card of Indian intelligence agencies for the last six decades has been positive when we also take into account their unreported successes besides noting their sub optimal performance. However, in some cases the intelligence agencies failed to connect the dots and draw out coherent assessments. Also, in some cases they couldn't coordinate the sharing of information amongst them; hence complete information wasn't available leading to incoherent evaluation. The same is being argued in this chapter with the help of a few case studies.

The sub optimal performance of intelligence agencies are widely and loosely referred to as 'intelligence failures'. Firstly, let us define 'intelligence failure' which the intelligence agencies are often held responsible for. "An intelligence failure is essentially a misunderstanding of the situation that leads a government (or its military forces) to take actions that are inappropriate and counterproductive to its own interests. Whether it is subjectively surprised by what happens is less important than the fact that the government or the military is doing or continues to do the wrong thing. Intelligence failure is defined, as the outcome of the inadequacies within the intelligence cycle. The intelligence cycle itself consists of six steps that are constantly in motion."

The Central Intelligence Agency (CIA) regards intelligence failure as a systemic organisational surprise resulting from incorrect, missing, discarded, or inadequate hypotheses. However, intelligence errors are factual inaccuracies in analysis resulting from poor or missing data.[4] This definition appears to be more rational and logical.

It is quite clear from above that intelligence agencies alone can't be blamed for intelligence failures which are actually systemic failures. They may be blamed at best for wrong analysis. There can be an inaccuracy at any stage in the intelligence process and thereby incorrect analysis is produced. Policy decisions based on this analysis are likely to be faulty. This inherent shortcoming of intelligence is by no means specific to India: they have been observed across countries. "Comparative studies also demonstrate that these are usually intractable. Intelligence failures are thus unavoidable".[5]

The intelligence agencies are used primarily as a device intended to provide early warning of enemy strength and intensions. They are also used as a supplier of raw information and considered assessment on the basis of which policies; strategies and tactics can be constructed. However, there have been instances where performance of our intelligence agencies has been sub optimal in either or in both of the above uses. These instances are being covered in this chapter as case studies of sub optimal performance of our intelligence agencies.

The 1962 War

The 1962 Indo China War is one of the most apt case studies of suboptimal performance of a country in war due to wrong and pre-conceived intelligence assessment. The 1962 War with China brought to light several problems with the then existing intelligence process. It became apparent that the IB had provided information from time to time, before the actual conflict on Chinese forces in Tibet and its September 7, 1962 report was one such. But by themselves these pieces of information were useless, unless properly collated and analysed".[6]

Most of the books pertaining to the 1962 War bring out a common observation that the IB which was the only intelligence agency worth its name at that time, prepared periodic assessments of Chinese disposition, movements, strength and build-up and forwarded it directly to the government. At that time, it was responsible for both internal as well as external intelligence. It also took upon itself the task of assessment as well, thus sidelining Joint Intelligence Committee (JIC). The same statement has been amplified by many analysts and is covered in succeeding paragraphs:

> "The JIC, however, was defunct. It continued to function only as principal but not exclusive assessment machinery of Government of India. Its Chairman, a senior ministry of external affairs (MEA) official, had no prior exposure to intelligence, and by his own admission he was unable to get the Committee to function in a coordinated manner. The directorate of military intelligence was a key component of the JIC. But it neither possessed independent intelligence sources nor was effective in producing threat assessments. In consequence, the IB's inputs were not subjected to rigorous analysis and their political and military import was not well understood".[7]

"The JIC it is said did not really question the veracity of the IB information. The IB abrogated to itself the task of intelligence collection and decided what to do with it".[8] "No one questioned the credentials of the IB to provide advice rather than provide information, or the unjustified jump in the logic of its argument, that Chinese reluctance to engage in confrontation in the past necessarily guaranteed such inactivity in the future."[9] The JIC accepted the conclusions of the IB and presented a report indicating the danger from Chinese Tibet.[10]

The IB was tasked not just to collect information but also to make assessments pertaining to prospective Chinese responses. The same agency was involved in intelligence collection as well as making an assessment of its own information. It led to violation of the fundamental principle that the reporting agency should not be the only agency involved in assessing its own reports. Much of the information provided by the agency was assimilated in a manner that matched its preconceptions. The intelligence collection was faulty and it was neither properly collated nor disseminated. There was also the problem of the attitude of its end users.[11]

"The most important factor which marred the performance of intelligence agencies was the political leadership's background assumptions about the unfolding crisis. At least since the end of 1950, Nehru had discounted the possibility of a major attack by China owing to international factors."[12] "Nehru as a user wouldn't allow China to attack India as that could compel India to move closer to the Americans."[13] He was relying on international intervention when he discounted the possibility of Chinese attack. From late 1959, Nehru also believed that the Soviet Union would act as a restraining force on China. The political environment at that time didn't pay much attention to possibility of war which induced intelligence agencies to a state of inertia. Furthermore, Nehru believed that by means of prudent management, the crisis could be prevented from going critical.[14]

Analysis of China War

It emerges from above that there was unprocessed information available with the intelligence agencies regarding a likely Chinese attack; however, they failed in assessing the intentions of the adversary. Many other organs of the State also, directly or indirectly, contributed towards faulty assessment of enemy intentions. It wasn't a case of 'intelligence failure' only but a systemic failure.

The Political leadership and IB fell into the trap of "Mirror Imaging" wherein both believed the view of each other which coincided with their own view that Chinese would not react sharply to Indian moves and would not like to escalate the situation. Post incident analysis has revealed that the intelligence was available but we failed in making a correct assessment. The major problem was lack of coordination of information amongst agencies, and regular input sharing with the JIC, the apex intelligence assessment agency. [15]

The Kargil War

During the summer of 1999, India and Pakistan fought a 10-week limited war in Kargil, a remote area of Kashmir. The post war analyses and Kargil Review Committee (KRC) constituted officially to examine the lapses during the Kargil intrusion, have widely reported that the indicators of heightened activity by Pakistan were available with the intelligence agencies, security forces and in turn, to policy makers yet; coherent intelligence assessment couldn't be arrived at. The available information and views of analysts is enumerated in succeeding paragraphs.

Leading security analyst Srinath Raghvan remarked that:

> "As early as June 1998, the IB reported 'increased activities at the border and continuing endeavour to infiltrate a large group of foreign mercenaries.' It also reported 'increased movement' of Pakistan Army opposite the Kargil sector. Importantly, this report was issued by the director IB; but bypassing the JIC (now subsumed under the National Security Council Secretariat) and the Research and Analysis Wing (R&AW) it was sent directly to the Prime Minister and the Home Minister as well as the Director General of Military Operations. The military intelligence assessed that the inputs were consistent with the heightened activity in the aftermath of the nuclear tests of May 1998."[16]

"In October, the R&AW reported that Pakistan appeared to be making all possible attempts to interdict Drass-Kargil highway resorting to sporadic shelling. The report also observed that 'a limited swift offensive threat with possible support of alliance partners cannot be ruled out.' However, when the Army Headquarters sought further details on possible locations where such an attack might be undertaken, neither the R&AW nor the JIC responded with clarifications or elaborations".[17]

Keki N Daruwalla, former Chairman, JIC wrote that, in Nov 1998, the IB had reported that Pakistan was training Talibans who were learning Balti and Ladakhi language besides undergoing military training and were likely to be infiltrated into Kargil area sometime during April 1999. This report was sent to only 121 Infantry Brigade. A fixed mindset worked towards swift offensive not an unorthodox encroachment holding operation directed towards changing the face of Line of Control and interdicting the highway. No further reports and assessment were sought by intelligence and security agencies. Coordination in intelligence has seldom been our strong point.[18]

B Raman writes that "Kargil was not only due to a lack of adequate intelligence inputs from the agencies, it was in equal measure due to the inability of the assessment machinery to make effective use of the even available inputs due to various reasons, some of which were beyond its control." [19]

The developments of 1998, as reported in various intelligence inputs, notably the increased shelling of Kargil, the reported increased presence of militants in the Force Commander Northern Area (FCNA) region and their training were assessed as indicative of a likely high level of militant activity in Kargil in the summer of 1999 and the consequent possibility of increased infiltration in this area.[20]

The Kargil Review Committee (KRC) Report, published in 2000, noticed serious deficiencies at various levels of the intelligence collection, operational process and coordinated sharing of inputs. JIC which was responsible for overall assessment couldn't connect the dots optimally.[21] Much of the information provided by the agencies was assimilated in a manner that fit their preconceptions. The function of intelligence agencies is not merely to inform, but to assess. But the evidence gathered by Kargil Review Committee shows that intelligence was available; what was missing was its assessment.[22] The KRC also remarked "There is a general lack of awareness of the critical importance and the need for assessment at all levels. JIC report doesn't receive the attention they deserve at the political and bureaucratic levels. The assessment process has been downgraded in importance."[23] The 1999 Kargil Crisis has been widely perceived as a failure of the Indian intelligence. However, little effort has been made to examine the analytical origins of this 'failure'.[24]

Analysis of the Kargil Intrusion

It can be concluded from above that there were inaccuracies and lack of coordination in the collection of information and its dissemination. It led to inaccurate, biased and inadequate analysis and assessment. The 'intelligence failure' in this case can also be attributed to inappropriate response to the produced intelligence. The political leadership and security agencies believed what they wanted to believe. The intelligence agencies did nothing substantial to make them believe otherwise. "Shortcomings in collection can be attributed to the intelligence agencies; but those in analysis and response tend to be as much failures of the political-strategic leadership as of any agency".[25] In both 1962 and Kargil War, the intelligence agencies could rightly claim to have provided several inputs germane to the attack.[26] The Indian intelligence agencies accurately assessed Pakistani intentions prior to the Kargil Crisis. Where they went wrong was in predicting the specific form in which these would be enacted.[27]

The intelligence agencies probably couldn't correlate the events preceding Kargil intrusion since the Pakistan Army made excellent use of stealth and deception in the run-up to the operation. The Pakistan ISI could manage a successful counter intelligence plan thereby putting our intelligence agencies off the track. Indian agencies could not pick up any of the tell-tale indicators which indicated preparation for attack such as induction of additional troops, logistics build-up, and improvement in communications. Our agencies were deceived in believing that the Pakistanis were conducting these activities as preparation for infiltration of militants since they were done in traditional infiltration areas. Indeed, even after the incursion was detected the Indians remained unclear about the composition of the intruding force.

The intelligence assessments prepared by our intelligence agencies remained focused on the possibility of Pakistan attempting increased infiltration. Our intelligence agencies probably did not anticipate an intrusion of this scale. This was presumed to be such since Pakistan has been mostly attempting only infiltration in that area. The inaccessible terrain in this area probably led our security agencies to believe that such an intrusion was not likely to succeed in the Kargil sector. The military also was surprised since infiltrators had never learnt to hold position and ground to fight proxy war. The agencies discounted the possibility of Pakistan misadventure in this area also under presumption that the Shiite population of Kargil was unlikely to support Pakistan. Our agencies overlooked the indicators and formed their assessment based on logic even though developments in that area defied logic.

The political leadership was upbeat with improved relations with Pakistan and assumed that the state of India Pakistan relations disregarded the possibility of such an intrusion. India's conventional and nuclear superiority also prompted our policy makers to confer to the assessment of our agencies.

Much of the information provided by the agencies was assimilated in a manner that fit their preconceptions.

From the case of Kargil, it appears that mirror-imaging can creep into warning analysis through inputs from intelligence consumers. When strong-minded consumers, such as military officials, develop fixed ideas about how the enemy will behave, intelligence analysts might end up internalising these ideas. The result is that intelligence producers fail to warn of threats which their consumers do not believe exist.[28]

There were four intelligence agencies involved in intelligence process relevant to this war namely R&AW, MI, IB and finally, the JIC. These agencies in some form or the other had assessed a likely attempt by Pakistan but they failed in predicting the specific form in which these would be enacted. All these agencies individually and collectively including security forces did not consider the possibility of a Pakistani miscalculation. This case study can be studied as a systemic failure not as a case of failure of intelligence only.

The 26/11 Mumbai Terrorists Strike

Terrorist strikes on 26 Nov 2008 at Mumbai, the economic capital of India, killing 164 people and wounding at least 308 once again exposed the gap in the Indian security set up. Once again, the unprocessed information indicating a terrorist strike at Mumbai was available with our intelligence agencies but processing of intelligence was off the mark. The same is amplified in succeeding paragraphs.

"The first intelligence inputs on impending 26/11 were received in mid-September by the liaison branch of R&AW. This input was not passed on to the analysis branch of the agency and was instead shared directly with other agencies without due processing or embellishment. Had this intelligence been analysed and processed by the production branch of the agency, perhaps greater focus and emphasis could have been added to the advisory that was sent out This flawed procedure was repeated when the second input arrived on November 13. Even then there was a systemic failure to process the information by the concerned branch. Once again a raw input, without context and analysis was immediately rushed to the other agencies.

Perhaps, this was a key reason why the input did not get the attention that it deserved". [29]

In December 2006, the Mumbai police had received an intelligence input that Pakistani terrorists could enter the city in the guise of fishermen.[30] In March 2007, based on the information of IB, Mumbai Police killed eight Pakistani (LeT) terrorists who had come for suicide attack at Mumbai.[31] Later, intercepts were again received by IB, that Pakistan has been making repeated attempts to attack lucrative targets and public places in Mumbai but nothing much was made of this information probably, being generic in nature.[32]

"A September 24th intercept with R&AW's signal intelligence indicated that an operation was being planned by the LeT. A few days earlier, the CIA station chief in Delhi had warned his R&AW counterpart that a terrorist group was planning a strike in Mumbai that would come from the sea. R&AW's international listening posts also picked up intercepts that the Taj Hotel would be one of the targets. The SIM cards recovered from the nine terrorists killed in the operation confirms this intelligence input. The cards were procured from various countries, including Austria (Vienna) and the US (New Jersey). Three were procured from Calcutta".[33]

Analysis of Mumbai Terrorist Strikes

It becomes clear from above that the agencies had apparently issued a stream of warnings in the months preceding the attacks: the latest one being given as late as 18 November 2008. However, they failed to look for indicators for a likely event and connect the dots to draw the complete picture and take requisite measures to avoid re-occurrence of incidents. The generic information of a likely terrorist strike was available with the intelligence agencies but they either ignored it or lacked imaginative mind to make correct assessment from these inputs. Even generic information was reluctantly shared by intelligence agencies and coordination to make holistic assessment was lacking. While there was a plethora of information from various security and intelligence agencies, an inability to connect the dots proved to be a fatal flaw.

Post incident analysis of almost all recent terrorist attacks in hinterland whether Mumbai, Jaipur, Ahmedabad, Bengaluru, New Delhi or Malegaon has revealed that information of impending attacks was available with intelligence agencies or their subsidiaries but we as a nation couldn't beat these incidents. A huge volume of information of generic nature was collected by intelligence agencies but they couldn't make the correct assessment. In some cases, even assessment was correct but we couldn't coordinate our timely response.

Conclusive Analysis

From the above case studies, it clearly emerges that there was ample information available with the intelligence agencies regarding a likely attack; however, they failed in making a holistic assessment. In many cases they did make an imaginative and correct assessment but failed to coordinate this assessment before approaching the decision makers.

The common trend across the countries in such cases of national security failures is that the public avoids blaming policymakers for their mishandling of the national security portfolio but conveniently starts blaming the intelligence community for their inability to effectively support the policy. However, a paradigm shift in nature of national security challenges facing the country today has to be acknowledged. The effective response to any unforeseen security challenge necessitates three prongs namely Intelligence, decision makers and reaction elements who respond to the produced intelligence to remain in the same grid and work as a team to read the situation continuously and react within the shortest possible time. The intelligence gathering and assessment making infrastructure, decision makers and reaction elements are recommended to be meshed into one single point of contact which could have reduced the reaction time of our response to such attacks.

An analyst, may assess an adversary's capability correctly, but may misjudge a particular intention of his adversary. It may happen not because of non availability of inputs, but because of what information is missing in between. The lack of intelligence coordination between intelligence agencies leads to 'information gaps'. The above analysis finds a strong supporter in American strategic analyst Rob Johnston when he comments, "The failure to determine an adversary's intention may simply be the result of missing information or, just as likely; it may be the result of missing hypotheses or mental models about an adversary's potential behavior".[34]

Notes

[1] Prem Mahadevan , "The Politics of Counter-Terrorism in India — Strategic Intelligence and National Security in South Asia"; I.B. Tauris & Co, London,2012 p.13

[2] Jeffrey Richelson, *U.S. Intelligence and the Indian Bomb,* http://www.gwu.edu/~nsarchiv/NSAEBB/NSAEBB187/index.htm

[3] B.Raman, " Did Musharraf Tell Nawaz About Kargil Plans?, Global Geopolitics Net , June 06, 2008 accessed online through http://ramanstrategicanalysis.blogspot.com/ on 17 Dec2011

[4] Official website of CIA accessed online at https://www.cia.gov/library/center-for-the-study-of-intelligence/csi-publications/books-and-monographs/analytic-culture-in-the-u-s-intelligence-co accessed online at 15 Mar 2011

[5] Srinath Raghavan "Intelligence failures and reforms" accessed online via http://www.india-seminar.com/2009/599/599_srinath_raghavan.htm on 17 Dec2011

[6] Srinath Raghavan, „ Intelligence failures and reforms" , #599, July 2009,p.3

[7] Srinath Raghavan, "Intelligence failures and reforms" , #599, July 2009,p.3

[8] General KV Krishna Rao , 'Prepare or perish' (Lancer 1991) pp104-105

[9] Dr Sarvapalli Gopal – the distinguished historian and biographer of Nehru as quoted by Dr Bhashyam Kasturi in "Intelligence services - Analysis, Organisation and Function", (Lancer Publication ,1995)p. 40

[10] V Longer, The Defence and Foreign Policies of India ,(Sterling ,1988), p.47

[11] Steve Hoffman, India and the China Crisis , (California,1991), p.18

[12] Srinath Raghavan "Intelligence failures and reforms" accessed online via http://www.india-seminar.com/2009/599/599_srinath_raghavan.htm on 17 Dec2011

[13] Srinath Raghavan, War and Peace in Modern India: A Strategic History of the Nehru Years, (Permanent Black, New Delhi, Delhi, 2009), p.91-97

[14] Srinath Raghavan "Intelligence failures and reforms" accessed online via http://www.india-seminar.com/2009/599/599_srinath_raghavan.htm on 17 Dec2011

[15] Dr Bhashyam Kasturi , Intelligence services - Analysis, Organisation and Function (Lancer,New Delhi , 1995) p. 40

[16] Srinath Raghavan , "Intelligence failures and reforms" accessed online via http://www.india-seminar.com/2009/599/599_srinath_raghavan.htm on 17 Dec2011

[17] Ibid

[18] Keki N Daruwalla , former Chairman , JIC , *The Hindustan Times*, 05 Sept 2001

[19] B. Raman, Intelligence: Past, Present, and Future, (Lancer, New Delhi, 2002),p .349

[20] Executive Summary of the Kargil Review Committee Report as presented in Rajya Sabha, 25 Feburary, 2000, accessed on line at http://rajyasabha.nic.in/25indi1.htm#8

[21] 'From Surprise To Reckoning,Kargil Committee Report' -Executive Summary accessed online via http://nuclearweaponarchive.org/India/KargilRCA.html On 20 Sept 2010

[22] Bhashyam Kasturi "Intelligence Process and Kargil" accessed online via http://www.ipcs.org/article/india/intelligence-process-and-kargil-359.html on 05 Jan 2012

[23] K Subrahmanyam, *Surprise to Reckoning: The Kargil Review Committee Report* (Sage, New Delhi, 2000),p.238

[24] Prem Mahadevan, " The Perils of Prediction: Indian Intelligence and the Kargil Crisis" (CLAWS, Manekshaw Paper number 29,2011),p.1

[25] Richard K. Betts, Enemies of Intelligence: Knowledge and Power in American National Security,(Columbia University Press, New York, 2007)p.37

[26] Srinath Raghavan "Intelligence failures and reforms" accessed online via http://www.india-seminar.com/2009/599/599_srinath_raghavan.htm on 17 Dec2011

[27] Prem Mahadevan, " The Perils of Prediction: Indian Intelligence and the Kargil Crisis" (CLAWS, Manekshaw Paper number 29,2011),p.1

[28] Richards J. Heuer, *Psychology of Intelligence Analysis*, Center For The Study of Intelligence, Central Intelligence Agency,1999, pp.111-115

[29] Interview with a senior Indian intelligence official, used by Saikat Datta in his article "Creating a successful intelligence and counter-terrorism matrix: Lessons from 26/11" published in CLAWS Journal Summer 2011

[30] "IB warned terrorists would interlude by sea" India Today, 28 NOV 2008, accessed online at http"//indiatoday.digitaltoday.in/index. php? option=com-content & task=view &id=21192 on 14 Oct 2011

[31] Praveen Swami, 'Mumbai: The road to Maximum Terror',SAIR,15Dec 2008,Vol VII/23, accessed online at http://satp.org/satporgtp/sair/archives/7-23.htm#assessment1 , on 13 Sept 2011

[32] The Politics of Counter-Terrorism in India — Strategic Intelligence and National Security in South Asia, Prem Mahadevan; I.B. Tauris & Co, London,2012 p.150

[33] Saikat Datta, Smruti Koppikar & Dola Mitra , "The Armies of The Night", Outlook issue dated December 15, 2008 accessed online at http://www.outlookindia.com/article. aspx? 239225 on 23 Nov 2011

[34] Dr. Rob Johnston, "Analytical Culture in the US Intelligence Community, An Ethnographic Study ",(Washington DC, 2005) , p.12

5

ASSESSMENT AND COORDINATION CHALLENGES

"To lack intelligence is to be in the ring blindfolded."

General David M. Shoup
Former Commandant of the Marine Corps

Analysing one's own mistakes and recommending remedial measures should not be considered as a negative and counterproductive activity. In the United States, intelligence coordination and assessment were highlighted as significant shortfalls after 9/11. Even American intelligence agencies (which are being looked at with awe and admiration by whole world post 'Operation Neptune Star' have also been criticised at one point of time to the extent as quoted below

"The 9/11 Commission found that the (American) intelligence community suffered from a lack of institutional imagination before the September 11 attacks. This made it impossible for most analysts and policymakers to accurately gauge the terrorist threat." [1]

However, American analysts in the same breath have noted some scope for improvement in our set up as well. James Burch comments "India's intelligence apparatus does not operate under a well defined set of laws and coordination between intelligence agencies remains an endemic problem. Its independent assessment capability has not been properly resourced and bureaucratic infighting greatly inhibits the ability of the executive to coordinate and direct intelligence efforts. Lastly, India's almost total lack of executive and legislative oversight severely limits accountability and the ability to reform the system."[2]

The above example must motivate us to take constructive 'fault finding' in a positive manner. Intelligence agencies need to look inwards to identify these challenges to intelligence assessment and coordination at the national level. An honest admission of ground realities will only pave path for self improvement in organisational and national interest.

On numerous occasions as discussed in the previous chapters, the intelligence assessment and coordination at the national level has been sub optimal. This has led to embarrassing situations and has been detrimental to the national security. A holistic and critical analysis of our intelligence assessment and coordination set up at the national level has been carried in this chapter to outline the challenges to coherent intelligence assessment and coordination.

Lack of Suitable Supervisory Mechanism

We have a number of intelligence agencies in the country today, each functioning in their own watertight compartment. The agencies prefer to share the information on a selective basis and follow a rigid chain of command of reporting. There is no single authority to coordinate the assessment of various intelligence agencies. The existing supervisory mechanism is often by passed and has gone through numerous stages of reorganisation and disbandment. As a result, intelligence assessment and coordination at the national level is not of the desired standards. The following example as observed by KRC related to Kargil says it all:

> "The Intelligence Bureau (IB) is meant to collect intelligence within the country and is the premier agency for counter-intelligence. This agency got certain inputs on activities in the FCNA region which were considered important enough by the Director, IB to be communicated over his signature on June 2, 1998 to the Prime Minister, Home Minister, Cabinet Secretary, Home Secretary and Director-General Military Operations. This communication was not addressed to the three officials most concerned with this information, namely, Secretary (R&AW), who is responsible for

external intelligence and had the resources to follow up the leads in the IB report; Chairman JIC, who would have taken such information into account in JIC assessments; and Director-General Military Intelligence. Director, IB stated that he expected the information to filter down to these officials through the official hierarchy. This did not happen in respect of Secretary (R&AW) who at that time was also holding additional charge as Chairman, JIC. The Committee feels that a communication of this nature should have been directly addressed to all the officials concerned."[3]

There is a need to appoint an appropriate nodal agency enjoying acceptance from all agencies. It would be based on the principle of primacy of Intelligence and establish a rule of accountability. The others will automatically follow and minor issues can be refined. This would also lead to enhancement of accountability of Intelligence agencies.[4]

Prior to the Kargil War the Joint Intelligence Committee (JIC) was tasked to coordinate the assessment from all intelligence agencies, but it did not have the requisite authority to task any of the agencies which made the whole system futile. The instructions issued after the Sino Indian War of 1962 had laid down that weekly and periodic meetings of JIC should be attended by officers of the rank of at least Joint secretary or its equivalent from the agencies and the user departments; and that the quarterly meetings on policy matters should be attended by the heads of the agencies and user departments. However, the instructions were reportedly not followed. The meetings of JIC were reportedly attended by the lower rank officers and every agency reportedly wanted direct access to the apex level political authority, the Prime Minister. [5]

JIC was merged with the National Security Council (NSC) and was made a secretariat of NSC in 1999 as per the recommendations of the Kargil Review Committee. However, it apparently lacks appropriate authority and each agency probably continues to report to its own political controllers, therefore, lacks in making comprehensive assessment. The coordinating agency without requisite authority and universal acceptance cannot achieve its target.[6]

There is a greater possibility of political misuse of a technical intelligence

(TECHINT) organisation than that of a human intelligence (HUMINT) organisation. Therefore, they have to be subjected to even more strict external controls than HUMINT organisations. JIC still lacks the teeth due to lack of unanimous and unambiguous authority.[7]

Presently, the supervisory mechanism for intelligence assessment related to terrorism is also not up to the mark. Refurbishing the terror combat infrastructure after the 26/11 Mumbai terrorist attacks, the government made the Multi-Agency Centre (MAC) nodal agency for intelligence assessment as well. However, the setting up of NCTC for overall supervision and coordination of intelligence related to terrorism has got delayed due to opposition from certain State Governments. It has made the need for supervisory mechanism for intelligence agencies an inescapable requirement.

Plethora of Intelligence Agencies

In 1947, India had only two intelligence agencies: the Intelligence Bureau (IB) and Military Intelligence (MI). Now, it has eight such agencies: the IB, the Directorate-General of Security, the R&AW, the Directorates-General of Military Intelligence, Air Intelligence, Naval Intelligence, the Defence Intelligence Agency (DIA) and the National Technical Research Organisation.[8] Multi Agency Centre (MAC), Joint Task Force on Intelligence (JTFI), National Investigation Agency (NIA), and proposed National Counter Terrorism Centre (NCTC) has been added in the last decade and are primarily dealing with terrorism. [9]

Narcotics Control Bureau (NCB), Directorate of Revenue Intelligence (DRI), Economic Intelligence Unit (EIU), Economic Offences Wing (EOW) of Delhi Police only adds to the long list above. The proposed setting up of a new Maritime Intelligence and Coastal Security Centre or a centre for Nuclear and Missile Intelligence will only add up to the list of the plethora of intelligence agencies. [10]

Today, almost every paramilitary and police force has its own intelligence network. The BSF (G) deployed along the borders of J&K is facing coordination problem with Military Intelligence and R&AW. Even the CRPF has unofficially created its own intelligence wing even though it has not been approved by the Ministry of Finance till date. The CRPF intelligence wing is further compounding the problem of intelligence coordination as IB,

State Police Intelligence Wing and at times, R&AW are already involved in intelligence collection on the same issues.[11]

Joint Intelligence Committee (JIC) and National Security Council Secretariat (NSCS) is responsible for making assessments at national level after taking inputs from all above agencies directly or indirectly.[12] 'It is natural that JIC has not been effective since there are too many cooks who can only spoil the broth'. The enormity of the task entrusted to JIC can be better understood if we analyse the wide canvas of roles of these agencies. The role of these intelligence agencies has been discussed in detail in Appendix E.

Intelligence agencies are reluctant to share actionable intelligence with each other. But, superfluous information of generic information is definitely shared with other agencies leading to information overload and making the task of assessment making and coordination more difficult.[13] "Certain external challenges to national security, infamous Kargil episode included have proved that the prime intelligence organisations and investigative agencies have failed to exchange, process and evaluate crucial intelligence continually.[14]

The observation of KRC related to the performance of intelligence agencies is quoted below to amplify the challenges of intelligence community. "While the intelligence agencies focused on ammunition dumping on the other side, they lacked adequate knowledge about the heavy damage inflicted by the Indian Artillery which would have required the Pakistani army to undertake considerable repairs and re-stocking. That would partly explain the larger vehicular movements reported on the other side. The Indian Army did not share information about the intensity and effect of its firing with others. In the absence of this information, R&AW could not correctly assess the significance of enemy activity in terms of ammunition storage or construction of underground bunkers. This provides another illustration of lack of inter-agency coordination as well as lack of coordination between the Army and the agencies.[15]

Owing to large number of agencies, the sharing of intelligence becomes difficult. Ideally, intelligence should be collected both horizontally and vertically, thus making the job more arduous. In any case, the information age of today has overloaded on our intelligence agencies.

It is observed that over a period, due to increased security challenges, a multiplicity of bodies have mushroomed, doing the same job. Numerous committees have been formed for periodic review of intelligence and security set up at the national level. This has led to an addition of new agencies at times borrowed from US or UK intelligence and security set up. However, the review committees probably overlooked the need to recommend the disbandment of previous agencies before recommending addition/creation of new investigative agencies. With the creation of additional organisations focused on intelligence, there has been a corresponding increase in bureaucratisation. This adds to the challenge of sharing information.

The large numbers of agencies also create a problem of intelligence coordination. As the number of agencies involved increase, the coordination amongst them becomes more complex. The large number of intelligence agencies also provides ideal ground for battle of turfs. These agencies have been added at different stages as piece meal reaction to the complex problem of national security. The decision makers have not taken a holistic view of the problem and hence the problem has got compounded. The remedy to the problem of inadequately performing institutions cannot be the creation of new institutions, but enabling the existing organisations to perform. A relevant quote from Maloy Krishna Dhar, Former Joint Director, IB is reproduced below

"Serious gap of communication between the IB and the State Police on one hand and the IB and the R&AW and CBI on the other had become apparent during security operations in Punjab, Kashmir, Assam and against the Pakistan sponsored jihadist element. The most glaring example of total intelligence failure was the Kargil adventure by Pakistan Army. The R&AW, the MI and to a lesser extent the IB had miserably failed to unearth the Pakistani design and warn the policy planners. Whatever intelligence was available was not coordinated to cull out a coherent collage .The rest is history".[16]

The 'Turf War'

"While the charter of agencies has been by and large well defined, undue obsession of the agencies over the sphere of activities sometimes leads to a loss of focus wherein the overall objective of safeguarding the national interests is sidelined to promote one's own agency." [17] Healthy competitiveness, which is so essential for excellence, must in fact be encouraged so that timely and accurate intelligence is available. But agencies at times get too possessive of their domain which is unhealthy.

The 'turf war' is one of the gravest systemic challenges the Indian intelligence faces today. The 'Turf War' between various intelligence agencies at times jeopardising national cause has been regularly voiced by defence analysts and media. Unfortunately, intelligence agencies themselves don't acknowledge it. Few reports are quoted below.

Admitting the 'Turf war' between intelligence agencies, CD Sahay, former Director, R&AW, comments "The 'turf war' between intelligence agencies will unfortunately continue to run which is a major lacuna in our intelligence set up." [18] Maloy Krishna Dhar, former Joint Director, IB notes that "There also exists the crying need for cooperation and coordination among Central Intelligence and investigation agencies".[19]

The newspaper *Mail Today,* in a column reports that "there is a clash between R&AW and NTRO". [20] "Turf war between NTRO and R&AW over the use of Unmanned Aerial Vehicle (UAV's) in the Left Wing Extremism affected area was reported by *Mail Today* on 28 June 2011. Despite the fact that the Aviation Research Centre (ARC) has aircraft and expertise for air borne surveillance, the government decided to authorise NTRO to purchase and operate the UAVs. The MI, however, is seeking interception power but it has been limited to gathering HUMINT". [21]

"DIA which reports to National Security Advisor (NSA) is also handicapped because of the lack of HUMINT mainly because resources for Human Intelligence (HUMINT) are with MI at present. MI and R&AW are also fighting over territorial jurisdiction. Official sources revealed that the MI wants to increase its intelligence gathering activity to 80 Km, across the border from current 20 Km. The external agency R&AW, however, insists that they have jurisdiction beyond 20 Km.[22]

Times of India observes "There are also serious differences of opinion among agencies such as the R&AW, IB, NTRO, DIA etc. NTRO is yet to be notified as a monitoring agency because of the objections from IB, while R&AW and IB have concerns about NTRO's efforts to develop analytical capabilities instead of limiting itself to mere collection of TECHINT".[23]

Praveen Swami writes "Though MAC and the JTFI exist; they are not in the best of health. These two bodies are under-staffed, over-worked and ill paid. There is also confusion as to whether the Union Home Ministry or the respective state governments should pay for the expenditure of MAC and JTFI staff." [24]

"This bureaucratic confrontation is attributable to the long standing infighting between the Indian Administrative Service officers who dominate the Home Ministry and the Indian Police Service officers, who constitute the majority of the IB." [25]

"Though the IB is tasked with internal intelligence, it is also responsible for counter intelligence, which frequently concerns the personnel serving in other intelligence agencies such as R &AW as well as the staff of foreign missions in India. This frequently brings it in conflict with the Ministry of External Affairs (MEA) and R&AW. Cross border terrorism, hawala transactions and smuggling of arms and narcotics are areas that concern both IB and R&AW, with each unwilling to let go of its jurisdiction."[26]

Lt Gen KS Khajuria, former DGMI notes "Whereas joint functioning or at least coordination is an essential ingredient to ensure that no single agency either becomes totally dominant or all powerful, there is also the aspect of intra agency competition and jealousy which effectively prevents joint functioning.[27] Maj Gen VK Singh, former R&AW officer endorses that "The confusion and overlap between various agencies is also an area of concern." [28]

Brig Gurmeet Kanwal, former Director, CLAWS, comments "India's intelligence coordination and assessment apparatus at the national level and counter-terrorism policies remain mired in the days of innocence".[29]

The above statements or excerpts have been included to drive home a point that over a period, the 'Turf War' between various agencies has become a major challenge for our intelligence mechanism at the national level. The first step to overcome the problem is to acknowledge it. Let us accept it as a challenge of whatever magnitude we may choose to accept.

Attitude of End Users

Intelligence has never been given requisite priority in our national policy. Theoretically, it may not be true but on ground, intelligence is not given due attention due to the reactive nature of our national security policy. In the US, the session of Congress begins with intelligence briefing to policy makers. In our country, we can't imagine such precedence being followed. The attitude of end users, both political and bureaucratic, greatly affects the utilisation of any information (intelligence). It has been noticed in the past that the attitude of the decision makers have varied widely in time and space based on the political compulsions. At times, such attitudes are expression of political compulsions over riding national interest.

In the words of Lt Gen R K Sawhney (Retd), former DGMI, "In India, intelligence is unfortunately treated with contempt; it is taken for granted and is misused. For intelligence agencies, there are only users not enablers."[30]It leaves intelligence agencies in a state of loss of focus and interest. Policy leaders determine the utility of intelligence they receive based on ideological and political factors. Hence, intelligence gets biased and judgment is altered to suit the view of their customers or further their own interests. [31] Several security analysts and former intelligence officers have pointed out this lack of requisite priority to intelligence by policy makers. Some of them are reproduced below.

Vikram Sood, former Director, R&AW observes with concern that "It is unfortunate that for a country like ours that has had to deal with insurgencies and unending terrorism for sixty years, the political leadership and a civil bureaucracy has viewed the business of intelligence collection with disdain. Efforts to control have usually meant putting roadblocks and reducing intelligence functions to bureaucratic practices." [32]

Maloy Krishna Dhar, former Joint Director, IB comments that "In the absence of a wider public debate, India's parliamentary members rarely discuss or understand the wider implications of India's intelligence issues."[33]

Additionally, abuse of the *Official Secrets Act of 1923* prohibits national security issues from coming into the forefront of public debate.[34]

"The ruling party ensures that a major portion of resources of Intelligence agencies are employed to provide them political intelligence on their rivals. It leads to loss of focus of intelligence agencies from national security duties".[35]

"The nation today suffers from an acute lack of awareness in matters of national security. This deficiency shows up most vividly in the political classes which are unable to comprehend the unified nature of security and intelligence".[36]

Praveen Swami comments "In fact, the IB and the RAW are not formally accountable to the parliament. The lack of an effective oversight structure leads to India's legislature being removed from the process. The Standing Committee on Home Affairs has received briefings on the IB's activities, but few of its members have a background in intelligence or are sufficiently staffed to exercise effective oversight."[37]

Maj Gen Dhruv Katoch, Director, CLAWS candidly points that "Even today, the intelligence gathering and assessment making infrastructure, decision makers and reaction elements have not been meshed into one single point of contact which could have reduced the reaction time of our response to various attacks." [38]

Prem Mahadevan in his book 'The Politics of Counter-Terrorism in India' comments "High consumer expectation and limited collection capabilities is one of the prime external shortcomings of Indian intelligence."[39]

B. Raman, former Additional Secretary, R&AW points "The tendency of our political class to politicise every debate on security issues has been the bane of our national security management".[40]

Lt Gen KS Khajuria, former DGMI comments that "The need for coordination at the highest level is an inescapable factor. It needs to be understood by the governing agencies in perspective and also practiced".[41]

Former R&AW official and Saxena Committee member B Raman

points that "Politicians, were cut off from the work of intelligence organisations, and most of them remained ill-educated about just what they were supposed to do, and were worse informed about what they actually did. Parliament's Standing Committee on Home did receive briefings about the functioning of the IB but few of its members had the requisite knowledge to ask tough questions and demand satisfactory answers. The situation suited everyone, including those in the intelligence world, who were happy with mediocrity."[42] Until the political process takes intelligence seriously, he suggested, Indian intelligence would never improve.[43]

The above quotes highlight the view of security analysts which can't be whisked away any longer. We have run into this problem earlier due to neglect of intelligence as a tool of statecraft and organ of maintaining national security. The attitudinal changes are required to grant requisite priority to intelligence at the national level.

Quality of Manpower

The volume of information, collated by various agencies and those available from open source is enormous; more than 80 percent of such information is available from open source. Processing, evaluation and dissemination of this voluminous data is a huge task. Personnel selected for intelligence tasks, therefore, should have an aptitude and flair for the job.[44] It is a known fact that intelligence is a special activity and we require special personnel for it with special qualities. It can't be treated as recruiting personnel for any other job. "Chaotic selection of personnel and poor human resource management is the main organisational shortcoming of the Indian intelligence."[45]

It has been observed that at numerous occasions, press reports have been used as intelligence without going into the details of the input. Artfully cloaked news reports from international publications are passed off as source reports. Many intelligence operatives would then source these news reports to their "non-existent human source assets" and even claim secret service funds.[46] Such malpractices are likely to be adopted by intelligence operatives who don't meet the desired standards.

"Unfortunately the required talent and expertise or commitment is no longer available in the civil service. The R&AW and the IB need many more professional intelligence officers who are home grown and are assisted by a never ending supply of qualified economists, scientists, computer whiz kids, mathematicians, and experts in international banking and finance".[47]

The above comments further supplement the observation that the job of an analyst is looked at with contempt within intelligence agencies. Everyone wants to work in an operational role due to the glamour attached with it. In any case, intelligence is not a lucrative job in India except when people come into it to look after their own interests. The intelligence operatives today lack analytical depth which is in turn responsible for the failure of intelligence agencies to 'connect the dots'.[48] We have acute shortage of quality analysts in intelligence agencies. The performance of analysts is hampered by their short tenures as they are frequently replaced and posted out in organisational interests.

The importance of analytical mindset can't be over emphasised. Its importance was aptly summed up by Michael Rogers, Chairman United States Intelligence Committee in the US House of representatives while reviewing the Bin Laden operation when he said "One of the most complicated searches for a terrorist in US history, the Bin Laden required years of intelligence collection, analysis and sharing small pieces of information which many officials said were meaningless on their own. However, once the courier was identified, the bits of information began to make sense".[49] It sums up the qualities which need to be imbibed in intelligence personnel in today's context.

Poor recruitment policies for intelligence operatives of today have eroded the ethos and high standards of the past. Bright officers are not opting for intelligence as a career thereby eventually affecting the quality of assessment being produced. The prime intelligence agencies suffer from the "tail-end syndrome" where UPSC bottom-rangers are offered the job.[50] The policy of selection of intelligence operatives needs a relook wherein language experts and personnel of all walks of life can be included in our intelligence community.

Lack of Specialised Training

The IB is facing acute shortage of manpower because it hasn't found the kind of staff it needs and also due to limited training capacity. It can train only 1200 personnel a year, barely covering for retirement[51]. The analyst's job is a specialist job which requires specialists training. However, the training curriculum in most of the intelligence agencies remains out-of-date and too investigative centric. Almost, every intelligence agency has its own training curriculum which doesn't lay down much stress on improving analytical skills. It also affects the coordination amongst intelligence agencies since there is no provision of centralised training for intelligence agencies. As every agency has its own training ethos, the analytical skills developed in intelligence operatives of each agency are sometimes at variance. Accordingly, assessments pertaining to a particular set of inputs also varies, which invariably compounds the problem of coordination amongst these agencies. Common training can be conducted at a national institute/academy of Intelligence which an intelligence operative would join after undergoing his basic training in his parent institute.[52]

The Indian intelligence community is also a victim of "groupthink" that adversely affects our analytical capabilities. Groupthink ushers in a "corporate judgement" which prevents any fresh or alternate thinking or analysis.[53] Intelligence analysts need to be taught analytical techniques in greater details using modern qualitative and quantitative techniques.

Lack of Accountability

> "*We're always trying to improve our intelligence gathering but these groups operate in an* immensely secretive way, it is very, very difficult often to track down exactly what they're *doing . . .*"

- Tony Blair,
Prime Minister of the United Kingdom 30 September, 2001

The above statement underlines the lack of accountability of intelligence agencies across the world, which is given the short shrift by quoting secrecy, leading to loss of efficiency. A greater degree of transparency without sacrificing national security needs has to be implemented similar to all other security agencies.

The damage being done by lack of accountability of intelligence agencies to intelligence assessment and coordination is enormous. The agencies keep sharing generic information without highlighting any worthwhile assessment since their performance is beyond evaluation by users. It may well be the case that success of intelligence agencies is also not reported due to lack of evaluation. The lack of accountability may generate complacency in intelligence agencies which is detrimental to the overall good health of intelligence agencies. Similar views have been echoed by many security analysts which are enumerated below.

"There is total lack of accountability in the operations of such intelligence agencies. Without an element of public scrutiny and parliamentary guidance, these organisations run their ship without much monitoring, thus permitting misuse of authority and functional disorganisation. Undoubtedly, secrecy is essential but the lengths to which people in India go to are ridiculous." [54]

"Unlike in other developed societies such as the USA, where the legislature acts as watchdog on every organ of the executive, including intelligence and security agencies, in India these organisations were beyond the pale of parliamentary review. There is very little information in the public domain. We know more about the CIA than about R&AW, because everything about the former is on their official website. Though, R&AW is modeled on the CIA of USA and Mossad of Israel, its detailed organisation, size and funding is not known to the Parliament. The organisational structure of both CIA and Mossad are in the public domain, and available in various publications as well as on the internet. The Right to Information act has been passed, but the intelligence agencies are beyond its purview. The only thing classified today is the mind of the commander i.e. the way he is going to fight the battle. Significantly, However, in India too much of stress is on secrecy which ultimately leads to loss of accountability. There is no yardstick for success and failure in any intelligence agency".[55]

"India has no appropriate legal framework to regulate its vast and growing communications intelligence capabilities. There is minimal institutional oversight by political institutions like parliament which means there is a clear and imminent danger that the technology could undermine the very democracy it was purchased to defend."[56]

Rana Banerji, head of the IDSA Task Force on Intelligence Reforms comments that "The intelligence community across the world is subject to parliamentary oversight in some form or the other. All major democracies have gone in for tiers of accountability and oversight...it empowers the intelligence agencies. There is a need to introduce legislation in Parliament laying out charters, functions and duties of intelligence organisations. We will have to address the practical problem of the qualifications of those doing the oversight."[57]

"There is no mechanism for tasking the agencies, monitoring their performance and reviewing their records to evaluate their quality. Nor is there any oversight of the overall functioning of the agencies. These are all standard features elsewhere in the world. In the absence of such procedures, the Government and the nation do not know whether they are getting value for money. While taking note of recent steps to entrust the NSCS with some of these responsibilities, the Committee recommends a thorough examination of the working of the intelligence system with a view to remedying these deficiencies."[58]

The above view of security analysts have again been included to highlight the magnitude of challenge posed due to lack of accountability and tasking of our intelligence agencies.

Over Reliance on Technical Intelligence (TECHINT)

"Intelligence is basically dependent on human resources. Intelligence is generated by trained professionals and the machines and gadgets contrived and deployed by them. The loveliest and purest diamond becomes the pride of a beauty queen's crown only when it is chiseled and polished by the master craftsman. Similarly, a raw piece of information is churned into intelligence by the trained and seasoned intelligence operators, before the same is used by the policy makers."[59]

Vikram Sood, comments that "No technical input will be enough without HUMINT and interpretation of this technical intelligence".[60]

"There is no substitute to excellent HUMINT in preventing terror strikes and taking proactive steps to target terror organisations. It is important to use technology but solely banking on TECHINT may be disastrous. Indian intelligence agencies have gradually become dependent on technical collection, and began to neglect traditional espionage."[61]

The above statements by former intelligence officers and defence analysts sums up the primacy of HUMINT in overall intelligence process which has been unfortunately relegated in lower order these days. Last few years have witnessed an over-reliance on TECHINT thereby making stereotypical assessments. The importance of 'beat constable and sources from all walks of life has gradually eroded. The TECHINT is to be analysed by a trained analyst based on his own 'hunch' which can't be replaced by technical gadgets.

Over reliance on TECHINT has blunted the sharp edge of intelligence operatives. Emphasis is still not being paid to sharpening the skill of HUMINT which has to be used in conjunction with TECHINT. The TECHINT can't be used as a sole tool of making analysis and assessment. The data bases of NATGRID whenever completed can be a useful tool but the assessment cannot be left to the computers.

Since the Indo-Pakistan conflict in the Kargil heights in 1999, there has been a major increase in the Technical Intelligence (TECHINT) capabilities of the Indian security community, which comprises the intelligence agencies of the Government of India and the intelligence divisions of the State Police.[62] It was done with a view to keep pace with the technologies being used by our adversaries and terrorists. However, excessive use over the last decade has made us rely solely on technical gadgets which can't always be relied upon. As stated above, it should be used to supplement the intelligence assessment of 'beat constable' who has traditionally been the focal point of local intelligence.

Loss of Focus

The intelligence agencies have often been accused of 'political orientation'. It is reported that a large part of IB's resources are directed at serving the ruling political party of the day. It naturally hampers the efficient and independent functioning of IB.[63] Praveen Swami stressed in his article in *The Hindu* on 05 Dec 11 that a large part of IB remains deployed on political tasks, not on national security duties. The former Director IB, Arun Bhagat reportedly admitted in a TV interview that he was told to conduct a survey on the food situation by the ruling political party which was an activity unrelated to national security.[64] The biggest dangers to intelligence services in India are subversion by external forces and the politicisation of the agencies where the internal agency assumes that security of the state is the same thing as the security of the government while the external agency gets policised.[65]

There are numerous such reports which have been deliberately not covered here. It suffices to say that intelligence agencies should not have 'political orientation'. The intelligence agencies should continue to maintain their apolitical orientation.

"Counter Intelligence and Covert action act as spoilers, often skewing the intelligence process and throwing it off track".[66] Intelligence agencies at times, deviate from their primary task and lay more stress on secondary and superfluous tasks. The drift in operational work of intelligence adversely affects the quality of assessment prepared by intelligence agencies. Counter intelligence and covert action have been at times used by intelligence agencies to divert attention in case of any sub optimal performance of intelligence agencies causing embarrassment to their top brass. The intelligence agencies at times lose their focus from primary role which is to be cautiously avoided.

Lack of Common Data Base

An analyst can perform his/her task much more efficiently if he/she has access to all possible information pertaining to any fresh input brought before him/her and collated information/database created over a period of time. However, presently no worthwhile progress has been made in our country in this regard. Each agency maintains its own database of whatever worth it is. However, it is not in a position to utilise the excellent database which other agency may have developed over a period of time. GC Saxena Committee had recommended creation of a shared information network between intelligence agencies. Similar recommendation was also made by 9/11 Commission in the US with regards to creation of an information network.

Post 26/11, the Central Government did indicate its intention of creating a common data base, but its implementation is still a long way behind schedule. 'Crime and Criminal Tracking Network System (CCNTS) which was conceived six months even before 26/11 to allow real-time sharing of information between the country's 14,000 plus police stations, as well as 6,000 police headquarters has missed even 2012 deadline.[67] National Intelligence Grid (NATGRID), Central Monitoring System (CMS) and Unique Identification Authority of India (UIDAI) are still in the pipeline. As a result, an analyst doesn't have complete information before him while making intelligence assessment. The same information may be available with other government agencies but he will not be able to access it till a common and shared data bank is not created.

Lack of Tasking and Evaluation of Intelligence Agencies

In our country today, there is little interface between the consumers and producers of intelligence. As a result, while the consumers don't know what to ask from the agencies, the latter furnishes whatever they could get to the consumers, irrespective of the actual requirements. In the absence of any conscious tasking by the consumers there can't be any realistic evaluation of the performance of the agencies.

There is a need to evolve a mechanism by which the consumer gets to forecast his requirement on quarterly/six monthly/annual basis and give to concerned intelligence agencies. The intelligence agencies performance needs to be evaluated by the supervisory authority in light of the requirement forecasted by the users. The same can be suitably moderated by the supervisory mechanism of intelligence agencies. The mechanism should also cater for immediate needs of the consumers. The central Government should take concrete steps to fulfill their agenda in the Election Manifesto of 2004 Elections which reads as under:

> "The Congress will ensure necessary connectivity between the intelligence agencies of the Government of India and the National Security Advisory Board, as well as between the intelligence agencies and the ministries of defence and ministry of external affairs."

Issues before the Nation: Security'
Defence and Foreign Policy, a Congress Agenda.[68]

It emerges from above that the challenges to intelligence assessment and coordination at the national level are interlinked and deep rooted. It would be foolish to presume that these challenges can be overcome in isolation. The attitudinal changes are more difficult to be implemented than organisational and structural changes. A holistic approach is mandatory to bring out such changes at the national level integrating all the organs of the government machinery. A road map to overcome these challenges would be attempted in the subsequent chapters.

Notes

1   Joshua Rovner and Austin Long, "Intelligence Failure and Reform: Evaluating the 9/11 Commission Report", Breakthroughs, Vol. 14, No. 1 (spring, 2005), pp. 1, accessed online via www.usnwc.edu/getattachment/ea6041fc-0260-4618.../Rovner-CV on 20 Sept 2010.

2   James Burch, Domestic Intelligence Agencies, Homeland Security Affairs vol. iii, no. 2 (June 2007) www.hsaj.org p. 15

3   Executive Summary of the Kargil Review Committee Report as presented in Rajya Sabha, 25 February, 2000, accessed on line at http://rajyasabha.nic.in/25indi1.htm#8

4   Interview of DC Nath, former Special Director, Intelligence Bureau on 24 Nov 10

5   B. Raman, Intelligence: Past, Present, and Future (New Delhi, India: Lancer Publishers & Distributors, 2002), p.343

6   Interview of Lt Gen R K Sawhney (Retd), former DGMI on 24 Nov 2010

7   B.Raman , "Possible Misuse of New Techint Capabilities" accessed online via www.southasiaanalysis.org/%5Cpapers48%5Cpaper4797.html on 06 Dec 2011

8   B. Raman, Intelligence: Past, Present, and Future (New Delhi, India: Lancer Publishers & Distributors, 2002), p.71

9   Saikat Datta , "Creating a successful Intelligence and Counter –Terrorism Matrix: Lessons from 26/11" The CLAWS Journal summer 2011 edition,p.102.

10 Maj Gen VK Singh, India's External Intelligence –Secrets of Research and Analysis Wing (R&AW), (Manas Publications ,2007),p.37

11 Bibhu Prasad Routray, Intel wing for the CRPF: Not the Right Move, CLAWS web article 17 Jul 2011

[12] Dr Bhashyam Kasturi, Intelligence services –Analysis, Organisation and function, p. 61

[13] Turf war in intel units hampers war on terror-Ajmer Singh, *Mail Today* July 16, 2011

[14] Maloy Krishna Dhar, Open Secrets: India's Intelligence Unveiled, New Delhi, Manas Publications, 2005,p.15

[15] Executive Summary of the Kargil Review Committee Report as presented in Rajya Sabha, 25 February, 2000, accessed on line at http://rajyasabha.nic.in/25indi1.htm#8

[16] Maloy Krishna Dhar, Open Secrets: India's Intelligence Unveiled, New Delhi, Manas Publications, 2005, p.15

[17] Mr. CD Sahay, former Director, R&AW, during Seminar on Intelligence Assessment and Coordination at National Level at CLAWS on 24 Nov 10

[18] Mr. CD Sahay, former Director, R&AW, during Seminar on Intelligence Assessment and Coordination at National Level at CLAWS on 24 Nov 10

[19] Maloy Krishna Dhar, Open Secrets: India's Intelligence Unveiled, (New Dehli, Manas Publications, 2005), p.15

[20] Ajmer Singh, "Turf war in Intel units hampers war on terror", *Mail Today*, 16 July, 2011

[21] Ibid

[22] Ibid

[23] "Demand grows for national intelligence Czar to end turf wars", Josy Joseph *Sunday Times of India* Oct 09 ,2011

[24] Rahul Bedi, "Indian intelligence gathering undermined by budget cuts," 2; Praveen Swami, "Stalled Praveen Swami, "Bureaucrats kill critical intelligence reforms," The Hindu, June 18, 2004, p.1

[25] Rahul Bedi, "Indian intelligence gathering undermined by budget cuts," 2; Praveen Swami, "Stalled reforms," Frontline 20, no. 9 (April/May 2003), Praveen Swami, "Bureaucrats kill critical intelligence reforms," The Hindu, June 18, 2004, p.1

[26] Maj Gen VK Singh, India's External Intelligence –Secrets of Research and Analysis Wing (R&AW), Manas Publications,2007, p.162

[27] Lt Gen KS Khajuria, former DGMI in his forward to the book Intelligence Services Analysis, Organisation and function by Dr Bhashyam Kasturi

[28] Josy Joseph "Demand grows for national intelligence Czar to end turf wars" , Sunday *Times of India* , 09 Oct,2011

29 Brig Guremet Kanwal (Retd), former Director, CLAWS, "Fighting terrorism -Policies mired in systemic weaknesses", accessed online at http://www.deccanherald.com/content/229625/indias-tough-choices-over-

30 Lt Gen R K Sawhney (Retd), former DGMI, during Seminar on Intelligence Assessment and Coordination at National Level at CLAWS on 24 Nov 10

31 Michael A. Turner, 'Why Secret Intelligence Fails', (Potomac Books Inc, 31 January, 2005), p.112

32 Vikram Sood,' Intelligence Reforms', : Indian Defence Review ,Vol 24.1 Jan-Mar 2009

33 Maloy Krishna Dhar, 'Open Secrets: India's Intelligence Unveiled'(Manas, New Delhi, 2005), p . 83

34 Praveen Swami, "Handicapped Intelligence" , Frontline , Volume 21 - Issue 14, Jul 03 - 16, 2004

35 'Praveen Swami, "New intelligence technology feeding surge in political espionage", Hindu, 05 Dec 11

36 Sunil Sainis, Intelligence Reforms, Bharat Rakshak Monitor - Volume 3(4) January-February 2001,p.22

37 Praveen Swami, "Stalled Reforms," Frontline ,Volume 20 - Issue 09, April 26 - May 09, 2003

38 Maj Gen Dhruv Katoch (Retd) , Director, CLAWS

39 Prem Mahadevan, 'The Politics of Counter-Terrorism in India — Strategic Intelligence and National Security in South Asia,; I.B. Tauris & Co, London,2012 p.37

40 B.Raman, "Control over TECHINT", accessed online at www.southasiaanalysis.org on 06 Dec2011

41 Lt Gen KS Khajuria , former DGMI, as quoted in Bhashyam Kasturi, Intelligence Services, Analysis, organisation and function,p.9

42 B. Raman, Intelligence: Past, Present, and Future (New Delhi, India: Lancer Publishers & Distributors, 2002), p.69

43 Praveen Swami, "For a paradigm shift' Frontline Volume 18 - Issue 07, Mar. 31 - Apr. 13, 2001

44 CD Sahay, former Director, R&AW, during Seminar on Intelligence Assessment and Coordination at National Level at CLAWS on 24 Nov 10

[45] The Politics of Counter-Terrorism in India — Strategic Intelligence and National Security in South Asia, Prem Mahadevan; I.B. Tauris & Co, London,2012 p.31

[46] Interview of Rana Banerji, former Special Secretary, R&AW on 10 Dec2011.

[47] Vikram Sood , former Chief of R&AW. *Indian Defence Review* Jul- Sep 2006

[48] Interview of Jayadava Ranade, former Additional Secretary, Cabinet Secretariat, Government of India on 24 NOV 2010.

[49] Hunting man-US int committee Chairman Michael Rogers reviews the Bin Laden operation, *Jane's Intelligence review* ,volume 23,Number 07 July 11, p. 58

[50] Interview of Rana Banerji, former Special Secretary R&AW.

[51] New Intelligence technology feeding surge in political espionage .Praveen Swami, Hindu 05 Dec 11

[52] Headquarters ARTRAC ,Intelligence application in Information age : The need to sharpen the gaze" May 2010

[53] Saikat Datta ," Creating a successful Intelligence and Counter –Terrorism Matrix: Lessons from 26/11" The CLAWS Journal summer 2011 edition,p.110

[54] Dr Bhashyam Kasturi , *Intelligence Services Analysis*, Organisation and Functions , P. 15

[55] India's External Intelligence –Secrets of Research and Analysis Wing (RAW), Maj Gen VK Singh, Manas Publications ,2007,p.14

[56] Praveen Swami "The Government 's listening to us" , Hindu, 02 Dec 11

[57] Interview of Rana Banerji, former Special Secretary, R&AW on 15 Dec 2011

[58] Executive Summary of the Kargil Review Committee Report as presented in Rajya Sabha, 25 February, 2000, accessed on line at http://rajyasabha.nic.in/25indi1.htm#8

[59] Maloy Krishna Dhar, Open Secrets: India's Intelligence Unveiled, New Delhi, Manas Publications, 2005,p.517

[60] Vikram Sood , *Indian Defence Review* Jul- Sep 2006

[61] Prem Mahadevan , "The Politics of Counter-Terrorism in India — Strategic Intelligence and National Security in South Asia" , (I.B. Tauris & Co, London,2012), p.39

[62] B.Raman, "Possible Misuse of New Techint Capabilities" accessed online via www.southasiaanalysis.org/%5Cpapers48%5Cpaper4797.html on 06 Dec 2011

[63] Saikat Datta, "War below the Radar," *New Delhi Outlook*, 31 July 2006, p.1; accessed

online via http://www.outlookindia.comon 18 Dec2011

[64] Interview given by Arun Bhagat to Hindi television station P7 and reported by special correspondent of *Hindu* on 07 Dec11

[65] Vikram Sood , former Director, R&AW, *Indian Defence Review* Jul- Sep 2006.

[66] Michael A. Turner, 'Why Secret Intelligence Fails', (Potomac Books Inc, 31 January, 2005), p.125

[67] Praveen Swamy , "National Police Network to miss 2012 deadline", *Hindu*,06Jun 2012

[68] Saikat Datta, 'Low on the IQ' accessed online via http://www.outlookindia.com/printarticle.aspx?227823 on 29 Dec 2010

6

GLOBAL TRENDS IN INTELLIGENCE AND SECURITY INFRASTRUCTURE

"In the difficult fight against the new menace of international terrorism, there is nothing more crucial than timely and accurate intelligence."

John Howard, Australian Prime Minister

By now, it has become evident that there is a need to infuse more life and variety in our intelligence assessment and coordination mechanism at the national level. This problem is not typical to our country. Almost all other countries face a similar situation. The next logical step is to analyse how other countries are coping up with this problem. Brig Gurmeet Kanwal comments 'While there is no need to blindly ape any country, there is no harm in learning from the best practices abroad and incorporating them into Indian policies.'[1] A holistic approach for improving intelligence assessment and coordination at the national level cannot be undertaken without an in depth analysis of intelligence and security structure of other countries that face similar challenges as us. The study should keep in mind the specific requirement of our country before recommending an intelligence model for adoption.

The US, UK, Australian and Israel Intelligence & Security structure have been covered in adequate detail in this chapter. It has been done to drive home a point that today we know more about the functioning of FBI, CIA, MI6 or Mossad as opposed to R&AW or IB for obvious reason of being over secretive. Even details of Pakistan's Inter Service Intelligence (ISI) are probably more known to us than any of our intelligence agencies.[2]

REGIONAL SCAN

Inter-Services Intelligence (ISI)

The Directorate for Inter-Services Intelligence is the premier intelligence agency of the State of Pakistan, operationally responsible for providing critical national security and intelligence assessment to the Government of Pakistan. The ISI is the largest of the three intelligence services of Pakistan, the others being the Intelligence Bureau (IB) and Military Intelligence (MI). The IB is the oldest intelligence agency and can be traced to Pakistan's creation in 1947. It was formed by the division of the pre-partition IB of British India. ISI was created in 1948, post turmoil in Jammu & Kashmir in 1947-48. Pakistan's ISI is primarily directed against India and the 'Asymmetric War' launched has impinged on India's national security and would continue to do so in the future. Over the years, the ISI has emerged as a powerful intelligence agency and enjoys wide international cooperation. While the IB comes under the Interior Minister, the ISI is a part of the Ministry of Defence (MoD). Apart from this, each wing of the Armed Forces has its own intelligence directorate for tactical military intelligence.[3] The ISI, which originally started as essentially an agency for the collection of external intelligence, has developed into an agency adept in covert actions and clandestine procurement of denied technologies as well.[4]

ISI's headquarters are located in Islamabad and the head of the ISI is called the Director General, who has to be a serving Lieutenant General in the Pakistan Army. Under the Director General, there are three Deputy Director Generals who report directly to him and are in charge in three separate fields of the ISI. The three main wings are internal wing (counter-intelligence and political issues inside Pakistan), the external wing (external issues), and Analysis and Foreign Relations wing.[5]

Departments

- **Joint Intelligence X** . It coordinates all other departments in the ISI. Intelligence and information gathered from other departments are sent to JIX which prepares and processes the information and prepares reports which are presented.

- **Joint Intelligence Bureau.** It is responsible for gathering political intelligence. It has three subsections, one devoted entirely to operations against India.

- **Joint Counter Intelligence Bureau.** It is responsible for surveillance of Pakistan's diplomats and diplomatic agents abroad, along with intelligence operations in the Middle East, South Asia, China, Afghanistan and the Muslim republics of the former Soviet Union.

- **Joint Intelligence (North).** It is exclusively responsible for the Jammu and Kashmir region and Northern Areas.

- **Joint Intelligence (Miscellaneous).** It is responsible for espionage, including offensive intelligence operations, in other countries.

- **Joint Signal Intelligence Bureau.** It deals with intelligence collections along the India-Pakistan border. The JSIB is the ELINT, COMINT, and SIGINT directorate that is charged to divert attacks from the foreign non-communications electromagnetic radiations emanating from events other than nuclear detonations or radioactive sources.

- **Joint Intelligence Technical.** It deals with the development of science and technology to advance Pakistan's intelligence gathering. The Directorate is tasked to take steps against the electronic warfare attacks in Pakistan. Without any exception, officers from these divisions are reported to be engineer officers and military scientists who deal with the military promotion of science and technology. In addition, there are also separate explosives and a chemical and biological warfare sections.

- **SS Directorate.** It monitors terrorist group's activities that operate in Pakistan against the state. The SS Directorate is comparable to the Central Intelligence Agency (CIA) Special Activities Division, and responsible for covert political action and paramilitary special operations.[6]

China

The Ministry of State Security (MSS) (Guoanbu) is China's official state security apparatus and main intelligence agency akin to the Central Intelligence Agency and the Federal Bureau of Investigation in the United States.[7] It is responsible for collection, monitoring, and investigation of information and intelligence pertaining to Chinese national security, domestically and internationally. According to Article 4 of the Criminal Procedure Law, the MSS has the right to detain and arrest people with the same procedure and precedence of regular police officers. [8]

Government reforms in 1983 created the MSS, restructuring the Chinese intelligence community and revising the mission of its predecessor agency to account for technological advances in intelligence tradecraft. The MSS utilises human, signals, remote, electronic, and communications intelligence in its varied operations. The main mission of the MSS is to protect national interests and preserve government stability. However, the MSS also aggressively targets the United States and European businesses and factories in a broad campaign of industrial and economic espionage.[9]

The MSS was founded in 1983, combining the functions of the Chinese Communist Party's investigation department with the intelligence, counterintelligence, and counterespionage components of the Ministry of Public Security (MPS). MSS headquarter is placed at the Ministry of Public Security Office in Beijing. Their stated mission is to ensure "the security of the state through effective measures against enemy agents, spies, and counter-revolutionary activities designed to sabotage or overthrow China's socialist system." MSS personnel are trained at the University of International Relations.

The MSS has been accused by the Western media of domestically harassing dissidents and interfering in the American political process in the 1990s as money was funneled from the ministry to various politicians in the United States through intermediaries. It is estimated that they have 170 intelligence offices in over fifty countries and utilise agents who purport to be industrialists, diplomats, students, and various other professions.[10]

In recent years, the MSS has utilised more advanced technology and has been accused of targeting high-tech and sensitive sites in the United States including Silicon Valley and Government Databases. In June 2008, Congressmen Frank Wolf and Chris Smith, who are critics of the Chinese government, claimed that their computers have been hacked by sources inside China in the past. The Chinese government maintains that the accusations are groundless and reflect a Cold War mentality. In addition, the Chinese also claim that they do not have such capabilities as a developing country.[11]

Chinese intelligence is believed to be highly active outside of the People's Republic of China. Chinese human-intelligence operations primarily rely on collecting a small amount of information from a large number of people. It is generally believed that Chinese employ academics or students who will be in their host country only for a short time, rather than spending years cultivating a few high-level sources or double agents.[12]

The Chinese military intelligence is divided into operational departments that fall under the administration of the central government and individual branches of the military. The People's Liberation Army (PLA), China's defence force, maintains trained intelligence, counterintelligence and security forces. The operations of these forces are highly secret, but most operations deal with domestic and regional threats to the government. PLA intelligence also guards military installations and key assets in the nation's nuclear weapons program. The PLA Navy has its own intelligence force, concentrating on surveillance at sea, signals, and communications intelligence. The PLA Air Force's intelligence forces are known as the Sixth Research Institute. Sixth Research conducts intelligence operations similar to other military and civilian organisations, but is also the primary agency for aerial surveillance.[13]

The Second Intelligence Department focuses on foreign intelligence and espionage against rival nations. In addition to monitoring foreign diplomats and foreign interests within China, the agency also conducts political surveillance of Chinese diplomats abroad. Recently, the Second Intelligence Department received a new mandate to work with the MSS to increase industrial, economic, scientific, and technological espionage efforts, especially in Western nations.[14]

Throughout China, there are municipal, regional, and national police forces. The Ministry of Public Security administers the national police force. A military trained police force, Unit 8341 General Security Regiment, provides security for government buildings and personnel, and conducts counterintelligence and anti-terrorism operations. The special police force and intelligence unit is maintained by the General Staff Department.[15]

The Chinese government also maintains secret police forces. These forces are mostly plain-clothes officers who use a network of informers to conduct surveillance and political espionage operations on behalf of the government. Some of these police forces have gained a bad reputation for arbitrary imprisonment of citizens and have garnered international criticism for use of excessive force and coercion.[16]

MSS conducts covert intelligence gathering operations overseas. It has established intelligence agencies in more than 170 cities and in nearly 50 countries and regions all over the world. These agencies are classified as general branches, branches, and sub-branches. MSS aggressively targets the United States, placing particular emphasis on California's high-tech sector. Cover for Beijing's espionage in the United States includes the 1,500 Chinese diplomats operating out of 70 offices, 15,000 Chinese students who arrive in the United States each year, and 10,000 Chinese who travel in some 2,700 visiting delegations each year.[17]

The MSS is divided into bureaus, which are as under:

- Domestic Affairs

- Foreign Affairs

- Hong Kong, Macau and Taiwan

- Technology

- Local Intelligence

- Counterintelligence

- Circulation

- Research (China Institute of Contemporary International Relations)

- Anti-Defection and Counter surveillance

- Scientific and Technological Information

- Personnel and Education

- Supervision and Auditing [18]

Nepal

Nepal's main intelligence agency is "National Investigation Department (NID)", headquartered in Singhadurbar, Kathmandu. The intelligence gathering module is mainly focused on national security, terrorism, narcotics, economic embezzlement and thriving organised crime. Besides, Crime Investigation Department of Nepal Police, Department of Military Intelligence (DMI) of Nepal Army and National Vigilance Centre are also carrying out the process of intelligence-gathering as per their respective working area. [19] Financial Information Unit (FIU) is Nepal's financial intelligence unit which has a major role to play in light of rampant financial offences in the country.[20]

Bangladesh

The National Security Intelligence, also known as the Directorate-General of National Security Intelligence, is the primary intelligence agency responsible for internal security (including internal political affairs), foreign intelligence and counterintelligence. The Directorate General of Forces Intelligence (DGFI) is the main military intelligence outfit, responsible for intelligence gathering for all military purposes. [21]

GLOBAL SCAN

Intelligence Community in USA

The US Intelligence Community is made up of 16 organisations whose activities are controlled and coordinated by the Director of National Intelligence (DNI), who reports to the President.[22]

The **DNI** is primarily charged with developing the overall intelligence budget, designing procedures to govern large intelligence acquisitions, setting priorities and coordinating policies/activities for the 16 intelligence agencies. It is also responsible for monitoring covert operations, setting policies for working with foreign intelligence services, authority to request information from non intelligence agencies, and performing joint planning for counterterrorism operations for the 16 intelligence agencies.[23]

Reporting to the DNI, besides the 16 intelligence agencies are the National Counterterrorism Center (NCTC),[24] which is staffed by terrorism experts from the CIA, FBI, and the Pentagon; the Privacy and Civil Liberties Board; and the National Counter Proliferation Center. These organisations display high degree of jointmanship.

A brief description of the 16 members of the current US Intelligence Community is provided below in succeeding paragraphs, with emphasis on their major intelligence responsibilities:-

1. **Central Intelligence Agency (CIA***)* - The CIA's major intelligence responsibilities are as under:-

   • To surreptitiously collect foreign intelligence.

   • To conduct counterintelligence and counterterrorism activities related to foreign intelligence and national security matters.

   • To develop the necessary technical collection systems required for carrying out the above responsibilities.[25]

2. **Federal Bureau of Investigation (FBI)** - The FBI's main intelligence responsibility is to conduct counterintelligence, counterterrorism and intelligence activities within the United States. These activities are under the direction of the head of the National Security Service, who in turn is hired by the FBI Director and the Attorney General but with the concurrence of the Director of National Intelligence.[26]

   In summary, the role of the FBI entails detection, penetration, prevention and neutralisation, by lawful means, of espionage, sabotage, terrorism, and other activities directed against the United States by hostile foreign persons and organisations.[27]

3. **Defence Intelligence Agency (DIA***)* - The DIA's main responsibility is to satisfy the foreign intelligence and

counterintelligence requirements of the Secretary of Defence, the Joint Chiefs of Staff, and the various other commands and components of Department of Defence (DOD) and other agencies.[28]

4. **National Security Agency (NSA)**- The NSA's major responsibility is to provide centralised coordination, direction, and performance of highly specialised technical operations to ensure that the US Government communications are protected and that foreign communications are a source of intelligence data.[29] It is overall responsible to coordinate TECHINT of the intelligence community. All the COMINT and SIGINT efforts of the USA are grouped under one single organisation, the NSA.[30]

5. **National Geospatial Intelligence Agency (NGA)** - This organisation, a support agency of the DOD, provides timely, relevant, and accurate imagery, imagery intelligence, and geospatial information in support of military and other users.[31]

6. **National Reconnaissance Office (NRO)** - An agency of the Department of Defence, the NRO reports to the Secretary of Defence, who in concert with the Director of Central Intelligence has the ultimate management and operational responsibility for NRO. The NRO manages the satellite reconnaissance programmes for the entire US Intelligence Community.[32]

7. **Air Force Intelligence**- The Air Force Intelligence's major responsibility is to conduct and manage the collection, processing, analysis and dissemination activities sufficient to meet worldwide Air Force and national needs.[33]

8. **Marine Corps Intelligence**- The Marine Corps Intelligence's major responsibility is to provide responsive and broad intelligence support for the worldwide Marine Corps organisation. The Intelligence Department is responsible for policy, plans, programming, budgets, and staff supervision of Intelligence and supporting activities within the United States Marine Corps.[34]

9. **Army Intelligence**- The Army Intelligence's major responsibility

is to provide specialised intelligence support to the Army worldwide and to the DOD.[35]

10. **Naval Intelligence**- The Naval Intelligence's major responsibility is to fulfill the intelligence, counterintelligence, investigative and security requirements of the Department of Navy.[36]

11. **Department of State**- The Department of State's Bureau of Intelligence and Research produces political and economic intelligence sufficient to meet the State Department's needs. It focuses on issues bearing on US national security, economic well-being, and promotion of democracy throughout the world.[37]

12. Department of Energy (DOE).

13. Department of Treasury.

14. **United States Coast Guard**- The United States Coast Guard deals with intelligence information relating to the US maritime borders and Homeland Security.[38]

15. **Department of Homeland Security**- The Department of Homeland Security prevents terrorist attacks within the United States, reduces America's vulnerability to terrorism, and minimises the damages and recoveries from attacks that do occur. It was created post 9/11 with an intelligence charter.[39]

16. **The Drug Enforcement Administration (DEA)**.[40]

Joint Structures

In US National Security Council Staff (NSCS) which assists NSC is organised into geographical, functional and support divisions. The NSC system consisting of NSC, its staff and the National Security Advisor acts as a glue that ties together various departments and agencies and makes them work as a single whole to achieve national security objectives and safeguard their national interests.[41]

Federal, state, local, and tribal governments in USA have also established several programs to protect the United States within their borders. These programs include Joint Terrorism Task Forces, the National Joint Terrorism

Task Force, the State and Major Urban Area Fusion Centers and the National Operations Center. These programs leverage the broad experience, knowledge, and skills of personnel from a wide variety of fields, such as intelligence, law enforcement, fire, and emergency services.[42]

Joint Terrorism Task Force (JTTF)

Joint Terrorism Task Forces (JTTFs) are small cells of highly trained, locally based, passionately committed investigators, analysts, linguists, SWAT experts, and other specialists from numerous US law enforcement and intelligence agencies. It is a multi-agency effort led by the Justice Department and FBI, designed to combine the resources of federal, state, and local law enforcement.

The National JTTF was established in July 2002 to serve as a coordinating mechanism with the FBI's partners. Some 40 agencies are now represented in the NJTTF, which has become a focal point for information sharing and the management of large-scale projects that involve multiple partners."[43]

JTTFs serve as the coordinated "action arms" for federal, state, and local government response to terrorist threats in specific US geographic regions. The FBI is the lead agency that oversees JTTFs. [44]

"The mission of a JTTF is to leverage the collective resources of the member agencies for the prevention, preemption, deterrence, and investigation of terrorist acts that affect United States interests, to disrupt and prevent terrorist acts, and to apprehend individuals who may commit or plan to commit such acts. To further this mission, a JTTF serves as a means to facilitate information sharing among JTTF members."[45]

"As of January 2011, there are 104 JTTFs based nationwide, including at least one in each of the FBI's 56 field offices. More than 600 state and local agencies participate in JTTFs nationwide. Federal representation includes representatives from the US Intelligence Community, the Departments of Homeland Security, Defence, Justice, Treasury, Transportation, Commerce, Energy, State, and Interior, among others."[46]

Fusion Centers. "A fusion center is a dedicated element, run by the applicable state or local jurisdiction that exchanges information and intelligence, maximises resources, streamlines operations, and improves the ability to disrupt, prevent, respond to, and recover from all threats by analysing data from a variety of sources. A fusion center is defined as a "collaborative effort of two or more agencies that provide resources, expertise, and information to the center with the goal of maximising a center's ability to detect, prevent, investigate, and respond to criminal and terrorist activity."[47] Fusion centers focus primarily on the intelligence and fusion processes through which information is gathered, integrated, evaluated, analysed, and disseminated.

State and major urban area fusion centers provide analysis and information-sharing capabilities that support the efforts of state and local law enforcement to prevent and investigate crime and terrorism. Fusion centers receive information from a variety of sources, including state and local tips and leads as well as federal information and intelligence. By "fusing" information from a wide variety of disciplines to conduct analysis, fusion centers generate products that are timely and relevant to their customers' needs. This allows state and local law enforcement to address immediate and emerging threat-related circumstances and events. It also supports risk-based, information-driven prevention, response, and consequence management.[48]

As of January 2011, there are 72 designated fusion centers (50 State and 22 Major Urban Areas). Fusion centers are designed to involve every level and discipline of government, private-sector entities, and the public—though the level of involvement of some participants will vary. Fusion centers are state and locally owned and operated. The Department of Homeland Security (DHS) has a statutory program to support fusion centers.[49]

JTTF Vs Fusion Center. "JTTFs are FBI-sponsored, multijurisdictional task forces established specifically to conduct terrorism-related investigations. Analytic and information-sharing efforts carried out by the JTTFs are done solely to support those investigative efforts. Also each FBI office contains a Field Intelligence Group which is the main interlocutor with the fusion center. **Fusion centers**, in contrast, are information sharing and analytic entities and do not focus solely on terrorism. They are state and locally owned and operated information analysis centers that analyse information and intelligence regarding a broad array of criminal and other activities related to homeland security." [50] Fusion centers focus on trend and pattern analysis that is intended to help the state and local law enforcement mitigate emerging crime problems, including terrorism and other threats to homeland security.[51]

Fusion Centers are run by state and local authorities, are state/local-centric, deal with terrorism, criminal and public safety matters and produce actionable intelligence for dissemination to appropriate law enforcement agencies but do not generally conduct investigations. JTTFs are sponsored by the FBI, regionally and nationally-focused, deal exclusively with terrorism matters and conducts investigations. [52]

National Joint Terrorism Task Force (NJTTF). The mission of the NJTTF is to enhance communication, coordination, and cooperation between federal, state, and local government agencies representing the intelligence, law enforcement, defence, diplomatic, public safety, transportation, and homeland security communities by providing a point of fusion for terrorism intelligence and by supporting the JTTFs throughout the United States. The NJTTF was established in July 2002 to serve as a coordinating mechanism with the FBI's partners. Forty-nine agencies are represented in the NJTTF, which has become a focal point for information sharing and the management of large-scale projects that involve multiple partners.[53]

National Operations Center (NOC). The mission of the NOC is to serve as the primary National level hub for domestic situational awareness, common operating picture, information fusion, information sharing, communications, and operations coordination pertaining to the prevention of terrorist attacks and domestic incident management.

"The NOC serves as the US's nerve center for information collection and sharing. The NOC is the principal operations center for Department of Homeland Security (DHS).[54] As the principal operations center, the NOC is tasked with performing two key responsibilities:

- "First, the NOC shall provide situational awareness and a common operating picture for the entire federal government, and for state, local, and tribal governments as appropriate, in the event of a natural disaster, act of terrorism, or other manmade disaster.

- Second, the NOC shall ensure that critical terrorism and disaster-related information reaches the government decision-makers. By performing its mission, the NOC enables the Secretary and other leaders to make informed decisions and identify courses of action during an event or threat. The Secretary has assigned the NOC to the DHS Office of Operations Coordination and Planning (OPS)."[55]

"The NOC serves as the primary national hub for situational awareness and operations coordination across the federal government for incident management and as the national fusion center, collecting and synthesising all-source information, including information from the state fusion centers, across all-threats and all hazards information covering the spectrum of homeland security partners."[56]

United Kingdom

The United Kingdom has three intelligence and security services, collectively known as the Agencies, the Secret Intelligence Service (SIS), Government Communications Headquarters (GCHQ) and the Security Service. Another important contributor to the UK's intelligence machinery is the Defence Intelligence Staff, which is an integral part of the Ministry of Defence (MoD). The funding for the three intelligence and security agencies is brought together in a single request for resources which is approved by the Parliament.[57]

The Intelligence Agencies

"The principal role of SIS sometimes known as MI6 is the production of secret intelligence on issues concerning Britain's vital interests in the fields of security, defence, foreign and economic policies in accordance with requirements established by the Joint Intelligence Committee (JIC) and approved by Ministers. SIS uses human and technical sources to meet these requirements, as well as liaison with a wide range of foreign intelligence and security services".[58]

The Government Communications Headquarters (GCHQ) deals with Signals Intelligence and Information Security. GCHQ also works closely with a number of foreign intelligence and security services. The tasking of GCHQ is done by the Joint Intelligence Committee (JIC).[59]

"The Security Service, also known as **MI5** is the UK's domestic security intelligence Agency. The Service's purpose is to protect against substantial, covertly organised threats, primarily from terrorism, espionage and the proliferation of weapons of mass destruction. Most recently, since the passing of the Security Service Act 1996, its role has been expanded to provide support to law enforcement agencies in fighting serious crime. The Security Service has no executive powers; cases likely to result in prosecution are coordinated closely with the police, or HM Customs and Excise, who take the necessary action."[60]

The Defence Intelligence Staff (DIS), part of the Ministry of Defence (MoD) and funded within Defence Votes, is also an essential element of the national intelligence machinery. Created in 1964, by the amalgamation of all three service intelligence staffs and the civilian Joint Intelligence Bureau, it forms an integrated body able to support the Ministry of Defence, the Armed Forces and other Government Departments. The DIS's task is to analyse information, from both overt and covert sources, and provides intelligence assessments, advice and strategic warning to the Joint Intelligence Committee, the MoD, Military Commands and deployed forces. The DIS controls, the Defence Geographic and Imagery Intelligence Agency (DGIA), and the Defence Intelligence and Security Centre (DISC), which are responsible for providing imagery, geographic products and intelligence training.[61]

The Supervisory Mechanism

JIC is the part of the British Cabinet Office responsible for directing the national intelligence organisations of the United Kingdom on behalf of the Cabinet of the United Kingdom and providing advice to the Cabinet related to security, defence and foreign affairs. It is the main instrument for advising on priorities for intelligence gathering and for assessing its results.[62]

It oversees the setting of priorities for the three intelligence and security agencies (Secret Intelligence Service, Security Service, GCHQ), as well as Defence Intelligence, and establishes professional standards for intelligence analysis in government.[63]

The JIC is subject to oversight by the Intelligence and Security Committee and is an element of the Intelligence, Security and Resilience organisation within Cabinet Office. The Committee is chaired by a permanent chairman, a member of the Senior Civil Services, who is supported by the Intelligence and Security Secretariat and assessment staff. The assessment staff is made up of experienced senior analysts drawn from across the government and the military and conducts all-source analysis on subjects of interest to the committee. JIC papers written by the staff draw input from across the intelligence and security agencies and other related bodies.[64]

Its membership includes the heads of the three collection agencies i.e. the Secret Intelligence Service, Security Service and GCHQ, the Chief of Defence Intelligence, Deputy Chief of Defence Intelligence Staff, the Chief of the Assessment Staff, representatives of the Ministry of Defence, Foreign and Commonwealth Office and other departments, and the Prime Minister's adviser on foreign affairs.[65]

The Chief of DIS, who is also Chief of Defence Intelligence (CDI), is responsible for overall coordination of intelligence collection of armed forces. The CDI reports to CDS and permanent secretary of MoD and also functions as Deputy Chairman of JIC.[66]

To summarise, the JIC is charged with the following responsibilities:-

- "Under the broad supervisory responsibility of the Permanent Secretaries' Committee on the Intelligence Services, to give direction to, and to keep under review, the organisation and working of British intelligence activity as a whole at home and overseas in order to ensure efficiency, economy and prompt adaptation to the changing requirements.

- To submit, at agreed intervals, for approval by Ministers, statements of the requirements and priorities for intelligence gathering and other tasks to be conducted by the intelligence Agencies;

- To co-ordinate, as necessary, interdepartmental plans for intelligence activity;

- To monitor and give early warning of the development of direct or indirect foreign threats to British interests, whether political, military or economic;

- On the basis of available information, to assess events and situations relating to external affairs, defence, terrorism, major international criminal activity, scientific, technical and international economic matters;

- To keep under review threats to security at home and overseas and to deal with such security problems as may be referred to it;

- To maintain and supervise liaison with Commonwealth and foreign intelligence organisations as appropriate, and to consider the extent to which its product can be made available to them.[67]

The Oversight Mechanism

The Intelligence and Security Committee (ISC) was established by the Intelligence Services Act 1994 to examine the policy, administration and expenditure of the Security Service, Secret Intelligence Service (SIS), and the Government Communications Headquarters (GCHQ).[68] The Committee has developed its oversight remit, with the Government's agreement, to include examination of intelligence-related elements of the Cabinet Office including the JIC, the Assessments Staff; and the Intelligence, Security and Resilience Group. The Committee also takes evidence from the Defence Intelligence Staff (DIS), part of the Ministry of Defence (MOD), which assists the Committee in respect of work within the Committee's remit.

The Prime Minister appoints the ISC Members after considering nominations from Parliament and consulting with the Leader of the Opposition. The Committee reports directly to the Prime Minister and through him to Parliament, by the publication of the Committee's reports.[69]

Parliament's Intelligence and Security Committee (ISC) also reviews the budget, administration, and policy of all three intelligence agencies. Its legislative oversight function, however, is much more limited that the US congressional committee system.[70]

The Information Sharing Mechanism

MI5 serves as an assessment agency as well as a collection entity. Its analysis directly supports the JIC which serves as the government's focal point for intelligence prioritisation and assessment. The JIC also provides regular assessments to ministers and other senior officials. The establishment of the Joint Terrorism Analysis Centre (JTAC) in June 2003 (under the supervision of MI5) brings analysts from the respective intelligence agencies under one umbrella to facilitate the sharing of intelligence and breaking down of cross-agency barriers. Underneath the JTAC structure, various Special Branches have pooled their resources to develop Regional Intelligence Cells that share responsibilities and support further information sharing.[71]

The United Kingdom also possesses several highly evolved mechanisms to coordinate the sharing of intelligence. The United Kingdom's strengths lie in its strong executive coordination and independent assessment process. Its domestic intelligence agency also operates under a well defined set of national laws, although the effectiveness of information sharing remains an issue.

Australia

The *Australian Security Intelligence Organisation (ASIO)* serves as Australia's domestic intelligence organisation. Similar to MI5, it is chartered to address a wide variety of threats. ASIO works closely with the Australian Protective Service (APS), with both agencies falling under Australia's Attorney General.

ASIO is also one of three tier-one intelligence organisations. The *Australian Secret Intelligence Service (ASIS)* functions as the foreign intelligence entity while the Defence Signals Directorate (DSD) is focused on signals intelligence. Heavily influenced by the British philosophy of separating domestic intelligence and law enforcement powers, ASIO does not have independent arrest powers. As such, ASIO must work closely with police entities particularly the APS on the lines of the FBI or the Royal Canadian Mountain Police (RCMP). The primary venue for APSASIO interaction is through the National Threat Assessment Centre, which serves as the focal point for collaboration with federal organisation and state police forces.[72]

ASIO also serves as an analytic assessment agency. The *Office of National Assessment (ONA)* serves as Australia's premier strategic assessment organisation. ONA, ASIO, ASIS, and DSD also enjoy close access to the Prime Minister's Office. The National Intelligence Group (NIG), which comes under ASIO, collates intelligence from multiple sources and disseminates products to governmental and law enforcement officials through Joint Intelligence Groups. Executive coordination of domestic intelligence and other matters is accomplished through the National Security Committee of Cabinet (NSC) and the Secretaries' Committee on National Security (SCoNS). The NSC consists of senior policy makers while the SCoNS consists of department secretaries who, like those in the United Kingdom, are professional bureaucrats.[73]

Israel

The Israeli Security Agency (ISA) popularly known in Israel and worldwide by the Hebrew acronym 'Shabak' and also as 'Shin Bet' was formed initially in 1948 as a unit in the Israel Defence forces (IDF) for internal security and counterespionage.[74]

All the domestic and foreign intelligence activity of the Israeli intelligence community is coordinated by the 'Committee of Directors of the Intelligence Services', known by its Hebrew acronym 'VARASH.' It was first convened in 1949. Its members currently are, the directors of the Mossad, Military Intelligence (MI), and the ISA. The inspector General of the Israel Police, the Director of the CPR in the Foreign Ministry, the counterterrorism adviser to the prime minister, and the director of Nativ were also members of VARASH earlier who were excluded later.[75]

The National Security Council (NSC) was established in 1999 according to the Israeli Government Resolution 4889, which was unanimously adopted on 7 March 1999. The NSC was designed to serve as a coordinating, integrative, deliberative, and supervisory body on matters of national policy; it operates as an arm of the Prime Minister's Office. The chairman of the NSC also serves as the national security adviser to the Prime Minister.[76]

MI is still considered the principal intelligence organisation in the Israeli intelligence community in assessing imminent threats. The main activity of the MI is to produce comprehensive national intelligence estimates for the Israeli prime minister and cabinet, including communications interception, target studies on the nearby Arab states, and intelligence about the chances of war. [77]

The Air Intelligence Squadron performs the function of data collection by means of aerial reconnaissance and signals intelligence, using an assortment of intelligence equipment, including remotely piloted and unmanned vehicles that are recoverable and recyclable after the first use.

The Naval Intelligence Squadron is a small unit of the Israel Navy that provides to the MI, on a consultative basis, assessments of sea based threats to Israel. The squadron is also responsible for coastal studies, naval gunfire missions, and beach studies for amphibious assaults.

The Institute for Intelligence and Special Operations (The Mossad)

The shadowy darkness of intelligence warfare has long been an Israeli domain. The intelligence agencies in Israel especially Mossad has been widely appreciated due to their 'reported and unreported successes'. Let us now take an overview of 'Mossad' to draw some inferences in the Indian context.

"Israel's redoubtable intelligence service (Mossad) is comparatively small, but has enjoyed much success as a result of experienced and brainy leadership coupled with skillful well trained officers in the field. Israel represents a special case: a small country, but with considerable wealth, technical acumen – and many nearby enemies. It probably spends a larger proportion of its wealth on strategic intelligence than most other countries for one central reason; the people of Israel feel under siege from the sea of enemies in which they find themselves."[78]

The Institute for Intelligence and Special Operations, otherwise known as the Mossad, has been appointed by the State of Israel to collect information, analyse intelligence, and perform special covert operations beyond its borders. [79]

"Mossad is one of the main entities in the Israeli Intelligence Community, along with Aman (military intelligence) and Shin Bet (internal security), but its director reports directly to the Prime Minister. Mossad is responsible for human intelligence collection, covert action, and counterterrorism."[80] "Its focus is on Arab nations and organisations throughout the world. Mossad is also responsible for the clandestine movement of Jewish refugees out of Syria, Iran, and Ethiopia. Mossad agents are active in the former communist countries, in the West, and at the UN".[81]

Mossad has a total of eight departments, though some details of the internal organisation of the agency remain obscure.

- Collections Department is the largest, with responsibility for espionage operations, with offices abroad under both diplomatic and unofficial cover.

- Political Action and Liaison Department conducts political activities and liaison with friendly foreign intelligence services and with nations with which Israel does not have normal diplomatic relations.

- Special Operations Division, also known as Metsada, conducts highly sensitive assassination, sabotage, paramilitary, and psychological warfare projects.

- LAP (Lohamah Psichologit) Department is responsible for psychological warfare, propaganda and deception operations.

- Research Department is responsible for intelligence production, including daily situation reports, weekly summaries and detailed monthly reports. The Department is organized into 15 geographically specialised sections or "desks", including the USA, Canada and Western Europe, Latin America, Former Soviet Union, China, Africa, the Maghreb (Morocco, Algeria, and Tunisia), Libya, Iraq, Jordan, Syria, Saudi Arabia, the United Arab Emirates and Iran. A "nuclear" desk is focused on special weapons related issues.

- Technology Department is responsible for development of advanced technologies for support of Mossad operations. [82]

The Analysis

Following the analysis of intelligence and security of some developed countries of the world, the observations are as under:-

- Synergy in all organs of state is an escapable requirement. Joint mechanism involving numerous agencies and experts from all walks of life has been adopted by almost all the countries.

- Centralised control of all intelligence agencies is another inescapable requirement.

- Intelligence agencies across the world are subjected to some form of oversight and accounting mechanism.

- Turf war, lack of requisite coordination and bureaucratic mangling of intelligence agencies is not specific to our country; it's prevalent across the countries albeit at varying proportion.

- Tasking of intelligence agencies by consumers and its periodic review is the norm in all the democratic countries.

- The intelligence agencies are becoming more open to the world and are looking for public/private participation in intelligence collection.

- Democracies across the world are paying more if not equal emphasis on intelligence analysis and assessment.

It is amply clear that most of the developed countries have robust and well organised intelligence and security structure in place. However, occasionally even their intelligence community has come under severe criticism. Review of the US intelligence and security structure post 9/11 is a glaring example even though the United States intelligence community had gone through a period of change between 1998 to 2000. The failure to predict or detect the May 1998 nuclear tests by India had led to a lot of soul searching within the US intelligence community. The muddling of Pakistan ISI in internal politics of the country is well known. At times, views have been expressed that our intelligence agencies should draw a leaf from ISI. In our anxiety for quick results against the ISI, we should not sacrifice time-tested principles as to how intelligence agencies should function in a democratic society.

In view of the aforesaid, none of the above intelligence set up is either perfect or can be used as a template in our country. The NCTC is a glaring example of adopting good model with incorrect procedure of adoption. The

NCTC was adopted from US National Joint Terrorism Task Force' (NJTTF) in December 2009, as part of post 26/11 reforms. The mission of the NJTTF is to enhance communication, coordination, and cooperation between federal, state, and local government agencies representing the intelligence, law enforcement, defence, diplomatic, public safety, transportation, and homeland security communities by providing a point of fusion for terrorism intelligence and by supporting the JTTFs throughout the United States. If we analyse the spirit with which it was adopted in our country, we will get to the bottom of the reasons why it has not been able to establish itself till today. With this as a backdrop, various viewpoints have been included in Appendix D of this book which helps us in understanding the background of the case. It also forces us to ponder over as to where we went wrong and help us in drawing lessons for not repeating the same mistake in future. These views were expressed by noted security analysts who participated in the national debate conducted by Chandigarh *Tribune* in Jan 2012 when the controversy related to it was at its peak.[83]

The United States and UK model can be used to a limited extent to draw relevant lessons for adoption in our country. While doing so, we must not overlook the difference in the type of the government between India and US/UK. The US and UK model is the most widely discussed model in our country by the strategic community. However, these models can't be blindly used as a template due to different ground realities of our country which are discussed below.

The Governance System

India is more similar to the United States since both possess a federalist type structure with the sharing of power between the federal government and state or provincial institutions. This difference is considerably less in the United Kingdom. India, the world's largest democracy, can be compared more readily with the United States since it also faces a large number of domestic intelligence challenges as is the case with US.

The UK and India have parliamentary systems where the power of the executive is divided between the head of state and head of government. The head of government, in this case the Prime Minister, is also dependent on the support of the parliament. This support is expressed through a vote of confidence or no confidence.

The powers of the President of India and USA, though both are heads of State, are poles apart. The distinction and separation between the executive and legislative branches of government is much clearer in the United States. The relation between the policy makers and intelligence agencies are less formal in the US. The intelligence agencies have far greater access to policy makers abroad than in our country. In the US, intelligence related matters are fast tracked to the President, unlike in India. In the US, the committees considering intelligence matters are presided over by the Director of National Intelligence (DNI) or his representatives. Recommendations of the DNI, goes to the NSC through the NSA after required vetting by the NSCS Division on intelligence Programmes. Such meeting of the NSCS on intelligence assessment is presided by the DNI hence; the DNI becomes the chief intelligence advisor to the President on intelligence related matters whereas the NSA becomes chief advisor to the President on National Security related matters.[84]

Other differences also include the wide differences in the language and culture within India versus the United States and the United Kingdom.[85] Our country today faces larger number of internal and external security challenges than any other democracy in the world. Its regional implications prohibit us to largely adopt either US or UK model.

Over a period, numerous intelligence agencies have been added in our country on the lines of agencies of either USA or UK. However, even that has not been done in a holistic manner. For example, all the COMINT and SIGINT efforts of the USA are grouped under one single organisation, the National Security Agency (NSA). But the NTRO in India doesn't have exclusive control over such resources even though it is the nodal agency for TECHINT collection. Almost all agencies including IB, R&AW and DIA continue to maintain their own TECHINT resources.

The DIA of the USA is the primary producer of foreign intelligence and fulfills a critically important need for central intelligence manager for DOD to support the requirements of the Secretary of Defence, the Joint Chiefs of Staff (JCS), and the military forces, as well as other policy makers.[86] We adopted DIA from US model but couldn't appoint Chief of

Defence Staff (CDS). As a result, this organisation is not being optimally used.

We adopted JIC from the UK model but it has no realistic control over the agencies. It has been primarily reduced to an assessment making body whose own existence has always been tempered with on numerous occasions.

It is imperative that we first keep in mind the challenges which our national intelligence mechanism faces today. A realistic model conforming to the ground realities of our country cannot be visualised without overcoming these challenges. These challenges have been identified in the previous chapter.

Notes

[1] Brig Gurmeet Kanwal (Retd), former Director, CLAWS, Fighting terrorism -Policies mired in systemic weaknesses, accessed online at http://www.deccanherald.com/content/229625/indias-tough-choices-over-

[2] B. Raman, Intelligence: Past, Present, and Future (New Delhi, India: Lancer Publishers & Distributors, 2002), p.62-67

[3] Matt Waldman, "The Sun in the Sky: The Relationship between Pakistan's ISI and Afghan Insurgents", June 2010 accessed online through http://eprints.lse.ac.uk/28435/ and http://www.crisisstates.com/index.htm on 16 Feb 2011

[4] Ibid

[5] B. Raman, Intelligence: Past, Present, and Future (New Delhi, India: Lancer Publishers & Distributors, 2002), p.62-67

[6] B. Raman, Pakistan's Inter-Services Intelligence (ISI), South Asia Analysis Group, http://www.acsa.net/isi/index.html

[7] Peter Mattis, 'Assessing the Foreign Policy Influence of the Ministry of State Security', The Jamestown Foundation, China Brief Volume: 11 Issue:1, January 14, 2011 accessed online via http://www.jamestown.org/programs/chinabrief/single/?tx_ttnews%5Btt_news % 5D=37368&cHash=0239321b02 on 15 Jan 2012

8   Gale Encyclopedia of Espionage & Intelligence: China, Intelligence and Security accessed online via http://www. /china-intelligence-and-security on 16 Mar 2011

9   Gale Encyclopedia of Espionage & Intelligence: China, Intelligence and Security accessed online via http://www. /china-intelligence-and-security on 16 Mar 2011

10 Howard O. DeVore, China's Intelligence and Internal Security Forces, (Couldson, UK: Jane's Information Group, 1999): Chapter 3.

11 http://secondchina.com/Learning_Modules/MIL/content/MIL_min_statesec.html

12 www.cia.gov/library/center-for-the-study-of-intelligence/csi-publications/csi-studies/studies/vol.-55-no.-3/

13 Gale Encyclopedia of Espionage & Intelligence: China, Intelligence and Security accessed online via http://www. /china-intelligence-and-security on 16 Mar 2011

14 Ibid

15 Ibid

16 Ibid

17 The US china Business Council, accessed online via www.uschina.org/public/china/govstructure/govstructure_part5/5.html on 01 Jun 2012

18 Nicholas Eftimiades, Chinese Intelligence Operations, 1994 accessed online via http://www.scribd.com/doc/45014640/Chinese-Intelligence-Operations on 26Feb 2011

19 Article on The National Intelligence Department (NID) by Kiran Nepal accessed online via http:/ The+National+Intelligence+Department+%28NID%29+by+Kiran+ Nepal&sap=dsp&lang=en&mid=3c198426ab9447d0a88bd1 on 16 Feb 2011

20 Official website of FIU accessed online via http://www.nrb.org.np/fiu/pdffiles/FIU_Annual_Report_2067-68.pdf on 16 Jun 2012

21 Bangladesh Intelligence and Security accessed online via http://lcweb2.loc.gov/cgi-bin/query/r?frd/cstdy:@field(DOCID+bd0146) on 20 June 2012

22 Jeffrey T Richelson, 'The US Intelligence Community, Fourth Edition, (Westview Press, 1999), p.12

23 Official website of DNI http://www.dni.gov/ accessed online on 17 Dec2011

24 www.nctc.gov/ accessed online on 17 Dec 2010

[25] Jeffrey T Richelson, 'The US Intelligence Community, Fourth Edition, (West view Press, 1999), p.16

[26] www.fbi.gov/ - United States, official website of FBI accessed online on 13 Oct 2011

[27] rt.com/usa/news/fbi-terror-report-plot-365-899/ accessed online 0n 13 Oct 2011

[28] Jeffrey T Richelson , 'The US Intelligence Community, Fourth Edition, (West view Press, 1999), p.55

[29] Ibid ,p.30

[30] India's External Intelligence –Secrets of Research and Analysis Wing (R&AW), Maj Gen VK Singh, Manas Publications ,2007, p.39

[31] https://www1.nga.mil/ accessed online on 20 Dec 2011

[32] Jeffrey T Richelson , 'The US Intelligence Community, Fourth Edition, (West view Press, 1999), p.36

[33] kh2hb.wordpress.com/.../us-air-force-security-service-air-intelligence accessed online on 20 Dec 2011

[34] Official website accessed via www.marines.mil/unit/hqmc/intelligence on 13 Oct 2010

[35] www.inscom.army.mil/ accessed online on 13 Oct 2010

[36] www.oni.navy.mil/ accessed online 20 Dec 2011

[37] Official web site of United States's Department of State www.state.gov/ accessed online on 20 Dec 2011

[38] www.uscg.mil/ accessed online on 20 Dec2011

[39] Official web site of Department of Homeland Security http://www.dhs.gov/index.shtm a ccessed online on 20 Dec 2011

[40] This section draws mainly on Jeffrey T Richelson, 'The US Intelligence Community, Fourth Edition ,(West view Press, 1999, p.112 -180 and http://www.angelfire.com/hi/ IntellCommunity/index.html pp1-130

[41] www.whitehouse.gov/administration/eop/nsc accessed online on 20 De 2011

[42] http://www.nctc.gov/docs/ITACG_Guide_for_First_Responders_2011.pdf accessed online 05 Jan 2012

[43] www.fbi.gov/about-us/.../terrorism/terrorism_jttfs - United States accessed online on 05 Jan 2012

[44] T Richelson , 'The US Intelligence Community, Fourth Edition , (West view Press, 1999), p.85

[45] publicintelligence.net/fbi-joint-terrorism-task-force-jttf-model-memo accessed online on 10 Jan 2012

[46] www.justice.gov/jttf/ - United States and www.fbi.gov/about-us/.../terrorism/terrorism_jttfs - United States accessed online on 05 Jan 2012

[47] Steven Aftergood, "Intelligence Fusion Centers Emerge Across the US" 25 April , 2006 accessed online at http://www.fas.org/blog/secrecy/2006/04/intelligence_ fusion_centers _em.html on 25 Feb 2012

[48] Interagency Threat Assessment and Coordination Group (ITACG) Intelligence Guide for First Responders, Mar 2011, pp.32-37

[49] Steven Aftergood, "Intelligence Fusion Centers Emerge Across the US" 25 April , 2006 accessed online at http://www.fas.org/blog/secrecy/2006/04/intelligence_fusion_ centers_ em.html on 25 Feb 2012

[50] Don Van Duyn, "Fusion Centers: Unifying Intelligence to Protect Americans",03 Dec 2009 accessed online via http://www.fbi.gov/news/stories/2009/march/fusion_031209 on 20 Feb 2012

[51] http://www.nctc.gov/docs/ITACG_Guide_for_First_Responders_2011.pdf accessed online 05 Jan 2012

[52] Tom Burghardt, Big Brother "Fusion Centers" Part of US Domestic Intelligence and Surveillance Apparatus" Global Research, September 26, 2009 accessed online at http://www.globalresearch.ca/index.php?context=va&aid=15386 on 20 Feb 2012

[53] www.fbi.gov/news/stories/2008/august/njttf_081908 - United States and www.justice.gov/ jttf/ - United States accessed online on 20 Feb 2012

[54] Interagency Threat Assessment and Coordination Group (ITACG) Intelligence Guide for First Responders, Mar2011, pp.32-37

[55] www.dhs.gov/xabout/structure/editorial_0797.shtm accessed online on 22 Feb 2012

[56] This section draws on http://www.nctc.gov/docs/ITACG_Guide_ for_First_ Responders_ 2011.pdf

[57] B. Raman, Intelligence: Past, Present, and Future (New Delhi, India: Lancer Publishers & Distributors, 2002),p.41

[58] Official website of MI 6 accessed via https://www.sis.gov.uk/ on 09 Sept 2011

[59] www.gchq.gov.uk accessed online on 19 Jan 2011

[60] www.mi5.gov.uk accessed online on 19 Jan 2011

[61] B. Raman, Intelligence: Past, Present, and Future (New Delhi, India: Lancer Publishers & Distributors, 2002), p.41

[62] http://www.fas.org/irp/world/uk/jic/ accessed online on 19 Jan20 11

[63] ibid

[64] http://www.fas.org/irp/world/uk/mi6/ accessed online on 20 Sept 2011

[65] http://isc.independent.gov.uk

[66] B. Raman, Intelligence: Past, Present, and Future (New Delhi, India: Lancer Publishers & Distributors, 2002),p.41

[67] http://www.fas.org/irp/world/uk/mi6/ accessed online on 20 Sept 2011

[68] Raman, Intelligence: Past, Present, and Future (New Delhi, India: Lancer Publishers & Distributors, 2002),p.42

[69] http://www.archive.official-documents.co.uk/document/caboff/nim/0114301808.pdf

[70] Masse, Domestic Intelligence in the United Kingdom, p.6

[71] Homeland Security Affairs Vol. Iii, No. 2 (June 2007) Www.Hsaj.Org

[72] Australian Government, Protecting Australia Against Terrorism 2006: Australia's National Counterterrorism Policies and Arrangements (2006), 40-41; http://www.dpmc.gov.au/publications/protecting_australia_2006/docs/paat_2006.pdf.

[73] Director-General of Security, ASIO Report to Parliament 2005-2006, 51.

[74] www.mossad.gov.il accessed online on 19 Dec 2010

[75] This section draws mainly on "Inside Israel's Secret Organisations" *Jane's Intelligence Review* October 1996

[76] Samuel M. Katz, " Soldier Spies: Israeli Military Intelligence" (Presidio Pr, May 1994), p.159

[77] Samuel M. Katz, " Soldier Spies: Israeli Military Intelligence" (Presidio Pr, May 1994), pp.109-117

[78] http://johnmccarthy90066.tripod.com/id858.html accessed online on 15 Feb 2011

[79] www.mossad.gov.il

[80] Mossad's official web site accessed online on 15 Feb 2011

[81] Ian Black and Benny Morris, " Israel's Secret Wars: A History of Israel's Intelligence Services" (Grove Press, 1992)pp.234-239

[82] http://www.fas.org/irp/world/israel/mossad/ accessed online on 15 Feb 2011 and Ian Black and Benny Morris, " Israel's Secret Wars: A History of Israel's Intelligence Services, pp.319-327

[83] 'The Tribune Debate on 'NCTC' accessed online via http://www.tribuneindia.com on 19 Jan 2012

[84] B. Raman, Intelligence: Past, Present, and Future (New Delhi, India: Lancer Publishers & Distributors, 2002), p.96

[85] James Burch, "A Domestic Intelligence Agency for the United States? A Comparative Analysis of Domestic Intelligence Agencies and Their Implications for Homeland Security", p.17

[86] India's External Intelligence –Secrets of Research and Analysis Wing (RAW), Maj Gen VK Singh, Manas Publications ,2007, p.39

7

SETTING THE STAGE: THE PRECURSOR TO THE RECOMMENDATIONS

"If you do not know others and do not know yourself, you will be in danger in every single battle."

Art of War, Sun Tzu

Intelligence information can be a powerful tool. It is most useful when the user has a clear understanding of what intelligence can and cannot do. Intelligence can assist in decision making, by presenting information and analysis that can improve the decision making process for consumers and partners while creating hindrances for the enemies. Intelligence also provides warning of threats in being. We as intelligence consumer should not lose sight of the fact that intelligence cannot predict the future. Intelligence provides assessments of likely scenarios or developments, but there is no way to predict what will happen with absolute certainty. It is also pertinent to note that the intelligence community can't violate the law. They have to operate within the laws which can be misused by our adversaries or anti national elements. Pragmatic expectations will help consumers plug their intelligence requirements.

Lt Gen R K Sawhney, former DGMI feels that "The success of intelligence agencies is owned by the Government, but failures are passed back. If we want our intelligence apparatus to improve, we have to invest in it and take responsibilities for failures collectively".[1] Vikram Sood, former Director, R&AW comments "There is no public recognition of achievements and there is general public skepticism about intelligence organisations[2].These statements represent the view point of the intelligence agencies' expectations from the nation as a whole. The public opinion and media outcry against intelligence agencies blaming it solely for national security failures during recent terrorist strikes in Indian hinterland is all well known. This side represents the consumer expectations from intelligence agencies which is probably unrealistic.

There is a need to educate people and policy makers on what intelligence agencies can do and what they can't.[3] It would be important to first set these expectations in correct perspective before making recommendations to improve intelligence assessment and coordination at the national level. Also, we must keep in mind the changed internal and external security threats facing our country in the last few decades or so. It will quantify the enormity of the challenges which the agencies have to face today. It will also give an insight into why piecemeal intelligence reforms have not been effective to the desired extent. This would set the stage for making any meaningful recommendations for bridging this gap. The same is being attempted in this chapter.

The nature of intelligence activity is such that successes achieved are rarely reported but intelligence failures are splashed across the visual and print media and remain in the public consciousness for a very long time. The contribution of intelligence community to the victory over Pakistan in 1971, successful counter intelligence programme before 1974 and 1998 nuclear tests, restoration of normalcy in Mizoram and Punjab has been scantly attributed to intelligence agencies but 1962 War or Kargil Intrusion or Mumbai Terrorist Strikes have been widely reported as 'intelligence failures'.[4]

Noted US scholar, Brian Johnson pointed that the reason to have intelligence agencies in first place was to gather information 'not related to the investigation of a known past criminal act or specific planned criminal activity'.[5] That is the job of police services; intelligence organisations must search for crimes no one has as yet, committed.[6] But more often than not intelligence agencies are presumed to be only investigative agencies. Creation of one more investigative agency NIA post 26/11 is one example of such presumption. The nation overlooked the fact that we have enough post-incident investigative agencies. We need an agency on the lines of FBI suitably armed, equipped and legally empowered to prevent terrorism, carry out counter-terrorism strikes and to prosecute captured terrorists under Indian Laws. But, based on public and media outcry post 26/11, an ill conceived consumer expectation, one more agency (NIA) was created.

In view of the above, we must keep the operational constraints of intelligence agencies in mind before evaluating their performance. We must also take into account the growing realms of intelligence such as cyber intelligence, economic intelligence, and information warfare/perception management etc, when we are putting the intelligence agencies to trial. The role of social media and internet has immensely increased the scope of intelligence which we often overlook while evaluating the performance of intelligence agencies. It is quite logical that intelligence agencies should be held accountable for the national security failures. However, if we pay attention to the inherent constraint of intelligence as a holistic process, the agencies can be engaged in constructive introspection and improvement. In essence, we must be fair to intelligence agencies and give them a fair trial.

Inherent Constraints of Intelligence Agencies

Time Bound The situation described by any given intelligence report is liable to change before the relevant information can be analysed and integrated into the decision making process. Consequently, most intelligence information is time bound and its usefulness depends upon the speed at which it can be transmitted and analysed. The pace of activities these days is too fast and the amount of available information is vast. Hence, there is always the possibility that the most crucial piece of information is the most mundane and thus overlooked. During the Kargil War, intelligence agencies did receive information pertaining to suspicious activities across the border but the information had changed its connotation between winter and summers of 1999.

Dynamic Threats. The security environment is fluid and constantly throws up new type of threats with which intelligence organisations must cope. Organisations provide the structures and processes that are necessary for effective analysis and exploitation of intelligence. Yet the building an organisation that is well suited to the effective collection, assessment, and distribution of intelligence is a constant challenge. It is imperative that intelligence organisation must be periodically reviewed and audited so that it can be suitably revamped to meet the constantly changing security environment. The concept of Joint Intelligence Committee was adopted after the 1962 debacle; however, it had also become redundant and non-functional over a period of time. It required a Kargil War to get us out of slumber and carry out a review of our intelligence structure.

Political Bias We must be conscious of the fact that the identification and interpretation of a threat is essentially a political activity. Policymakers are subjective consumers of intelligence, with strong political incentives to disregard unsettling estimates. Unsurprisingly, leaders have a long history of ignoring such intelligence inputs.[7]

The possibility that intelligence information will be distorted by political bias is present at every stage of the intelligence process. From the outset, political assumption determines what is considered a threat and what is not. The intelligence agencies must be insulated from political environment and granted legal protection. However, some form of parliamentary oversight is also necessary to induce requisite checks and balances within and amongst the intelligence agencies.[8]

Human Errors It is pertinent to mention that the human mind is inclined to search for, and seize upon information that confirms existing beliefs and desires. The same trend can also be identified as a marked tendency among military intelligence agencies, in particular, to formulate "worst case" estimates of the intentions and especially the capabilities of potential enemies. In such cases intelligence operatives tend to 'situate the appreciation' instead of appreciating the situation. This tendency was quite obvious in assessment of intelligence agencies which coincided with assessment of Pandit Jawaharlal Nehru and they both believed in each other's assessment which was proved wrong. We must not forget that intelligence operatives are also "human beings", prone to obvious human tendencies. Let us not treat them as "supermen" who can only be hanged.'

Intelligence: The Growing Realms

Cyber Intelligence

Cyber Intelligence constitutes new data and information gathering resources, technologies, capabilities and techniques. Many of the current intelligence gathering platforms offer little or no cyber threat intelligence gathering capabilities. This is because unlike nuclear weapons and other weapons of mass destruction, cyber weapons and attacks require far less infrastructure and do not require restricted materials or knowledge that is in limited supply. It is extremely difficult to cloak the return path for information obtained from the cyber bugs that compromised the computer systems.

Cyber Warfare Intelligence addresses the process of gathering data and information about a cyber enemy or threat. This represents the data collection, analysis and interpretations that lead to insight and understanding that is specific to the cyber threat operational environment. The defence forces for obvious reasons are one of the prime targets of cyber warfare. The collection of cyber threat intelligence presents the most significant challenge for the defence intelligence community. Developing cyber intelligence requires digital trespassing on foreign networks and the computers operated by foreign governments, corporations and individuals which is a time consuming and risky affair. This underlines the importance of availability of suitably trained operatives for cyber intelligence. [9]

Economic Intelligence

"The economic intelligence is also of great importance. One component is the strength and vulnerabilities of national economies. The knowledge of strength may be important in understanding their capabilities for conflict while knowledge of vulnerabilities may be important in assessing threats to stability".[10] Economic crimes in India, like in other countries, are linked to several other offences, or even organised crimes, having a bearing on national security. A greater degree of sophistication is being noticed in the activities of smuggling, tax evasion and commercial frauds.

Economic Intelligence has added a new dimension to the paradigm of intelligence process. The importance of economic intelligence in the current world order cannot be over emphasised. This has only added to the problem of overloaded intelligence operatives. The amount of data now being presented to an analyst has increased many folds. This makes the task more daunting.

Perception Management

Perception management is considered the fourth instrument of power, besides diplomatic, economic and the military power. Expressions such as psychological warfare (psy war), perception management, precision guided propaganda, etc refer to same techniques of influencing the minds of the people. Perception Management revolves around using 'soft' (positive) and 'hard' (negative) images to influence the minds of a target population. The new information age permits precision guided propaganda, much as modern technology permits precision guided bomb. Perception management can be both, defensive as well as offensive. In defensive techniques, we are actually countering the enemy's propaganda in a reactive mode. The offensive or pro active mode deals with attacks on enemy's mind before it subverts the minds of 'target audience'.[11]

Social Networking and National Security

We are living in an age of information abundance. Information has an impact to a large extent on all aspects of life and spheres. The impact in the political and military spheres has connotations with respect to the national security issues. We need to understand the key facets of the information age and the strategies required to manage the abundance of information at our disposal.

In earlier times, the sources of information were few. We had the print media and a few channels, but communication was one way. The senders and the channels were powerful but the receivers were powerless and unconnected. This situation has dramatically changed now. The number of sources and channels has increased dramatically and we have a surfeit of information and many way communication. While the senders and channels are still powerful, for the first time the receivers too have been empowered and are increasingly getting better and better connected to the media and to each other. The requirement is to achieve narrative dominance in this environment. Where earlier the narrative was about rationing scarcity, information control, censorship and propaganda, the shift now is towards managing abundance. This information abundance has enhanced the scope of intelligence agencies many folds.[12]

Computers have changed our life and how we do almost everything. They have in fact started managing national security. There is a lot more on the information superhighway these days than just information. There is overload of information facilitated by E-mail, Facebook, MySpace, YouTube, Wikipedia, LinkedIn, Twitter, and other social networking tools. Social networking involves linking individuals together as part of a voluntary group. Persons join groups because they share common attributes, interests, activities, or causes. Within the group they exchange information, goods, services, and opinions. As the group grows it forms a network. Social networks are not limited to the Internet. Computer technology, however, has greatly expanded the capacity and speed for establishing networks of people. [13]

This has thrown new challenges for national security managers in particular intelligence agencies. They may be expected to monitor/intercept all transmission or communication which is impossible in the world of social net working.

The intelligence agencies can no longer monitor the huge volume of data being transmitted via social networking sites which can be easily exploited by anti national elements. However, the onus of keeping a track of trends and new developments on the social networking sites lies on the intelligence agencies. This in itself is a challenging responsibility which throws open a new challenge for intelligence agencies on a daily basis.

There has been a sea change in the perception of what constitutes our 'national space'. The definition is much broader now and issues (such as economics, social media, science) that were for some time removed from the realm of intelligence targeting are now indivisible parts of it.

There is a change in the tone of the revisionist feeling within the country. Revisionists today are able to use all possible resources to aggressively project their viewpoints. In some cases, this leads to advanced forms of terrorism. Urban terrorism has become a major challenge for our security agencies. LWE is becoming another major challenge which has exploited the existing fissures and divisions in the society i.e. the economic disparity. The fissures of divisions based on caste, religion and ethnicity are also being exploited by these elements. Intelligence agencies today, are under a lot of pressure to predict and thus help contain revisionism.

The nature of organised crime has changed and its infiltration into the society is growing. The joining of local crime syndicates with narcotics distributors and arms smugglers has increased their destabilising influence on the society. This element often joins hands with the revisionist elements and produces extremely serious threats to national security. Intelligence targeting of these indefinable, politically connected and dangerous criminals is a difficult task especially as it involves crossing national borders.

The nuclear threat from our 'nuclear neighbours' has added a new dimension to intelligence targeting. Increased nuclear and missile technology proliferation to India's hostile neighbours has imposed more demanding requirements on all three aspects of intelligence targeting, i.e. collection, collation and dissemination. It may require special training, equipment and techniques of intelligence gathering and analysis. The need to provide accurate and actionable intelligence assessments regarding these threats is paramount. Our intelligence agencies have to prepare themselves for this new type of intelligence targeting.[14]

This brings us to a conclusion that the intelligence agencies definitely be held accountable for intelligence and security failures along with other organs of statecraft. At the same time, we as a nation must understand that the function of intelligence is multi-faceted and is a challenging task. The task of Intelligence agencies, whether handling external or internal intelligence, is extremely demanding and testing. It is pertinent to note that such failures are inevitable as the intelligence agencies have to function under certain constraints and ever changing security dynamics as enumerated above. With this as a backdrop, we can now make certain recommendations which if implemented with strong political will can prepare our intelligence agencies for challenges of the 21st century.

Notes

[1] Interview with Lt Gen R K Sawhney (Retd),former DGMI on 24 Nov 2010

[2] Vikram Sood , former Chief of R&AW, *Indian Defence Review* Jul- Sep 2006.

[3] Michael A. Turner, 'Why Secret Intelligence Fails', (Potomac Books Inc, 31 January, 2005), p.11

[4] Prem Mahadevan , "The Politics of Counter-Terrorism in India — Strategic Intelligence and National Security in South Asia"; I.B. Tauris & Co, London,2012 p.13

[5] Brian A. Jackson, "Considering the Creation of a Domestic Intelligence Agency in the United States", accessed online via http://www.dtic.mil/dtic/tr/fulltext/u2/a494510.pdf on 15 Mar 2012

[6] Praveen Swami, " New intelligence technology feeding surge in political espionage", accessed online at http://www.thehindu.com/news/national/article2687373.ece on 06 Dec2011

[7] Joshua Rovner and Austin Long, "Intelligence Failure and Reform: Evaluating the 9/11 Commission Report" , Breakthroughs, Vol. 14, No. 1 (Spring , 2005), pp. 1, accessed online via www.usnwc.edu/getattachment/ea6041fc-0260-4618.../Rovner-CV on 20 Sept 2010

[8] Peter Jackson and Jenifer Siege, ' Intelligence and Statecraft – The Use and Limits of Intelligence in International society' (Praeger Publishers , 2005) p.27-57

[9] http://www.technolytics.com/Cyber_Warfare_Doctrine_Public_Version.pdf accessed online on 11 Jan 12

[10] Jeffrey T Richelson, 'The U.S. Intelligence Community, Fourth Edition ,(West view Press, 1999), p.6

[11] B. Raman, Intelligence: Past, Present, and Future (New Delhi, India: Lancer Publishers & Distributors, 2002),p.295

[12] Nitin Pai, 'The Impact of Social Media on the Management of National Security' CLAWS , 07 Feb 2012

[13] http://knol.google.com/k/social-networking-and-national-security#Introduction accessed online on 19 Dec 2011

[14] Sunil Sainis, "Intelligence Reforms" Bharat Rakshak Monitor - Volume 3(4) January-February 2001,p.3

8

THE RECOMMENDATIONS

"Our enemies live in the seams of our jurisdictions. No single agency or nation can find them and fight them alone. If we are to protect our citizens, working together is not just the best option, it is the only option."

- Robert Mueller, Director, FBI in Global Terrorism Today and the Challenges of Tomorrow

The above statement sums up the requirement of synergised integrated and cohesive efforts to deal with multi dimensional challenges to national security facing the world today. The same yardstick should also apply to our intelligence efforts to complement our national security. In the last decade or so, a few review committees were constituted to bring about synergy in the working of our intelligence agencies. The results have been mixed. The score card of our intelligence efforts at the national level has not been very encouraging, necessitating a review.

The aim of this study is not to delve into inter-agency issues or 'turf battles', but to draw out a roadmap and formulate long-term plans to improve our intelligence coordination and assessment at the national level. The ingredients of 'successful coordination' are trust (no personality clash), transparency, information sharing, 'glory sharing', taking successes and failures in stride. The intelligence must be shared by very regular interaction amongst all agencies. In case, we can achieve a right mix of above ingredients, the lack of coordination amongst intelligence agencies can be improved. This chapter will highlight those issues that require more attention and focus than they have received before.

In India, we are obsessed with 'new/out of the box recommendations'. Most recommendations are rejected on the ground that they do not contain anything novel. It is not the new recommendation which is important. The spirit and will to implement these recommendations are more important. After every debacle, a commission of inquiry is appointed to investigate the matter, determine the reasons for the failure, and recommend improvements. However, recommendations are not taken in the correct spirit and the will to implement them has been lacking. Previous recommendations which were not carried out earlier can become more effective, if they are implemented in the true spirit. With this as a backdrop the recommendations are outlined below.

National Resolve to Accord Priority to Intelligence

The task of Intelligence agencies, whether handling external or internal intelligence, is extremely demanding and testing. Intelligence has never been given its due priority in our country. In the words of Lt Gen R K Sawhney, former DGMI, "In India, intelligence is unfortunately treated with contempt; it is taken for granted and is misused. For intelligence agencies, there are only users not enablers. Policy leaders determine utility of intelligence they receive based on ideological and political factors. Hence, the intelligence gets biased, and they alter judgments to suit the view of their customers or to further their own interests." [1]

India's national security policy is mostly threat reactive than pro-active. Our security policy is predominantly defensive in nature. As a result, our political leadership remain satisfied as long as situations are met with a response. The role of intelligence agencies is much beyond as perceived today. Intelligence services have to be given the wherewithal to formulate predictive strategic assessments of long and short term threats. Intelligence assumes even more relevance in our present security environment with unresolved boundary disputes with Pakistan and China. There is a need for arriving at faster intelligence collation and assessment. As India is growing at a faster rate, intelligence should get more prominence.

A national consensus has to be reached through various means to accord requisite priority to intelligence and treat it as a special activity. Intelligence agencies should be provided with adequate budgetary support to ensure their optimal functioning. The policy makers should avoid perceiving world events, and lean toward analysis that supports their own predispositions which at times could be against the cautious advice rendered by intelligence agencies. A high degree of rapport and faith must be built amongst policy makers and intelligence agencies. Unrealistic expectations from intelligence agencies should be avoided at all costs.

Our perception towards intelligence has to change. Intelligence should not be treated as part of the bureaucratic system. We have to realise that attitudinal changes are needed to accept Intelligence gathering as a special activity. Attitudinal changes are most difficult to bring about; hence this point has been covered in the beginning of the list of recommendations.

The Intelligence Reforms

It is the need of the hour to appoint an Indian Intelligence Reform Commission on the lines of Administrative Reforms Commission to refurbish the ongoing intelligence mechanism at the national level. Reforms have been undertaken in the past but most of these have been in isolation and crises driven. The intelligence reforms have to be implemented with a strong will from the point of view of both the consumer and the producer.

Legal Status

The first reform should focus on giving intelligence agencies the backing of legislative enactments. Law should provide a degree of independence as well as the responsibilities which frees intelligence from bureaucratic shackles. The financial management of intelligence agencies has to be streamlined. The administrative functions of intelligence agencies have to be defined by an act of Parliament. It is recommended that intelligence agencies function under some sort of a legal cover. The legislation should provide for an institutionalised mechanism wherein grievances of intelligence agencies/personnel should be addressed on priority. At the same time, the legislation should also cater for a system in which complaints against intelligence agencies /personnel can be speedily investigated.

Audit and Accountability

There is a need to bring all organs of the state under the supervision of the Parliament, without exception.[2] Laws should also hold intelligence agencies accountable to a supervisory committee. Given the importance of intelligence, and especially the possibility of failures, oversight is essential. The supervisory committee would provide legality to the functioning of intelligence agencies which in turn would enhance their effectiveness and efficiency.

The supervisory committee would ensure accountability of intelligence agencies in their functioning and actions. The supervisory committee would ensure avoidance of alleged human right violations thereby enhancing the image of intelligence agencies. A supervising mechanism on the intelligence agencies would also improve the administration of intelligence agencies. Transparency in the system is a must to ensure a high morale of intelligence agencies. As brought out previously in this book, intelligence agencies in almost all developed countries are accountable to some form of supervisory and audit mechanism.

In US, the legislative oversight function is efficiently carried out by the Congressional Committee System.[3] The Senate Intelligence Committee is charged with overseeing and making continuing studies of the intelligence activities and programs of the United States Government. It is responsible to submit to the Senate, appropriate proposals for legislation and report to the Senate concerning such intelligence activities and programs. It provides vigilant legislative oversight over US intelligence activities to assure that they are Constitutional.[4]

In the UK, the Parliament's Intelligence and Security Committee (ISC) reviews the budget, administration, and policy of all three intelligence agencies. MI5 also has a legal framework and a charter of duties. It produces an annual report, which is placed before Parliament. It provides details of its budget and the manner of its utilisation. Even the JIC is subject to oversight by the Intelligence and Security Committee and is an element of the Intelligence, Security and Resilience organisation within the Cabinet Office.[5]

In case of Israel, parliamentary oversight is exercised by the Knesset

Subcommittee for Intelligence and Secret Services, a subcommittee of the Foreign Affairs and Defence Committee, which supervises the entire Israeli Security Forces.[6] The list of Knesset members per Knesset includes all Knesset members that served for any time, including part time, on the Subcommittee for Intelligence and Secret Services during the tenure of each Knesset.[7]

It is recommended that selected appointments in Parliament such as the Speaker, Leader of Opposition, members of Cabinet Committee on Security (CCS) and one or two nominated experts on intelligence from other walks of life should constitute a Parliamentary Standing Committee on Intelligence Set Up. The committee should periodically review the functioning of intelligence agencies and review their budget allotment without jeopardising national security to exercise requisite control over the intelligence agencies.

Manish Tewari, Member of Parliament, introduced a Bill in the Lok Sabha to regulate the functioning and use of power by the Indian intelligence agencies within and outside India and to provide for the coordination, control and oversight of such agencies on 29 March 2011.[8]It would be in the national interest to debate such a bill and pass it on priority. More than a year after tabling of the Bill, no progress has been made.

National Intelligence Authority

It is recommended that a national intelligence authority be created to improve the quality of intelligence assessment and more importantly to coordinate the intelligence efforts at national level. There is a need for a centralised supervisory mechanism for intelligence agencies as has been done in USA post 9/11. The office of the Director National Intelligence (DNI) was created to oversee the intelligence community in USA. The Director of National Intelligence (DNI) serves as the head of the US Intelligence Community overseeing and directing the implementation of the National Intelligence Program and acting as the principal advisor to the President, the National Security Council, and the Homeland Security Council for intelligence matters related to national security.[9]

The need of the hour is to provide strong leadership with unity of command to enhance intelligence assessment and coordination at the national level. It is imperative that more authority is vested with national intelligence authorities. There is a need to appoint an appropriate nodal intelligence agency to assess and coordinate intelligence at the national level. It should be based on principle of primacy of intelligence and establish the rule of accountability. Of course, there would be resistance to creation of such a mechanism but with strong political will to implement; such minor issues can be overcome.

The emergence of an 'Intelligence Czar' due to unity of command would be argued by some experts. However, it is recommended that adequate safeguards be built into the system to ensure accountability of intelligence agencies. The unity of command is required to facilitate coordination of intelligence efforts at national level at the same time accountability, audit and oversight is essential to ensure efficiency.

A Recommended Model of Intelligence and Security Set up at National Level

In order to achieve the above requirements, it is recommended that a National Intelligence Assessment and Coordination Council (NIACC) be created. The Council members would include Director of IB, R&AW and DIA immediately on retirement from their post with requisite staff (Secretariat) to support them. The senior serving officers of these agencies can also be appointed as members; however, before appointment they will have to resign from active service. It would replace Intelligence Coordination Group (ICG) and Joint Intelligence Committee which have become almost non functional over a period of time. The long list of intelligence agencies as covered in Chapter Two and appendix E (approximately 25) has to be reduced to just three. The rest of the agencies should be amalgamated in the above three intelligence agencies. A separate study can be conducted to recommend the agencies which can be disbanded altogether and some of them would continue to work under any of the three agencies. The NIACC would act as Joint Analysis Centre comparable to J-TAC (Joint Terrorism Analysis Centre) of UK except the fact that it would not restrict itself to intelligence related to terrorism only.

A National council would help in improving the working of inter-agency organisations such as the Multi Agency Centre (MAC) and the proposed

National Counter Terrorism Centre (NCTC). As brought out previously in this book, most democracies have independent machinery for assessment, coordination and follow up. The setting up of NIACC will assist in overseeing the functioning of a plethora of intelligence agencies which exist today. The above recommended structure brings analysts from the respective intelligence agencies under one umbrella to facilitate the sharing of intelligence and breaking down of cross-agency barriers.

However, such a structure would first necessitate a system like Chairman, Joint Chiefs of Staff of US or the Chief of Defence Staff (CDS) of UK. A pre requisite to the above recommended intelligence restructuring is that CDS as recommended by KRC be appointed immediately after discussing various models amongst political parties. The CDS would invariably attend the meetings of Cabinet Committee on Security (CCS) to bring about synergy between assessment makers, decision makers and reaction elements who respond to the produced intelligence.

The Proposed Structure of NIACC

- The three members of NIACC would have equal status and would be personally represented in all meetings with National Security Advisor (NSA).

- NSA is mostly from diplomatic background and hence may not have adequate intelligence and security background knowledge. The NIACC would assist NSA by providing him consolidated intelligence assessments.

- The NSA in consultation with National Security Council Secretariat (NSCS), Strategic Policy Group (SPG) and National Security Advisory Board (NSAB) would prepare its own assessment for CCS, where as NIACC based on the inputs of these three intelligence agencies would prepare its independent assessment for NSA. Hence, NSA would now have independent recommendations of NIACC which he will communicate to CCS.

- NIACC would be created as a new and separate office in the PMO, on the lines of the Director of National Intelligence (DNI) of the US except that it would have three members of equal status.

Flow Chart of Recommended Intelligence Assessment and Coordination Mechanism at National Level

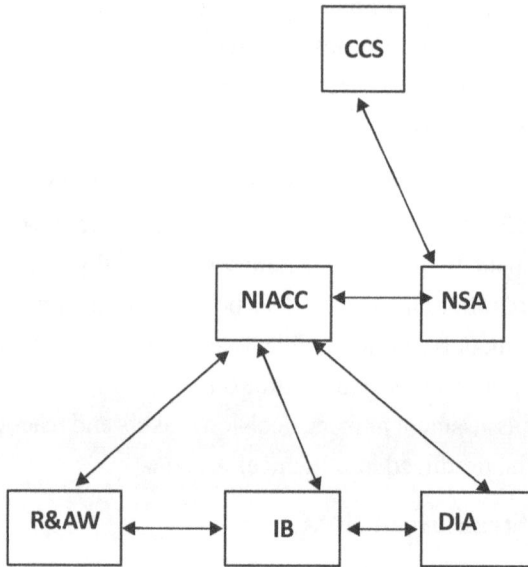

```
                          ┌──────┐
                          │ CCS  │
                          └──────┘
                              ▲
                              │
              ┌───────┐    ┌──────┐
              │ NIACC │◄──►│ NSA  │
              └───────┘    └──────┘
           ▲    ▲    ▲
          /     │     \
    ┌───────┐ ┌──────┐ ┌──────┐
    │ R&AW  │◄►│  IB  │◄►│ DIA  │
    └───────┘ └──────┘ └──────┘
```

Action Plan for Restructuring

- Only three intelligence agencies namely IB (Internal Security), R&AW (External and Strategic intelligence) and DIA (Defence and Technical intelligence) with their formalised charter of duties ratified by legislation in Parliament be allowed to operate.

- The domestic intelligence agency, IB would provide coordinated inputs pertaining to internal security matters perpetuated by elements within the state. The functioning of MAC, JTFI, and NCTC would be coordinated by IB which in turn would provide coordinated assessment related to terrorism and other internal security threats to NIACC. The assessment related to economic intelligence would be prepared by IB which would then be submitted to NIACC for overall assessment.

- The external intelligence agency R&AW would provide coordinated inputs on threats emanating from external actors .The agency would also be exclusively responsible for generating strategic intelligence inputs and provide consolidated assessment to NAICC. R&AW would also be responsible for maintaining interface with foreign intelligence agencies.

- DIA with existing expertise of Signal Intelligence Directorate and Defence Image Processing and Analysis Centre (DIPAC) would be provided with technical intelligence gathering assets presently with NTRO. The manpower of NTRO will be amalgamated into R&AW and IB. These civil personnel will not be shifted to DIA. The technical intelligence gathering assets of NTRO are recommended to be amalgamated into DIA. NTRO can be effectively amalgamated into DIA only after appointment of CDS. The assets required for functional technical intelligence would also be transferred to IB and R&AW from NTRO. DIA will also have IB and R&AW representatives to act as liaison officers for their parent agency.

- Intelligence agencies of paramilitary forces would be required to appoint intelligence liaison or nodal officers to interact on a regular basis with the above main intelligence agencies.

- A separate study can be ordered to finalise the details of amalgamation and transfer of resources of all other intelligence functioning in the country today. The agencies, if necessary, can have their integral intelligence mechanism upto the state level .However, all such agencies would finally operate under any of the three intelligence agencies at the national level as recommended above.

The Power and Duties of NIACC

- It would take a holistic view of all intelligence from different sources, evaluate accuracy, synthesis to obtain a cohesive picture, arrive at a final assessment after discussing amongst the three members.

- The NIACC would provide a coordinated input in the form of an assessment to the Cabinet Committee on Security (CCS).

- It would have powers comparable to a judicial committee ratified by the legislation of Parliament.

- NIACC would be briefed on a weekly basis by directors of IB, R&AW and DIA. Its most senior member would chair the meetings. It can summarily ask for additional information from intelligence agencies and it would be obligatory for them to comply with its directions.

- This council will have budgetary and personnel authority, enabling it to reward compliance and punish non-compliance. The NIACC would have summary powers to recommend allotment of funds to the parliament based on the response of intelligence agencies to the tasking done by it.

- It would be responsible for monthly, quarterly and annual tasking of the intelligence units. The intelligence units would be tasked to submit their consolidated inputs to NIACC in a time bound manner.

- It would also be responsible to prepare an all source assessment with recommendations for follow up action, there on. It would be responsible for developing strategic assessments and categorising domestic threats.

- It would identify and assess short, medium and long term threats to national security. It would facilitate a coordinated flow of intelligence assessment to political decision makers and help them in formulating an adequate policy and/ or action response.

- NIACC would exercise leadership and management over the intelligence community in terms of controlling resources, implementing cross organisational information sharing initiatives.

Improving Quality of Human Resources

The tapping of suitable human resources for intelligence agencies cannot be over emphasised. This has to be attested by the very high bar that should be to be crossed by candidates wishing to enter the ranks of the Indian intelligence community. We have to select the best and bright people including experts from other walks of life who can do "out of the box" thinking. Open recruitment system is recommended to be followed to ensure that the most talented professionals are recruited. It is the current practice in frontline intelligence agencies of countries like the US, the UK and Israel.

"An intelligence agency can be effective in its national effort only if it is manned by men and women of talent, ability, commitment and expertise. The intelligence operatives making assessment at the national level should interact regularly with the policy makers". Essentially, India's intelligence agencies must learn the art of self improvement".[10]The above remarks of Vikram Sood, former Director, R&AW is recommended to be followed by any intelligence agency as a guiding principle for human resource management.

Analysis is the heart of the intelligence process, its success boils down to the skill and expertise of the individual analyst. However, in India an analyst's job is considered to be a mundane activity without any glamour. As a result, there are few takers for this job. The intelligence agencies have no option but to assign this job to whatever quality of manpower they can lay their hands on. Unfortunately, those analysts who have had long tenures with intelligence agencies are leaving since it is no secret that analysts can make more money in the private sector. They also have more freedom of operation without any fear of being scrutinised.

In the present circumstances, we need more of intelligence analysts than intelligence operatives. The intelligence community must address the problem of retaining good analysts on priority. The analysts should be given long tenures and focus on their specialisation to maintain continuity which could be very demanding. This has to be done deliberately to ensure that the job of analysts becomes equally if not more attractive than the intelligence operatives.

The personnel selected for intelligence tasks, therefore, should have an aptitude and flair for the job. The government policies need to be suitably modified to make the intelligence profession more lucrative as a career option by offering incentives. The training and grooming of intelligence personnel need improvement and their morale should be kept high. "Linguistic skill of intelligence personnel have assumed greater importance in today's world".[11] The intelligence operatives have to operate in different type of areas with a vast difference in language. An analyst cannot analyse the input based on translation done by amateur translators who have no background knowledge about the input. If we have dedicated language experts with intelligence agencies, the quality of analysis can be improved. The language experts if required must be hired to facilitate the task of intelligence agencies.

Promotions and stagnation should be strictly performance based. We have to provide a long tenure to intelligence personnel to maintain continuity. Similar incentives are being offered to intelligence agencies in USA. The same can be done if Intelligence agencies are well looked after and have proper redressal system in their own set up. The intelligence agencies need more and more professional intelligence officers who are recruited as intelligence being their career option and have long tenures with intelligence agencies. The officers on deputation should be limited and that too selected on their merit, not otherwise.

The manpower in intelligence agencies should also be absorbed from experts in other walks of life. The intelligence officers should be assisted by qualified economists, scientists, mathematicians, and experts in international banking and finance.

Technologically savvy personnel are also recommended to be employed in these agencies to exploit the boom in technology. Gone are the days, when intelligence was so secretive and functioned in isolation. Today, nothing is classified information except your adversary's mind. One has to learn to analyse and reason out to read your adversary's mind.

Cross-pollination between military and civil intelligence agencies would improve the quality of assessment and coordination. Bright officers should be selected for deputation to other intelligence agencies like R&AW who would in turn facilitate improved inter agency coordination. There is a requirement of Military intelligence personnel including Air and Naval intelligence to have an exposure with a civil intelligence agency. The Army Intelligence officers should go to R&AW and come back to the Army to pass on their experiences. Similarly, there is also a requirement of civil intelligence personnel to have an exposure to the military intelligence agency. All the three major intelligence agencies, viz IB, R&AW and the DIA require inter-agency postings of each other's officers for better coordination.

Training

One of the prime measures to improve inter-agency coordination is to have a common training facility for intelligence personnel. A common and improved professional training programme would foster better inter personal relations amongst intelligence operatives and also improve inter-agency coordination. It will resolve the various issues of "Turf war "and will also provide an opportunity to understand the methods and capabilities of all intelligence agencies. Common training can be conducted at a national institute /academy of Intelligence which an intelligence operative would join after undergoing his basic training in his parent institute.

The intelligence community should be trained with the aid of war gaming. For instance, we can assign analytical teams to play the role of terrorists. These "red teams" can stimulate creative thinking and assess the nature of the threat, thereby making correct assessment. The analysts should also be given field tours and attend these training courses to remain in touch with the current environment. Additional analysts hired can act as their replacements and free these analysts for training and courses. It is recommended that concerted efforts be made to improve the training facilities for intelligence operatives on priority. Cross-training among intelligence agencies can further solve the problem of shortage of training facilities.

National Intelligence Grid (NATGRID)

Assessment can be done best only by the professional analysts, who have the subject and area knowledge. For quality assessment, the professional analysts should have the background data at their disposal. It is recommended to shape a 'Shared Information Environment' amongst various intelligence and security agencies which will assist in the creation of a 'Trusted Information Network'. It is essential to create a decentralised network that would allow all national security agencies to access one another's databases. This network would be highly secure and allow some retention of information rights by specific agencies, but its overall purpose would be to break down barriers between agencies. In theory, this would allow the intelligence community to utilise the benefits of the "information revolution" to prevent failures of operational coordination.

A project to centralise data from multiple sources for better intelligence analysis was announced after 26/11. Setting up of NATGRID which was approved by CCS in Nov 2010 should be expedited as it would ease the pressure of information overload on intelligence agencies as the sharing will become faster and automated. The information can be accessed by different users on need to know basis which can be controlled by the software. The grid when established would facilitate better synergy amongst intelligence agencies as it would make possible exchange of information between security agencies across the country.

NATGRID when created, will have access to about 21 categories of databases (railway, air travel, income tax, bank accounts, credit cards, visa and immigration records).However, we cannot solely rely on NATGRID for analysis and must make judicious use of databases of each other agency. It is recommended to have built in firewall to prevent the access of database to unauthorised agency.

We can explore the use of developing a project on the lines of "Total Information Awareness (TIA)" in US. It aims to create the tool that would permit analysts to "data mine" data bases by using softwares that translates analyst queries into usable form and applies specific "business rules" to sort out relevant information. It can assist analysts to go back to databases and find patterns of behavior that are associated with a particular person or event.

TIA is the name of a massive US data mining project focused on scanning travel, financial and other data from public and private sources with the goal of detecting and preventing trans-national threats to national security. TIA has also been called Terrorism Information Awareness. The program was part of the Homeland Security Act and, after its creation in January 2003, was managed by the Defence Advanced Research Projects Agency (DARPA).[12] Even though this project is also likely to be accused of transgressing into privacy rights as is with 'Aadhaar' (UIDAI) in India, the same can be explored for implementation.

National Counter Terrorism Centre (NCTC)

It is recommended that the Government should expedite setting up of NCTC which should be suitably armed, equipped and legally empowered to prevent terrorism, carry out counter-terrorism strikes and to prosecute captured terrorists under Indian Laws. NCTC should be set up with control over intelligence, operations and investigation of all matters pertaining to terrorism. However, the attempt to bring all intelligence agencies under it should be discouraged as intelligence/investigation/security agencies have a far wider mandate than just terrorism.

Counter terrorism is part of the overall ambit of intelligence and security operations but is not the only mandate of intelligence agencies. .The ultimate aim should be to bring about synergy and cohesion in counter-terrorism efforts, by doing away with overlapping, duplications, bottlenecks and unnecessary hurdles. To achieve this objective, it is enough if NCTC functions as an umbrella organisation with representations from intelligence, investigation and security agencies. It should be in a position to integrate all instruments of national power, including diplomatic, economic, social, political, military, intelligence, and law enforcement to ensure unity of effort. It should happen at central, state and local levels. The tentacles of the NCTC should penetrate deep down to the district levels instead of being another top-heavy organisation. Personnel for NCTC could be pooled from relevant intelligence, investigation and security agencies headed by the senior most experienced officer on rotation basis with a simple command structure. In this way, turf wars could be avoided, with the potential and efficacy of the agencies maximised. There is a need to create such modules at state and District level as well. A detailed backgrounder on NCTC has been included in Appendix D.

Public Private Partnership

There is no dearth of 'Nationalistic Sentiments' in our nation. In fact, Indians are rated as one of the highest on 'Emotional Quotient' in the world. Thus, the system must harness this important segment in the intelligence field and explore avenues for incorporating them. We must take advantage of the advancement in management techniques in the corporate sector to improve intelligence management. a vast majority of global diaspora is Indian. They too can be systematically incorporated in our intelligence mechanism.

For example, JASON is an independent scientific advisory group that provides consulting services to the US government on matters of defence science and technology. It was established in 1960. It has conducted a number of studies even for US intelligence agencies and most of its reports are unclassified.[13]

It is recommended that we must make use of various private institutions and think tanks for analytical study of national and security issues. At the same time for think tanks to participate freely, they should have access to Intelligence. Outsourcing of selected analytical tasks can be done to tap the potential of experts of other walks of life. Filtered inputs without jeopardising security issues should be made available to think tanks and experts in their fields albeit not part of the intelligence mechanism.

The concept of Public-Private Partnership is being used by intelligence agencies of many countries. "Although the *Government* has not acknowledged it, there exists within the United States a major, secret, broad-based surveillance network consisting primarily of retired and ex- Intelligence Community personnel, retired and ex- military personnel, citizens from all walks of life, current Intelligence Community employees, intelligence officers from nations friendly to the US., elements of community emergency services (police, fire, ambulance, etc.), and employees of the US Postal Service".[14] In April 2001, the Mossad published a "help wanted" ad in the Israeli press seeking electronics engineers and computer scientists for the Mossad technology unit.[15]

The aspect of public-private partnership needs to be explored in intelligence assessment. Project Argus in UK can be cited as an example in this regard. Project ARGUS is an initiative of the UK National Counter Terrorism Security Office, which explores ways to aid the common man in preventing, handling and recovering from a terrorist attack. Argus is a free event which takes participant through a terrorist attack using a desk top multi-media simulation. Participants work in small syndicate groups to answer a series of questions and the challenges put to them, and develop their responses to the attack.[16]

Project Griffin of UK is another example of successful public-private partnership. Project Griffin is a police initiative to protect cities and communities of UK from the threat of terrorism. It brings together and coordinates the resources of the police, emergency services, local authorities, business and the private sector security industry.Project Griffin was developed by the City of London Police and formally introduced in London in April 2004 as a joint venture between the City and Metropolitan police forces. Its remit was to advise and familiarise managers, security officers and employees of large public and private sector organisations across the capital on security, counter-terrorism and crime prevention issues.[17] There is no way that there can be any effective functioning of intelligence agencies in the future without some involvement and reliance on the private sector.

Tapping the Potential of Defence Attaché

A major portion of holistic assessment can be extracted from them since they interact with various forums in the country of their posting. Unfortunately their potential has never been exploited in our country. Ministry of External Affairs (MEA) should also share the intelligence which comes to it from diplomatic channels with appropriate users.

The Intelligence Budget be Declassified

As brought out earlier, in most democratic nations, intelligence agencies are under the executive control of the elected government but are finally accountable to the legislature, which in most cases approves not only their funding but also their charter. In our country, there is no financial accountability for intelligence agencies. The misuse of Secret service funds has been widely reported. The government should look at strengthening financial accountability of intelligence agencies without jeopardising their functioning as a measure to prepare Indian intelligence agencies for the challenges of the 21st century. It is recommended that intelligence spending be declassified which is currently hidden in the overall budget. It is pertinent to mention that no informed public debate over priorities can occur as long as the public is kept unaware of the total spending and basic distribution of funds in the intelligence community.

Research and Development (R&D)

The intelligence agencies have to invest in their R&D facilities to devise new techniques to improve the quality of intelligence assessment, training and TECHINT capabilities which in turn would go a long way in improving the intelligence advice to policy makers. The intelligence agencies across the world have been relying heavily on their own R&D capabilities and have immensely benefitted from them. There are technical firms in our country who want to enter into producing technical gadgets for our intelligence agencies. However, the intelligence agencies have not been encouraging them in their endeavour due to fear of loss of 'secercy'. It is recommended that intelligence agencies should have 'single window system' wherein we could provide civil manufacturer with all the information. Intelligence agencies should appoint contact officers who could be contacted by these firms. It would encourage availablilty of 'state of art' technical equipment to intelligence agencies.

Use of Analytical Tools in Intelligence Assessment

For any intelligence community to operate effectively in support of national security policy, it needs analysts who can analyse information and turn it into intelligence and use it at the operational and tactical level. In US and abroad, post 9/11, there has been a rapid growth in the number of professional intelligence training and educational programmes. Universities as well as colleges and high schools are developing programmes and courses in homeland security and intelligence analysis. However, it has not been given the required impetus in India.

The Scarecrow Professional Intelligence Education Series (SPIES) first developed for intelligence personnel but now educates public as how to conduct intelligence assessment in the United States. The analysts can be effectively trained to use analytical tools to sharpen their analytical abilities. The intelligence agencies can get into collaboration with the corporate sector with requisite experience in analytical training to train intelligence analysts. Few of the recommended tools for training are as under:-

- **Deductive Reasoning** It is an act of drawing conclusions from previously formulated premises.

- **Induction** It is the process of arriving at a generalisation on basis of one or more observations.

- **Classification** It is the process of assigning information into classes or categories.

- **Link Analysis**- Analytical technique for making relationship explicit. It can be effectively used by analyst to study the linkage between terrorist groups across the world.

- **Sociometry** – Analysis of relationship within the group.[18]

Annual Tasking and Evaluation of Intelligence Agencies

It is recommended to institutionalise a system of annual tasking of the agencies as well as of their evaluation. One of the most significant achievements of the NSCS post 1999 was to put in place a system of annual tasking and evaluation of the agencies. This was further fine tuned in the Intelligence Coordination Group (ICG). Unfortunately, this mechanism has been discontinued for quite some time now. It is strongly recommended that this system of annual tasking and evaluation should be reinstated forthwith. This system of annual tasking and evaluation would ensure greater accountability of the agencies. They would be specifically tasked and the same can be used to evaluate the performance of an agency. In turn, intelligence agencies would conduct more focused collection and assessment of intelligence in accordance with the requirements of the consumers. As recommended earlier, National Intelligence Assessment and coordination council (NIACC) be entrusted with the responsibility of annual tasking and evaluation of intelligence agencies at the national level.

State Intelligence Mechanism Every State has its own intelligence set up primarily consisting of State Special Bureau(SIB), Central Intelligence Department(CID),State Police Intelligence Wings, Subsidiary Multi Agency Centre(SMAC) . Every state even calls them by different names. They lack in coordination in their nomenclature what to talk of their joint functioning. It is recommended that State-level intelligence mechanisms also be transformed and networked into the national grid simultaneously.

Revitalise HUMINT Mechanism The technology/TECHINT can give us lead but the confirmation of the input and its accurate analysis can be done only by robust HUMINT. In the second Lebanon war of 2006 the importance of HUMINT of Hezbollah against TECHINT of Israel was clearly highlighted. The CIA proved the importance of human intelligence over technical intelligence in Operation 'Neptune Star'. At the operational level, credit should be given to the CIA, which on the basis of a Guantanamo interrogation report, was able to build upon it, brick by brick, and get to the target. The technology assisted the CIA operatives to track their target but the ultimate work was done by the human brain. The fact that the target was being shielded by its own ally (Pakistan), had made the task more difficult. In such a mission, human intelligence played a much greater role than technical intelligence and ensured greater chances of success in the execution of the mission.

Over a period we have come to rely solely on TECHINT (ELINT, COMINT and SIGINT). It is not a foolproof technique to base our assessment only on TECHINT. Within organisations there has been an increasingly greater reliance on TECHINT in preference to HUMINT capabilities. No amount of TECHINT is a substitute for an intelligence operative or a shrewd and experienced analyst. TECHINT will give facts but not intentions. It is recommended that over reliance on TECHINT needs to be curtailed.

It is imperative that we rejuvenate the age old and reliable concept of 'beat constable', since no one can sense the pulse of his locality better than him. We as a nation have to focus more on strengthening the HUMINT gathering activities if we want to successfully prevent terror strikes and eliminate people who promote terrorism in our country.

Police Reforms and Modernisation

"Intelligence reforms without police reforms are pointless because the local policeman develops the strategic intelligence given by the central agencies. Police reforms without civil service reform are equally meaningless. And civil service reforms without political reform are similarly meaningless." The above remarks of Vikram Sood, the former Director, R&AW outlines the need for police reforms to improve intelligence assessment and coordination at national level. The Intelligence Community cannot develop in isolation. India's security structure is not strong due to the lack of police reforms and modernisation. Policies to revive policing and intelligence gathering need to factor in the critical need of improving the quality of police personnel at the lowest level of the system. The recommendations of the Police Reform Commission (1979) and the Padmanabhaiah Committee on Police Reforms set up in Jan 2000 need to be implemented on priority. Radha Vinod Raju, former Director General of the NIA in his interview in Jane's Intelligence Review noted that unless the national police service is strengthened, setting up new counter-terrorism structures "at the top" will be futile.[19]

Openness in Intelligence Community

The secrecy hampers quality analysis and efficacy. In today's world nothing is classified other than commander's mind which intelligence operatives have to analyse themselves. The secrecy may be used as a cover to shield incompetency. It is recommended that the intelligence community has to strike a balance between openness and secrecy. However, it should not jeopardise the operational effectiveness. We can draw a few lessons from US intelligence community in the field of openness. In US , Interagency Threat Assessment and Coordination Group (ITACG) Intelligence Guide for First Responders has been published which is designed to assist first responders in accessing and understanding Federal intelligence reporting and to encourage the sharing of information.

The Department of Homeland Security in US also helps first responders nation-wide by ensuring that emergency response professionals are prepared, equipped and trained for any situation, and by bringing together information and resources to prepare for and respond to a terrorist attack, natural disaster or other large-scale emergency. In this way we heap rich dividends of expertise of professionals in all walks of life that can assist the intelligence community in refining their assessment skills. By grading and spreading the intelligence inputs, more minds and talent get to work and improve an intelligence input.[20]

Israel Intelligence community follows "the Siman-Tov Procedure", which involves the grant of permission to even junior intelligence officers to express their views and assessments to a higher-ranking officer if their immediate commander was reluctant to accept their opinions. A new unit known as the Control Unit was added to MI in Israel whose purpose is to take the stance of devil's advocate. The officers of this unit are directly subordinate to the director of Military Intelligence (DMI). The aim was a pluralistic system of intelligence that uses more than just the single assessment prepared by MI. This is not an Israeli innovation, but it was adopted by Israeli intelligence.[21]

Summary of Recommendations

- **National Resolve to Accord Priority to Intelligence** A National consensus has to be reached through various means to accord requisite priority to intelligence and treat it as special activity.

- **Intelligence Reforms** It is recommended that an Indian Intelligence Reform Commission is appointed on the lines of the Administrative Reforms Commission to overhaul the ongoing system which would give Intelligence the backing of legislative enactments. It would ensure accountability of intelligence agencies thereby enhancing their efficiency. The Intelligence budget needs to be declassified.

- **National Intelligence Authority** It is recommended that a National Intelligence Authority be created to improve the quality of intelligence assessment and more importantly to coordinate the intelligence efforts at national level. The setting up of National Intelligence Assessment and Coordination Council (NIACC) as discussed above will assist in overseeing the functioning of a plethora of intelligence agencies which exist today.

- **Improving Quality of Human Resources** Personnel selected for intelligence tasks, therefore, should have an aptitude and flair for the job. Assessment can be best done only by the professional analysts, who have subject and area knowledge. Cross-pollination between military and civil intelligence agencies would improve the quality of coordination and assessment.

- **Training** One of the prime measures to improve inter-agency coordination is to have common training facility with common training programme at a national institute /academy of Intelligence for intelligence personnel.

- Expediting setting up of National Intelligence Grid (NATGRID) and National Counter Terrorism Centre (NCTC).

- **Public-Private Partnership** We must take advantage of advancement in management techniques in corporate sector to improve intelligence management. It is recommended that we must make use of various private institutions and think tanks and experts for analytical study of national and security issues.

- **Use of Analytical Tools in Intelligence Assessment** The analysts can be effectively trained to use analytical tools such as Deductive Reasoning and Link analysis to sharpen their analytical abilities.

- **Annual Tasking and Evaluation of Intelligence Agencies** It is recommended to institutionalise a system of annual tasking of the agencies as well as of their evaluation. NIACC is recommended to be entrusted with responsibility of annual tasking and evaluation of intelligence agencies at national level.

- **State Intelligence Mechanism** It is recommended that State-level intelligence mechanisms also be transformed and networked into the national grid simultaneously.

- **Revitalise HUMINT Mechanism** It is recommended that over reliance on TECHINT needs to be curtailed. The technology/ TECHINT can give us lead but the confirmation of the input and its accurate analysis can be done only by robust HUMINT. It is imperative that we rejuvenate the age old and reliable concept of 'beat constable', since no one can sense the pulse of his locality better than him.

- **Police Reforms and Modernisation** Policies to revive policing and intelligence gathering need to factor in the critical need of

improving the quality of police personnel at the lowest level of the
system.

• **Openness in Intelligence Community** It is recommended that
intelligence community has to strike a balance between openness
and secrecy. It has to be done without jeopardising the operational
effectiveness. At the same time they must exploit the advantages
of being open to the environment. Intelligence community must
encourage innovative and 'out of the box thinking'.

Conclusion

The diplomacy, intelligence, military technology and economic power are
important components of statecraft. The ideal situation for a state is to have
a right combination of the above ingredients. The same could not have been
more applicable than today. No single instrument is powerful enough in the
pursuit of national interests and all instruments have to be sharp and powerful
but intelligence is an important function at all times, peace or war or between
the two stages.

Intelligence is an expanding business. Its scope is increasing in multiple
dimensions. Cyber and economic intelligence, perception management are
the indicators of growing realms of intelligence. The social networking sites
aided by the information explosion have opened the floodgates of new
challenges for intelligence and security agencies.

Unfortunately, Intelligence has not been given the due priority in our
country. The success of Intelligence agencies is owned by the Government,
but failures are passed back. Along with the impressive successes, Indian
intelligence, like every intelligence community, has failed in many instances,
and these are the activities most talked about. The report card of Indian
intelligence agencies for last six decades has been positive when we also
take into account their unreported successes besides noting their sub optimal
performance.

The Intelligence agencies have on occasions fallen short of
expectations in their analysis or in coordinating this analysis amongst them.
The analytical capabilities of intelligence agencies have been on the decline
and needs to be given a fillip to restore it. The day-to-day functioning of

intelligence agencies is satisfactory but assessment making capability needs a fresh impetus. The lack of coordination results in information gaps when complete information is not brought before the intelligence analyst. This in turn lowers the quality of intelligence assessment. It can be safely concluded after this study that there is no dearth of information but analysis and assessment at national level requires fine tuning.

The situation can no longer be allowed to remain at status quo. The need, therefore, for intelligence coordination at the highest level is an inescapable factor. It needs to be understood by the governing agencies in perspective and also practiced. This brings us to the main recommendation that our intelligence and security structure be reconstituted to prepare our intelligence and security agencies to meet the challenges of the 21st century. In the end, it is once again reiterated that a concerted and holistic approach to improve intelligence assessment and coordination at national level is needed rather than a crisis driven and piecemeal approach. Intelligence being collected by strategic assets of the Indian Air Force as well as by the three services unmanned armed vehicles (UAVs)/drones should be shared real time with the DIA who also must share with IB and R&AW, and thence the NIACC for making the larger picture.

The government had constituted a task force in June 2011 to carry out a holistic review of national security and the country's preparedness to face the myriad challenges. The Task Force is being headed by former cabinet secretary, Naresh Chandra. This task force was constituted a decade after the Kargil Review Committee carried out a similar assessment in the wake of the Kargil conflict of 1999. The review has been completed and the task force submitted its recommendations in June 2012.[22]   It is hoped that the recommendations of the Task Force will be implemented on priority in national interest.

Notes

[1]   Interview of Lt Gen R K Sawhney (Retd),former DGMI on 24 Nov 2010

[2]   India's External Intelligence –Secrets of Research and Analysis Wing (RAW), Maj Gen VK Singh, Manas Publications ,2007,p.15

[3]   usgovinfo.about.com/od/uscongress/a/committees.htm accessed online on 12 Mar2012

[4]   http://uspolitics.about.com/od/usgovernment/tp/senate_intelligence.htm accessed online on 12 Mar2012

[5]   http://www.fas.org/irp/world/uk/mi6/ accessed online on 20 Sept 2011

[6]   B Raman ,Intelligence : Past ,Present and Future, pp. 364-377

[7]   www.knesset.gov.il/.../eng/CommitteeHistoryByCommittee_eng.asp accessed online 15 Mar 2011

[8]   Official website of Observer Research Foundation accessed online on 31 mar 2011 http://www.observerindia.com/cms/sites/orfonline/modules/report/ReportDetail.html? cmaid= 22080&mmacmaid=22081

[9]   http://www.dni.gov/who.htm accessed online on 23 Feb 2011

[10] Vikram Sood , former Chief of R&AW, Indian Defence Review Jul- Sep 2006

[11] Lt Gen Kamal Davar, PVSM, AVSM (Retd), former DG DIA during CLAWS seminar on 'National Security Reforms: A Decade After The GoM Report' on 12 May 2011

[12] http://searchsecurity.techtarget.com/definition/Total-Information-Awareness accessed online on 17 Jan 2012

[13] http://www.fas.org/irp/agency/dod/jason/ accessed online on 13 Feb 2012

[14] http://www.angelfire.com/hi/IntellCommunity/index.html p.2 accessed online on 12 Dec 2011

[15] http://www.fas.org/irp/world/israel/mossad/

[16] http://www.nactso.gov.uk/OurServices/Argus.aspx accessed online on 12 Dec 2011

[17] http://www.projectgriffin.org.uk/ accessed online on 12 Dec 2011

[18] Jerome Clauser, 'An introduction to Intelligence research and Analysis ,revised and edited by Jan Goldman ,(Pentagon Press ,2010),Pp. 105-129

[19] Urmila Venugopalan , Jane's Intelligence Review November 2011 ,p.58

[20] Interagency Threat Assessment and Coordination Group (ITACG) Intelligence Guide for First Responders, Mar2011,pp.1-6

[21] "Inside Israel's Secret Organisations" Jane's Intelligence Review ,October 1996

[22] http://articles.timesofindia.indiatimes.com/2012-07-11/india/32631950_1_intelligence-agencies-national-technical-research-organisation-intelligence-front accessed online on 01 July 2012

INTELLIGENCE: A BACKGROUNDER

'Nothing should be as favourably regarded as intelligence; nothing
should be as generously rewarded as intelligence; nothing should be as
confidential as the work of intelligence.' Sun Tzu, The Art of War

This book caters even for readers who may not have requisite background
knowledge to assimilate the nuances of the intelligence process and its direct
linkages with multifarious dynamics of national security. Before embarking
on a journey to analyse issues related to intelligence, it is prudent that ground
rules are set and readers are brought up to date with terminologies used
frequently by the intelligence community. A note on key terminologies used
frequently in this book and in the intelligence process as a whole has been
appended below. The new realms of intelligence in today's changing world
and ever increasing challenges for intelligence community has also been
included below for readers with inadequate background knowledge.

Key Terminologies of the Intelligence Community

An in depth analysis of impediments to the lack of requisite intelligence
assessment and coordination necessitates complete understanding of
nuisances of the intelligence process. The study as a precursor to
recommendations to improve intelligence assessment and coordination can
be hampered by various fallacies connected to the intelligence process as a
whole. One of the common fallacies is to confuse the tasks of law
enforcement agencies with intelligence agencies. Law enforcement and
intelligence operate in different worlds – one seeks to prosecute, the other
to gather information. In view of aforesaid, it is imperative that terminologies
of intelligence community are put in correct perspective in the beginning of
the study attempting to recommend measures to improve intelligence
assessment and coordination at national arena.

The Intelligence Community is an assemblage of separate agency intelligence organisations which gather, evaluate, and distribute information, most of which is secret.[1]

TYPES OF INTELLIGENCE

Strategic Intelligence. It involves long term assessment of the threat that an opponent poses to national security .The purpose of strategic intelligence is to alert policy makers to changes in the nature. The strategic intelligence looks at long term perspective whereas tactical intelligence limits itself to current perspectives.

The strategic intelligence can be of four varieties as under:-

- **Capability Intelligence** – It relates to collecting intelligence about capabilities of other militaries.

- **Acquisition Intelligence** – It concerns itself with latest acquisition by security forces of other countries.

- **Perception Intelligence**- This strategic intelligence relates to perception and its management of other militaries.

- **Advance Warning Intelligence** – It provides advance warning of events related to other militaries.[2]

Tactical Intelligence. It is the acquisition of highly perishable information for consumption by local security forces. The strategic intelligence looks at long term perspective whereas Tactical intelligence limits itself to current perspectives.

The tactical intelligence is basically an actionable intelligence. It is used primarily as value addition to strategic intelligence. It is used as 'rethink intelligence which forces users to take a second look at conventional wisdom and current assessment.[3]

"Any intelligence, strategic or tactical, that is of interest to the defence capabilities of a country, which influences, in peace or war the military security of a nation, may be termed Military Intelligence (MI). It is possible that this intelligence may arise from a variety of sources. Wherever this intelligence is of relevance to an Air Force, Army or Navy it can be categorised as MI. For example, if India were to find out from photographic aerial reconnaissance that Pakistan has moved two divisions close to our borders, it should alert the defence planners to this move. Of course, like in any other intelligence organisation there has to be collection, analysis and dissemination of information in MI, but the point is that certain specific categories of intelligence are of greater interest to MI than others".[4]

SOURCES OF INTELLIGENCE

Geospatial Intelligence (GEOINT) is the exploitation and analysis of imagery, Imagery Intelligence (IMINT), and geospatial information to describe, assess, and visually depict physical features and geographically referenced activities on the Earth.

Human Intelligence (HUMINT) is intelligence derived from information collected and provided by human sources. This information includes overt data collected by personnel in diplomatic and consular posts as well as otherwise unobtainable information collected via clandestine sources, debriefings of foreign nationals who travel abroad, official contacts with foreign governments, and direct observation.[5]

Measurement and Signature Intelligence (MASINT) is technically derived data other than Imagery and Signals Intelligence (SIGINT). The data is analysed and results in intelligence that locates, identifies, or describes distinctive characteristics of targets. It employs a broad group of disciplines including nuclear, optical, radio frequency, acoustics, seismic, and materials sciences. Examples include the distinctive radar signatures of specific aircraft systems or the chemical composition of air and water samples.

Open-Source Intelligence (OSINT) is intelligence produced from publicly available information collected, exploited, and disseminated in a timely manner to an appropriate audience for the purpose of addressing a specific intelligence requirement. OSINT draws from a wide variety of information and sources, including the following:

- **Mass Media.** It includes newspapers, magazines, radio, television, and computer-based information.

- **Public Data.** It includes government reports, official data such as budgets and demographics, hearings, legislative debates, press conferences, speeches, directories, organisation charts, marine and aeronautical safety warnings, environmental impact statements, contract awards, and required financial disclosures.

- **Gray Literature.** It is open-source material that usually is available through specialised access for a specific audience is referred as gray literature. The gray literature can include, but is not limited to, research reports, technical reports, economic reports, trip reports, working papers, discussion papers, unofficial government documents, proceedings, preprints, studies, dissertations and theses, trade literature, market surveys, and newsletters. The material cuts across scientific, political, socio economic and military disciplines.

- Observation and Reporting — includes significant information not otherwise available that is/has been provided by amateur airplane spotters, radio monitors, and satellite observers among many others. The availability of worldwide satellite photography, often high resolution, on the Web (e.g., Google Earth) has expanded open-source capabilities into areas formerly available to major intelligence services only.[6]

Signals Intelligence (SIGINT) is information gathered from data transmissions, including Communications Intelligence (COMINT), Electronic Intelligence (ELINT), and Foreign Instrumentation Signals Intelligence (FISINT). SIGINT includes both the raw data and the analysis of the data.

- COMINT is the capture of information for the purposes of tracking communications patterns and protocols (traffic analysis), establishing links between intercommunicating parties or groups, and/or analysis of the meaning of the communication.

- FISINT is information derived from the intercept of foreign electromagnetic emissions associated with the testing and operational deployment of non-U.S. aerospace, surface, and subsurface systems including, but not limited to, telemetry, electronic interrogators, and video data links.

- ELINT is information derived primarily from electronic signals that do not contain speech or text (which are considered COMINT). The most common sources of this type of information are radar signals.[7]

THE INTELLIGENCE CYCLE

The intelligence cycle is the process of developing raw information into finished intelligence for policy makers, military commanders, and other consumers to use in making decisions. The cycle is highly dynamic and never-ending and often includes a sixth stage of evaluation. Evaluation occurs for each of the stages individually and for the cycle as a whole. It is sometimes referred to as feedback. Intelligence cycle includes the following:

- Planning and Direction: Establish the Intelligence Requirements of the consumer.

- Collection: Gather the raw data required to produce the desired finished product.

- Processing and Exploitation: Convert the raw data into comprehensible form that is usable for producing the finished product.

- Analysis and Production: Integrate, evaluate, analyse, and prepare the processed information for inclusion in the finished product.

- Dissemination: Deliver the finished product to the consumer who requested it and to others as applicable.

- Evaluation: Acquire continual feedback during the cycle that aids in refining each individual stage and the cycle as a whole.[8]

Intelligence Analysis. Intelligence analysis is the application of individual and collective cognitive methods to weigh data and test hypotheses within a secret socio-cultural context.[9]

Intelligence Assessment. Intelligence assessment is an examination or analysis of a collation of accepted intelligence in order to draw conclusions as to what they portend for the future and whether any follow up action on them is called for.[10] Intelligence assessment is one of the most vital segments of intelligence cycle. Intelligence Assessments are finished intelligence products resulting from the intelligence analysis process. Assessments may address tactical, strategic, or technical intelligence requirements. Analysis and production requires highly trained, specialised personnel—analysts to give meaning and priority to the information. Synthesising the processed information into an actionable finished intelligence product allows the information to be useful to the customer.

Intelligence Coordination The process by which producers gain the views of other producers on the adequacy of a specific draft assessment, estimate, or report; it is intended to increase a product's factual accuracy, clarify its judgments, and resolve or sharpen statements of disagreement on major contentious issues. The process of seeking concurrence from one or more groups, organisations, or agencies regarding a proposal or an activity for which they share some responsibility and that may result in contributions, concurrences, or dissents.[11]

INTELLIGENCE: THE GROWING REALMS

Cyber Intelligence

Cyber Intelligence constitutes new data and information gathering resources, technologies, capabilities and techniques. Many of the current intelligence gathering platforms offer little or no cyber threat intelligence gathering capabilities. This is because unlike nuclear weapons and other weapons of mass destruction, cyber weapons and attacks require far less infrastructure and does not require restricted materials or knowledge that is in limited supply. It is extremely difficult to cloak the return path for information obtained from the cyber bugs that compromised computer systems.

Cyber Warfare Intelligence addresses the process of gathering data and information about a cyber enemy or threat. This represents the data collection, analysis and interpretations that lead to insight and understanding that is specific to the cyber threat operational environment. The defence forces for obvious reasons are one of the prime targets of cyber warfare. The collection of cyber threat intelligence presents the most significant challenge for the defence intelligence community. Developing cyber intelligence requires digital trespassing on foreign networks and the computers operated by foreign governments, corporations and individuals which is a time consuming and risky affair. This underlines the importance of availability of suitably trained operatives for cyber intelligence. [12]

It has been experienced that most cyber attacks leave behind forensic evidence that can be used to assess the capabilities of the attacker and we can get an insight into the entities behind the attack. Most of the time we get significant evidence pertaining to techniques, cyber weapons, and strategies used in these cyber assaults. This evidence should be exercised, processed and turned into intelligence.

One of the unique aspects of cyber weapons is their ability to be launched from anywhere. Computers that are physically located in other countries can be compromised and used as a cyber attack launch platform. We need to develop forensic investigative capabilities that can trace these attacks to the origination point, but establish the parties behind the attack.

Counter Intelligence (CI). Information gathered and activities conducted to identify, deceive, exploit, disrupt, or protect against espionage, other intelligence activities, sabotage, or assassinations conducted for or on behalf of foreign powers, organizations, or persons, or their agents, or international terrorist organizations or activities.[13]

Cyber Counter Intelligence (CCI). *CCI* covers the measures to identify, penetrate, or neutralize adversarial operations that use cyber means as the primary tradecraft methodology. [14]CCI activities in cyberspace include those forensics examinations of information systems and other approved virtual or on-line activities to identify, disrupt, neutralise, penetrate, or exploit hostile adversaries. [15]

Cyber counter-intelligence are measures to identify, penetrate, or neutralise foreign operations that use cyber means as the primary tradecraft methodology, as well as foreign intelligence service collection efforts that use traditional methods to gauge cyber capabilities and intentions.[16]

The challenges of cyber intelligence will require rethinking of our intelligence infrastructure as well as the development of new intelligence assets and technologies. Challenges in the public and private sectors are common to both as they have been equally affected by cyber attacks. The educated human resources to collect cyber intelligence are in short supply and needs immediate corrective measures. The computer literacy has to be further enhanced. More is needed, however, in terms of understanding what's at stake in cyber security, improving intelligence regarding adversaries' capabilities, intentions and activities, and creating the mechanisms to couple the public sector's capabilities to the private sector's needs. The government should consider how best to improve our cyber intelligence, so that our capabilities of cyber intelligence can contribute to a global cyber strategy that defends our national and economic security interests.[17]

Economic Intelligence

The economic intelligence is also of great importance. One component is the strength and vulnerabilities of national economies. The knowledge of strength may be important in understanding their capabilities for conflict while knowledge of vulnerabilities may be important in assessing threats to stability.[18]   With the process of economic liberalisation having gathered momentum there have been significant changes in the nature of smuggling and tax evasion. While there has been reduction in conventional smuggling due to liberalisation of import regime and reduction in rates of duty, there is no respite in commercial frauds by way of misdeclaration/undervaluation of imported goods and misuse of export promotion schemes. Further, we now face an increased threat of smuggling of narcotic drugs, foreign currency, arms and explosives etc. due to growing nexus between smugglers and anti-national elements. Problems such as international terrorism, narco-terrorism, money laundering, IPR violations, cyber crimes, import of hazardous substances etc. will occupy centre stage in the future as the emerging global threats. There are also issues like dumping of goods which cause more concern to developing economies like India and will, therefore, engage attention of the policymakers and enforcement agencies alike.

Economic crimes in India, like in other countries, are linked to several other offences, or even organised crimes, having bearing on national security. A greater degree of sophistication is being noticed in the activities of smuggling, tax evasion and commercial frauds and there is a growing recognition in the world that the economic offences are, many times, part of other serious crimes posing serious threat to the security of the nation. Any doubts on this score have been dispelled by the events of Sept 11 and Dec 13.[19]

Economic Intelligence Targeting

Economic Intelligence has added a new dimension to the paradigm of intelligence process. The importance of economic intelligence in the world order of today can't be over emphasised. It will not be out of place to recapitulate the activities involved in economic intelligence processing. Economic intelligence targeting by a nation consists of four main branches of activity:

- Collection of information related to the internal state of the nation's economy, this includes subjects like tax collection, illegal trading practices, traffic in controlled substances and specially taxed goods.

- Collection of information related to external influences on the economy, especially attempts by other countries to undermine the nation's economy as a whole or attempts to wrongfully dominate economic institutions.

- There is also the task of collecting and collating data about other economies of hostile countries and economic competitors of nationally sensitive business interests.

- Targeting relating to international economic organizations, i.e. the detailed nature of their functioning, and their perceptions of the nation's economy[20].

Failure of Intelligence

"An intelligence failure is essentially a misunderstanding of the situation that leads a government (or its military forces) to take actions that are inappropriate and counterproductive to its own interests. Whether it is subjectively surprised by what happens is less important than the fact that the government or the military is doing or continues to do the wrong thing.[21] Wikipedia defines intelligence failure, as the outcome of the inadequacies within the intelligence cycle. The intelligence cycle itself consists of six steps that are constantly in motion."

The Central Intelligence Agency (CIA) regards intelligence failure as a systemic organisational surprise resulting from incorrect, missing, discarded, or inadequate hypotheses. However, intelligence errors are factual inaccuracies in analysis resulting from poor or missing data.[22]

There are broadly three types of intelligence failures: those pertaining to the collection of information, to its analysis, and to the response to the produced intelligence. Shortcomings in collection can be attributed to the agencies; but those in analysis and response tend to be as much failures of the political-strategic leadership as of any agency. Three categories of factors, either singly or in combination, account for these failures: external, organisational and innate.[1]

The external factors relate to our adversaries who would want to conceal or misrepresent their intentions and capabilities. A principal challenge of intelligence is to operate against forces that actively seek to outwit us. The organizational factors could include negligent intelligence agents, rivalry between agencies or their leadership, and firewalls between different agencies. These are the issues that tend to be the focus of efforts at intelligence reform. The innate factors are certain key aspects of intelligence that are inherently problematic and not amenable to being 'fixed'. Indeed, these innate factors render intelligence failures inevitable.[23]

Notes

[1] http://www.angelfire.com/hi/IntellCommunity/index.html pp1-3 accessed online on 15 Jan 2011

[2] B. Raman, Intelligence: Past, Present, and Future (New Delhi, India: Lancer Publishers & Distributors, 2002),p.20-21

[3] Ibid

[4] Bhashyam Kasturi, Military Intelligence in India: An Analysis, The Indian Defence Review, © 1995 by Lancer Publishers & Distributors.

[5] Jeffrey T Richelson, 'The U.S. Intelligence Community, Fourth Edition , (West view Press, 1999), p.5

[6] Interagency Threat Assessment and Coordination Group (ITACG) *Intelligence Guide for First Responders pp.1-6 Mar2011*

[7] Ibid

[8] Jeffrey T Richelson, 'The U.S. Intelligence Community, Fourth Edition ,(West view Press, 1999, p.1-3

[9] Michael Warner, "Wanted: A Definition of 'Intelligence'," Studies in Intelligence 46, no. 3 (2002): 15–22.

[10] B. Raman, Intelligence: Past, Present, and Future (New Delhi, India: Lancer Publishers & Distributors, 2002), 333

[11] Interagency Threat Assessment and Coordination Group (ITACG) *Intelligence Guide for First Responders pp.1-6 Mar2011 p.86*

[12] http://www.technolytics.com/Cyber_Warfare_Doctrine_Public_Version.pdf accessed online on 11 Jan 12

[13] http://www.nctc.gov/docs/ITACG_Guide_for_First_Responders_2011.pdf accessed online 05 Jan 2012

[14] Jeff Bardin, Cyber Counterintelligence Doctrine - Offensive CI, , 02 Jun 11

[15] Ibid

[16] www.*publicserviceeurope.com/.../cyber-counter-intelligence-a-new-realm... accessed online on 13 Jan 2011*

[17] Cyber Tasks Intelligence Community - Robert K. Ackerman, SIGNAL Magazine- March 2010

[18] Jeffrey T Richelson, 'The U.S. Intelligence Community, Fourth Edition ,(West view Press, 1999), p.6

[19] The official web site of DRI accessed online at dri.nic.in on 11 Dec 2011

[20] Sunil Sainis, Intelligence Reforms, Bharat Rakshak Monitor - Volume 3(4) January-February 2001,p.14

[21] Abram N. Shulsky and Gary J. Schmitt, Silent Warfare: Understanding the World of Intelligence (Dulles, Virginia: Brassey's, 2002), 63.

[22] Official website of CIA accessed online at https://www.cia.gov/library/center-for-the-study-of-intelligence/csi-publications/books-and-monographs/analytic-culture-in-the-u-s-intelligence-co accessed online at 15 Mar 2011

[23] Srinath Raghavan "Intelligence failures and reforms" accessed online via http://www.india-seminar.com/2009/599/599_srinath_raghavan.htm on 17 Dec2011

Appendix B

FROM SURPRISE TO RECKONING
KARGIL COMMITTEE REPORT
EXECUTIVE SUMMARY

25 February 2000

Against the backdrop of an animated public discussion on Pakistan's aggression in Kargil, the Union Government vide its order dated July 29, 1999 constituted a Committee to look into the episode with the following Terms of Reference:

- To review the events leading up to the Pakistani aggression in the Kargil District of Ladakh in Jammu & Kashmir; and

- To recommend such measures as are considered necessary to safeguard national security against such armed intrusions."

The Committee comprised four members namely, K. Subrahmanyam (Chairman), Lieutenant General (Retd) KK Hazari, BG Verghese and Satish Chandra, Secretary, National Security Council Secretariat (NSCS) who was also designated as Member-Secretary.

FINDINGS

Developments Leading to the Pakistani Aggression at Kargil

The Review Committee had before it overwhelming evidence that the Pakistani armed intrusion in the Kargil sector came as a complete and total surprise to the Indian Government, Army and intelligence agencies as well as to the J&K State Government and its agencies. The Committee did not come across any agency or individual who was able to clearly assess before the event the possibility of a large scale Pakistani military intrusion across the Kargil heights. What was conceived of was the limited possibility of infiltrations and enhanced artillery exchanges in this Sector.

A number of former Army Chiefs of Staff and Director Generals of Military Operations were near unanimous in their opinion that a military intrusion on the scale attempted was totally unsustainable because of the lack of supportive infrastructure and was militarily irrational. In the 1948, 1965 and 1971 conflicts, the Indian Army was able to dominate the Pakistani forces on these heights. This area has been the scene of fierce artillery exchanges but minimal cross-LOC military activity. These factors, together with the nature of the terrain and extreme weather conditions in the area, had generated an understandable Indian military mindset about the nature and extent of the Pakistani threat in this sector.

The developments of 1998 as reported in various intelligence inputs, notably the increased shelling of Kargil, the reported increased presence of militants in the Force Commander Northern Area (FCNA) region and their training were assessed as indicative of a likely high level of militant activity in Kargil in the summer of 1999 and the consequent possibility of increased infiltration in this area. The Pakistani reconnaissance mission in August 1997 in Gharkun village was noted and a patrol base established in Yaldor. An operation was also planned to apprehend the infiltrators if they returned in the summer of 1998. They apparently did not do so. Intrusions across the LOC are not uncommon. Pakistan had in the past intruded into the Indian side of the LOC and the Indian Army had responded adequately. There had, however, been no intrusions since 1990. The terrain here is so inhospitable that the intruders could not have survived above 4000 meters for long without comprehensive and sustained re-supply operations. Such an assumption would be totally unsustainable in purely military terms.

The Committee has not come across any assessment at operational levels that would justify the conclusion that the Lahore summit had caused the Indian decision-makers to lower their guard. This has been confirmed by the discussions the Committee had with a number of concerned officials. Nonetheless, there was euphoria in some political quarters, among leaders in and out of office, though some others saw serious pitfalls in the Lahore process.

Intelligence

It is not widely appreciated in India that the primary responsibility for collecting external intelligence, including that relating to a potential adversary's military deployment, is vested in R&AW. The DGMI's capability for intelligence collection is limited. It is essentially restricted to the collection of tactical military intelligence and some amount of signal intelligence and its main role is to make strategic and tactical military assessments and disseminate them within the Army. Many countries have established separate Defence Intelligence Agencies and generously provided them with resources and equipment to play a substantive role in intelligence collection. For historical reasons, the Indian Armed Forces are not so mandated. Therefore, it is primarily R&AW which must provide intelligence about a likely attack, whether across a broad or narrow front. Unfortunately, the R&AW facility in the Kargil area did not receive adequate attention in terms of staff or technological capability. The station was under Srinagar but reported to Leh which was not focussed on Kargil but elsewhere. Hence intelligence collection, coordination and follow up were weak.

The Intelligence Bureau (IB) is meant to collect intelligence within the country and is the premier agency for counter-intelligence. This agency got certain inputs on activities in the FCNA region which were considered important enough by the Director, IB to be communicated over his signature on June 2, 1998 to the Prime Minister, Home Minister, Cabinet Secretary, Home Secretary and Director-General Military Operations. This communication was not addressed to the three officials most concerned with this information, namely, Secretary (RAW), who is responsible for external intelligence and had the resources to follow up the leads in the IB report; Chairman JIC, who would have taken such information into account in JIC assessments; and Director-General Military Intelligence. Director, IB stated that he expected the information to filter down to these officials through the official hierarchy. This did not happen in respect of Secretary (R&AW) who at that time was also holding additional charge as Chairman, JIC. The Committee feels that a communication of this nature should have been directly addressed to all the officials concerned.

Such lapses, committed at one time or the other by all agencies, came to the notice of the Committee. These illustrate a number of deficiencies in the system. There is need for greater appreciation of the role of intelligence and who needs it most and also more understanding with regard to who must pursue any given lead. It further highlights the need for closer coordination among the intelligence agencies.

There were many bits and pieces of information about activities within the FCNA region. Very few of these could be considered actionable intelligence. Most of them tended to indicate that Kargil was becoming a growing focus of Pakistani attention which had been clearly demonstrated by the marked increase in cross-LOC shelling in 1998. The reports on ammunition dumping, induction of additional guns and the construction of bunkers and helipads all fitted into an assessment of likely large scale militant infiltration and yet more intensive shelling in the summer of 1999. The enhanced threat perception of Commander 121 Infantry Brigade, Brigadier Surinder Singh also related to increased infiltration. R&AW assessed the possibility of "a limited swift offensive threat with possible support of alliance partners" in its half-yearly assessment ending September 1998 but no indicators substantiating this assessment were provided. Moreover, in its next six monthly report ending March 1999, this assessment was dropped. In fact, its March 1999 report emphasised the financial constraints that would inhibit Pakistan from launching on any such adventure.

No specific indicators of a likely major attack in the Kargil sector such as significant improvements in logistics and communications or a substantial force build-up or forward deployment of forces were reported by any of the agencies. Information on training of additional militants with a view to infiltrating them across the LOC was not sector-specific. There was an increase in shelling in 1998 both in the Neelam Valley (in POK) and Kargil (India). The Indian side resorted to heavy firing since it was necessary to suppress Pakistani fire aimed at disrupting the traffic on NH-1A from Srinagar to Leh. While the intelligence agencies focused on ammunition dumping on the other side, they appeared to lack adequate knowledge about the heavy damage inflicted by Indian Artillery which would have required the Pakistani army to undertake considerable repairs and re-stocking. That would partly explain the larger vehicular movements reported on the other side. The Indian Army did not share information about the intensity and effect of its past firing with others. In the absence of this information, RAW could not correctly assess the significance of enemy activity in terms of ammunition storage or construction of underground bunkers. This provides another illustration of lack of inter-agency coordination as well as lack of coordination between the Army and the agencies.

The critical failure in intelligence was related to the absence of any information on the induction and de-induction of battalions and the lack of accurate data on the identity of battalions in the area opposite Kargil during 1998. The responsibility for obtaining information on the Order of Battle (ORBAT) was primarily that of RAW and, to a much lesser extent, that of DGMI and the Division or Brigade using their Intelligence and Field Surveillance Unit (I&FS) and Brigade Intelligence Team (BIT) capabilities.

It could be argued that given the nature of the terrain, the climatic conditions and the unheld gaps in existence since 1972, there was no way of anticipating the intrusion during the winter provided Pakistan accepted the risk of incurring casualties in avalanches, which it did. However, since Pakistan was focusing upon Kargil, information regarding the induction of two additional battalions in the FCNA region and the forward deployment of two battalions could have proved to be an indicator of the likely nature of Pakistani activity in this sector.

The Kargil intrusion was essentially a limited Pakistani military exercise designed to internationalise the Kashmir issue which was tending to recede from the radar screen of the international community. It was, therefore, mainly a move for political and diplomatic gain. The armed forces play their war games essentially within military parameters. Unlike other countries, India has no tradition of undertaking politico-military games with the participation of those having political and diplomatic expertise. If such games had been practised, then the possibility of limited military intrusions to internationalise the Kashmir issue might have been visualised.

As mentioned earlier, WASO did not provide intelligence inputs of significant value. Those of the Aviation Research Centre (ARC) of R&AW were no doubt extremely valuable. The Army makes six-monthly indents and, wherever necessary, special indents on the ARC. These indents and their prioritisation depend on the nature of the threat perception which, in turn, is shaped by inputs from RAW. This circular process entails the Army having to depend upon inputs from R&AW for its own threat assessment. In other words, the Indian threat assessment is largely a single- track process dominated by R&AW. In most advanced countries, the Armed Forces have a Defence Intelligence Agency with a significant intelligence collection capability. This ensures that there are two streams of intelligence which enables governments to check one against the other.

The Indian Intelligence structure is flawed since there is little back up or redundancy to rectify failures and shortcomings in intelligence collection and reporting that goes to build up the external threat perception by the one agency, namely, R&AW which has a virtual monopoly in this regard. It is neither healthy nor prudent to endow that one agency alone with multifarious capabilities for human, communication, imagery and electronic intelligence. Had RAW and DGMI spotted the additional battalions in the FCNA region that were missing from the ORBAT, there might have been requests for ARC flights in winter and these might have been undertaken, weather permitting. As it happened, the last flight was in October 1998, long before the intrusion, and the next in May 1999, after the intrusions had commenced. The intruders had by then come out into the open.

The present structure and processes in intelligence gathering and reporting lead to an overload of background and unconfirmed information and inadequately assessed intelligence which requires being further pursued. There is no institutionalised process whereby R&AW, IB, BSF and Army intelligence officials interact periodically at levels below the JIC. This lacuna is perhaps responsible for R&AW reporting the presence of one additional unit in Gultari in September 1998 but not following it up with ARC flights on its own initiative. Nor did the Army press R&AW specifically for more information on this report. The Army never shared its intelligence with the other agencies or with the JIC. There was no system of Army minorities at different levels from DGMI downwards providing feedback to the Agencies.

There is a general lack of awareness of the critical importance of and the need for assessed intelligence at all levels. JIC reports do not receive the attention they deserve at the political and higher bureaucratic levels. The assessment process has been downgraded in importance and consequently various agencies send very junior officials to JIC meetings. The DGMI did not send any regular inputs to the JIC for two years preceding the Kargil crisis. The JIC was not accorded the importance it deserved either by the Intelligence agencies or the Government. The Chairmanship of JIC had become the reserve of an IPS officer who was generally a runner- up for the post of Secretary (R&AW) or DIB. The post was in fact left unfilled for 18 months until December 1998. During this period, Secretary (R&AW) doubled as Chairman, JIC.

There are no checks and balances in the Indian intelligence system to ensure that the consumer gets all the intelligence that is available and is his due. There is no system of regular, periodic and comprehensive intelligence briefings at the political level and to the Committee of Secretaries. In the absence of an overall, operational national security framework and objectives, each intelligence agency is diligent in preserving its own turf and departmental prerogatives. There is no evidence that the intelligence agencies have reviewed their role after India became a nuclear weapon state or in the context of the increasing problems posed by insurgencies and ethnic-nationalist turbulences backed with sophisticated hi-tech equipment and external support. Nor has the Government felt the need to initiate any such move.

Recommendations

Kargil highlighted the gross inadequacies in the nation's surveillance capability, particularly through satellite imagery. The Committee notes with satisfaction that steps have been initiated to acquire this capability. Every effort must be made and adequate funds be provided to ensure that a capability of world standards is developed indigenously and put in place in the shortest possible time.

Institutionalised arrangements should be made to ensure that the UAV imagery generated is disseminated to the concerned intelligence agencies as quickly as possible. UAVs could also prove effective in counter-insurgency operations. They may replace WASO patrols in the long run. However, in the interim, the possibility of using more stable WASO platforms than Cheetah helicopters and equipping them with thermal imaging sensors should be explored.

The communication intelligence equipment needs to be modernised in keeping with the advances made by Pakistan in inducting advanced communication technologies. There has also been a gross shortage of direction-finding equipment which could contribute significantly to counter-insurgency operations. The United States has grouped all its communication and electronic intelligence efforts within a single organisation, the National Security Agency (NSA). The desirability of setting up a similar organisation in India with adequate resources for this extremely important and non-intrusive method of gathering technological intelligence calls for examination. While the effort to build up adequate communication and electronic intelligence capability should be tailored to suit India's particular needs, parochial departmental interests should be effectively countered.

In many advanced countries, technological intelligence collection is undertaken by an integrated Defence Intelligence Agency with adequate resources. In India, the defence intelligence effort is limited in relation to the role assigned to the external intelligence agency (RAW) except for limited tactical and signal intelligence. The resources made available to the Defence Services for intelligence collection are not commensurate with the responsibility assigned to them. There are distinct advantages in having two lines of intelligence collection and reporting, with a rational division of functions, responsibilities and areas of specialisation. The Committee is of the view that the issue of setting up an integrated defence intelligence agency needs examination.

The Committee has drawn attention to deficiencies in the present system of collection, reporting, collation and assessment of intelligence. There is no institutionalised mechanism for coordination or objective- oriented interaction between the agencies and consumers at different levels. Similarly, there is no mechanism for tasking the agencies, monitoring their performance and reviewing their records to evaluate their quality. Nor is there any oversight of the overall functioning of the agencies. These are all standard features elsewhere in the world. In the absence of such procedures, the Government and the nation do not know whether they are getting value for money. While taking note of recent steps to entrust the NSCS with some of these responsibilities the Committee recommends a thorough examination of the working of the intelligence system with a view to remedying these deficiencies.

All major countries have a mechanism at national and often at lower levels to assess the intelligence inputs received from different agencies and sources. After the 1962 debacle, the then existing JIC under the Chiefs of Staff Committee was upgraded and transferred to the Cabinet Secretariat. It was further upgraded in 1985 with the Chairman being raised to the rank of Secretary to the Government. The Committee finds that for various reasons cited in the Report, the JIC was devalued; its efficacy has increased since it became part of the National Security Council Secretariat. However, its role and place in the national intelligence framework should be evaluated in the context of overall reform of the system. [1]

Note The extract of only the portion related to 'Intelligence' has been included here even though the committee had a very wide scope of study.The other portions have deliberately not been included here as they are not directly linked to the scope of this book. The other details can also be accessed at links below

- From Surprise To Reckoning, Kargil Committee Report'(Sage Publication,2000)

- From Surprise To Reckoning, 'Kargil Committee Report' Executive Summary accessed online via http://nuclearweaponarchive.org/India/KargilRCA.html 0n 20 Sept 2010

- D Ramana , 'Kargil Review Committee: A Commentary', **Bharat Rakshak Monitor - Volume 2(6) May-June 2000**

- Bhashyam Kasturi,The Subrahmanyam Committee on Kargil, Institute of Peace and Conflict Studies via

- http://www.ipcs.org/article/military/the-subrahmanyam-committee-on-kargil-259.html

Notes

[1] B. Raman, Intelligence: Past, Present, and Future (New Delhi, India: Lancer Publishers & Distributors, 2002), p.44-57

Appendix C

GC SAXENA TASK FORCE REPORT

The government in May 2000 instituted four task forces to concentrate on border management, intelligence apparatus, internal security, and higher defence management, as a follow-up measure of KRC. The recommendation of his task force along with recommendations of other three task forces was compiled into a document "Reforming the National Security System". Unlike KRC report, the GC Saxena Task Force report was 'classified' by the Government; hence, its exact recommendations are not available in the open domain. Thus, Chapter III, Intelligence Apparatus, only has the title and nothing else.[1] A large number of media articles, however, gave a fair idea of the recommendations of the Task Force. Media articles by Praveen Swami, Saikat Datta and V Sudarshan immediately after these recommendations were made have been used below to prepare a brief on the recommendations of the Task Force.[2]

Governor, J&K, Girish Chandra Saxena's report on the area of intelligence is without doubt the most substantial of the four documents the GoM has accepted. The members included former Foreign Secretary, K Raghunath, and former IB chief, MK Narayanan, former Special Secretary, Home, P P Shrivastava, former Additional Secretary, R&AW, B Raman, and R Narsimha of the National Institute of Advanced Studies. The report calls on India's intelligence establishment to take "an honest and in-depth stock of their present intelligence effort and capabilities to meet challenges and problems". The report calls for a wholesale upgrading of technical, imaging, signals, electronics counter-intelligence and economic intelligence capabilities, as well as a system-wide reform of conventional intelligence gathering.[3]

The report gives the IB, a formal charter for the first time in its history. It will now have responsibility for the collection and dissemination of all intelligence on internal security, making it the nodal organisation for counter-terrorist and counter-intelligence work. The organisation has also been tasked with ensuring the security of information systems. In six months, the organisation should also have created India's first dedicated police computer network and terrorism database. Among the major paradigm shifts envisaged in the IB's functioning is that the gathering and generation of intelligence and its analysis will be separated.

Until, now the R&AW has been the only organisation permitted to conduct espionage operations abroad. Now the IB will be empowered to conduct covert work relevant to its new charter, including deep penetration operations. The Saxena report points out, that the IB will have to upgrade considerably the quality of its personnel and their training, and that the Ministry of Home Affairs will have to stop treating the organisation as an "appendage or subsidiary unit".

The R&AW, like the IB, should emerge from the restructuring a leaner and more focused organisation. Much of its deadweight could be cut away including organisations like the Shanti Suraksha Bal (SSB) and the Indo-Tibetan Border Police (ITBP). This will free officer level personnel for the organisation to concentrate on its main job, gathering external intelligence and running trans border operations.

The GoM agreed that R&AW should retain the high-profile Aviation Research Centre (ARC), set up with the assistance of the United States in the wake of the 1962 India-China border conflict. The Army had demanded that it be given control of the ARC, which operates a fleet of aircraft especially equipped for high altitude operations and precision imaging equipment. At the moment RAW designs a year-long agenda for the ARC, based on broad assessments by the Army of the kinds of surveillance flights that are required. Now the Army will have more direct representation in the ARC, in the form of a Military Intelligence Advisory Group which shall be involved in day-to-day operations. Control of the organisation, however, remains firmly in R&AW's hands. This is because the organisation is best equipped to assess broad threat perceptions.

While R&AW will retain primacy in external intelligence, the new DIA will be empowered to conduct trans border operations. The DIA's head will have more power than any military intelligence bureaucrat of the past. The General will be the principal military intelligence advisor to the Chief of Staff's Committee and the Defence Minister. The DIA chief will also directly control two of the military intelligence establishment's most powerful institutions, the Signals Intelligence Directorate and the Defence Image Processing and Analysis Centre (DIPAC).

The influence of the DIA will also be felt at the field level, where it will participate in intelligence support groups, run jointly with the IB and the R&AW to provide coordinated information to the Army Corps Commanders in areas where the Armed Forces Special Powers Act is in force.[4]

"The Task Force drew attention to our failure to address the problem of pan-Indian terrorism in a professional manner and suggested the creation of a Counter-Terrorism Centre (CTC) in the Intelligence Bureau to deal with terrorism in a coordinated manner.

The CTC suggested by it was patterned after the CTC of the USA's Central Intelligence Agency (CIA), which was then responsible for counter-terrorism in the US, since the terrorist threats to the US before 9/11 mainly emanated from abroad and were largely directed at US nationals and interests abroad. Since terrorism in India — whether regional or pan-Indian-was largely directed at homeland targets, the Saxena Task Force, of which I was a member, suggested that the proposed CTC should be part of the Intelligence Bureau and should work under the direction of the Director, Intelligence Bureau (DIB).

The CTC, as proposed by the Saxena Task Force, was essentially a preventive architecture responsible for introducing the principle of jointness in preventing terrorism. Jointness meant counter-terrorism experts from different agencies of the Government of India working together under the leadership of the DIB for analysing and assessing the intelligence collected by different agencies and the Police and giving directions for follow-up action. The idea was that the follow-up action would still be taken by the State Police, but on the guidance and directions of the CTC, which was not given any executive powers of its own. The Vajpayee Government set up the CTC in the IB, but named it the Multi-Agency Centre (MAC). Since it was not given any executive powers to act independently on its own in the jurisdiction of the State Police, there was no objection to its creation from the States".[5]

The suggestions made by the Saxena Committee Report on reforming the Indian intelligence apparatus remain unimplemented in the face of bureaucratic resistance and an unenthusiastic political leadership.[6]

Well-placed sources say the report points out the glaring absence of a body at the highest level that could provide direction to the agencies on what intelligence they have to gather and evaluate their work. It also noticed complete lack of coordination, cooperation and sharing of intelligence between different agencies. The report points to the pervasive unhappiness among those whom the agencies serve. The user of intelligence information also doesn't project their requirements to the agencies. It observes that our HUMINT capabilities have degraded. The Task Force remarks at the absence of a process that would ensure the agencies are working in the interest of the nation, but doesn't make any specific proposal in this regard. It urges a proper process to brief the political leadership. The Saxena Committee suggests streamlining and rationalising of the built-up assets for cutting down costs. It advises ironing out of glitches in sharing technical intelligence outputs. It recommended RAW's Science and Technology division to be strengthened, both in terms of technology and manpower.

Chapter III of the report then goes on to ask intelligence agencies to acquire state-of-the-art equipment and advises collaborative efforts between them and the Defence Research and Development Organisation (DRDO) to create these indigenously as well. In fact, the task force on intelligence found the intelligence apparatus lacking in UAVs, sensors, scanners, jammers and other such equipment.[7]

Chapter III underlines the immediate need to acquire/develop the necessary equipment for space-based surveillance and reconnaissance systems including satellites capable of imagery with requisite resolution. During such time as the Unmanned Aerial Vehicles (UAVs) are unavailable, the report advises a more enduring aerial platform for surveillance purposes than the practice of employing helicopters with thermal sensors. The task force was so keen to acquire UAVs that it even suggested a six-monthly report on the progress made in this regard.

The report apparently cautions that it would be unrealistic to expect imagery from an indigenous satellite-based surveillance system to compare with those available from the best in the world. It says that the reason for this is that the proposed indigenous system (permission for developing this has been given) lacks in the Synthetic Aperture Radar (SAR) capability. This has wide applications in terms of reconnaissance, targeting and surveillance because of its all-weather day-or-night capability. Low-frequency SARs can also penetrate optically-opaque materials, including, under some conditions, foliage and even soil, consequently enabling imaging of targets camouflaged by trees, etc. SAR can even image underground targets such as utility lines, arms caches, bunkers, mines, etc. It has the capacity to read moving targets and determine location, speed, size and other relevant attributes.[8]

Notes

[1] V. Sudarshan, 'What's Wrong With Our Intelligence? ', 'Outlook' July 2002 accessed online via http://www.outlookindia.com/article.aspx?216296 on 19 Dec 1010

[2] Praveen Swami, "For a paradigm shift' Frontline Volume 18 - Issue 07, Mar. 31 - Apr. 13, 2001

[3] Saikat Datta ," Creating a successful Intelligence and Counter –Terrorism Matrix: Lessons from 26/11" The CLAWS Journal summer 2011 edition,p.102.

[4] Praveen Swami, "For a paradigm shift' Frontline Volume 18 - Issue 07, Mar. 31 - Apr. 13, 2001

[5] B Raman, former Additional Secretary, R&AW, Cabinet Secretariat "Inadequate consultation is the bane" accessed online at 'The Tribune Debate on NCTC' online via http://www.tribuneindia.com/ on 15 Mar 2012

[6] Praveen Swami, "Stalled Reforms," Frontline ,Volume 20 - Issue 09, April 26 - May 09, 2003

[7] V. Sudarshan, 'What's Wrong With Our Intelligence? ', 'Outlook' July 2002 accessed online via http://www.outlookindia.com/article.aspx?216296 on 19 Dec 1010

[8] http://www.outlookindia.com/article.aspx?216296 accessed online on 19 Dec 2010

Appendix D

NATIONAL COUNTER TERRORISM CENTRE (NCTC): VARIOUS VIEWS

While reviewing our national intelligence set up, there is no harm in learning from the best practices abroad and incorporating them into Indian policies. But, there is no need to blindly ape any country.None of the above intelligence set up is either perfect or can be used as a template in our country. The NCTC is a glaring example of adopting good model with incorrect procedure of adoption. The NCTC was adopted from US National Joint Terrorism Task Force (NJTTF) in December 2009, as part of post 26/11 reforms. The mission of the NJTTF is to enhance communication, coordination, and cooperation between federal, state, and local government agencies representing the intelligence, law enforcement, defence, diplomatic, public safety, transportation, and homeland security communities by providing a point of fusion for terrorism intelligence and by supporting the JTTFs throughout the United States.

If we analyse the spirit with which it was adopted in our country, we will get to the bottom of the reasons why it has not been able to establish itself till today. With this as a backdrop, various viewpoints have been appended below which helps us in understanding the background of the case. It also forces us to ponder over as to where we went wrong and help us in drawing lessons for not repeating the same mistake in future. These views were expressed by noted security analysts who participated in the national debate conducted by Chandigarh Tribune in Jan 2012 when the controversy related to it was at its peak.

The Way Forward – NCTC

Union Home Minister, P Chitambaram, while delivering the 22nd Intelligence Bureau Centenary Endowment Lecture on 23 Dec 2009 proposed radical restructuring of security architecture. The extract of his speech related to National Counter Terrorism Centre (NCTC) is enumerated in succeeding paragraphs.[1]

"Another major idea is the proposal to set up the (NCTC). As the name suggests, the goal is to *counter*terrorism. Obviously, this will include preventing a terrorist attack, *containing* a terrorist attack should one take place, and *responding* to a terrorist attack by inflicting pain upon the perpetrators. Such an organisation does not exist today. It has to be created from scratch. I am told that the United States was able to do it within 36 months of September 11, 2001. India cannot afford to wait for 36 months. India must decide now to go forward and India must succeed in setting up the NCTC by the end of 2010

Once NCTC is set up, it must have the broad mandate to deal with all kinds of terrorist violence directed against the country and the people. While the nature of the response to different kinds of terror would indeed be different and nuanced, NCTC's mandate should be to respond to violence unleashed by any group – be it an insurgent group in the North East or the CPI (Maoist) in the heartland of India or any group of religious fanatics anywhere in India acting on their own or in concert with terrorists outside India. NCTC would therefore have to perform functions relating to intelligence, investigation and operations. All intelligence agencies would therefore have to be represented in the NCTC. Consequently, in my proposal, MAC would be subsumed in the NCTC. Actually, MAC with expanded authority will be at the core of the new organisation and will transform itself into NCTC. The functions that will be added to the current functions of MAC are investigation and operations. As far as investigation is concerned, Government has set up the National Investigation Agency, and that agency would have to be brought under the overall control of NCTC. The last function – operations – would of course be the most sensitive and difficult part to create and bring under the NCTC. But I am clear in my mind that, without 'operations', NCTC and the security architecture that is needed will be incomplete. It is the proposed 'operations' wing of the NCTC that will give an edge – now absent – to our plans to counter terrorism.

The establishment of the NCTC will indeed result in transferring some oversight responsibilities over existing agencies or bodies to the NCTC. It is my fervent plea that this should not result in turf wars. Some agencies would naturally have to be brought under NCTC and what come to my mind readily are NIA, NTRO, JIC, NCRB and the NSG. The positioning of

R&AW, ARC and CBI would have to be re-examined and a way would have to be found to place them under the oversight of NCTC to the extent that they deal with terrorism. The intelligence agencies of the Ministry of Defence and the Ministry of Finance would, of course, continue to remain under the respective Ministry, but their representatives would have to be deputed mandatorily to the NCTC. NATGRID would obviously come under NCTC. So also, CCTNS would have to be supervised by the NCTC.

Given the overarching responsibility of NCTC and its mandate, it will be obvious that it must be headed by a highly qualified professional with vast experience in security related matters. Considering the structure of our services, it is natural to expect that the head of one of our organisations will be appointed to the post, by whatever name it may be called. He/she could be a police officer or a military officer. He/she must be one who has impeccable professional credentials and the capacity to oversee intelligence, investigation and operations. He/she will be the single person accountable to the country on all matters relating to internal security. At the Government level, and in order to be accountable to Parliament, it would be logical and natural to place the NCTC under the Ministry of Home Affairs".[2]

The NCTC was finally to become operational from 01 Mar 2012, three years after it was announced to be set up. However, it has met with serious resistance from Chief Ministers of non UPA States. It was opposed by States on the ground that it violates the federal principles. The view of some of the important commentators, strategic analysts and intelligence experts related to NCTC has been appended below.

NN VOHRA

While a host of issues are involved in any discussion on national security I shall focus essentially on certain aspects of the core issue: are the obtaining Union–State understandings adequate for the effective management of national security?

In this context I feel that it may be useful to make a few introductory observations. In the past decades there have been serious internal disturbances and communal conflagrations in several parts of the country. The affected States have not been able to timely and effectively deal with such developments on their own. Consequently, the Union has been deploying Central Police Forces, and even the Army, to restore normalcy in the disturbed areas. In certain cases, as for instance in the North-East States, such deployments have been on an extensive scale and for prolonged periods. This has led, among many other consequences, to prolonged agitations for the repeal of the Disturbed Areas Act and the Armed Forces Special Powers Act on the ground that the enforcement of these laws has resulted in large-scale violations of Human Rights of the affected populations. The Government of India has had the aforesaid laws examined by several Committees in the past years. It has, however, not so far been possible to arrive at any clear cut decision regarding the amendment or repeal of these laws.

In the past three decades, the States have been questioning the Union's constitutional authority to take pre-emptive action to deal with an emerging internal disturbance in any part of the country. Without detailing the arguments raised by the States I would briefly state that, as of today, the Union does not have the authority to suo motu deploy Central Police forces in any State or part thereof to prevent or pre-empt an arising serious disturbance. As per the practice which has evolved over the years, the Armed Forces of the Union have been deployed only after consultation with the affected State Governments or at the latter's specific requests.

Do States have a case?

Considering the enormous cost paid by the country for the State Government's failure to prevent the demolition of Babri Masjid, questions have continued to be asked as to what exactly is the Union's responsibility in such matters. And more recently, after the gruesome terrorist attack in Mumbai in November 2008, serious questions have arisen even about the inherent capacity of the Union to deal with such situations.

Time has come to arrive at clear agreements, within our federal arrangements, to lay down the respective responsibilities of the Union and the States for effective security management. If such agreements cannot be secured then, in my opinion, we need to urgently bring about the required constitutional amendments to ensure that, between the Union and the States, the country can be effectively protected from terrorist and other attacks which may arise from within or beyond our frontiers.

In the context of these introductory observations I would state that, since the advent of terrorism in our country, the safeguarding of national security has emerged as perhaps the most crucial area of governance. It has been realised that endeavours to promote the welfare of our people would have little meaning if the very unity and integrity of the country is threatened and the security of all our people cannot be fully assured.

Not just physical security

The Mumbai terrorist attack has warned us that no more time can be lost in reorganising, enlarging and strengthening the national security management apparatus for effectively preventing and, as necessary, successfully encountering every threat to the Indian State, from anywhere across its land or sea borders or from across the air space. National security could be defined, in simple terms, to comprise external security, which relates to safeguarding the country's territorial integrity against war or external aggression, and internal security, which concerns the maintenance of peace and public order within the entire country.

Security experts and analysts have generally found it convenient to separately address issues relating to the management of internal and external security. In my view, such a sectoral approach is no longer tenable. Ever since Pakistan launched a proxy war in Jammu and Kashmir and Jihadi terrorist networks started operating in India, the traditional distinction between internal and external security got obliterated and, as we have seen, issues relating to these two arenas have got growingly intertwined. It is no longer practical to deal with them separately.

It also needs to be recognised that, over the past years, the arising security threats and their sources have geographically spread far and wide, far beyond our immediate and extended neighbourhoods, to countries in the Middle East, South East Asia and even in the Western hemisphere.

Consequently, our internal security concerns have also spread to cover myriad issues and, today, it would just not do to merely focus on the threats to physical security. Internal security management is now required to be viewed holistically and, for this reason, it has become essential to provide security in respect of almost all areas and particularly in respect of food, water, energy, nuclear power, economy, environment and ecology, science and technology, cyber security and so on.

For effective internal security management it would also require to be kept in view that our country represents an immense cultural and geographical diversity and the well over one billion of our people comprise multi-religious, multi-lingual and multi-cultural societies in which certain socio-religious practices, traditions and customs are rooted in thousands of years of recorded history.

Further, it needs to be remembered that the free interplay of cultural and religious identities in our vast and unfettered democracy generate disagreements and confrontations, which have the potential of leading to conflicts and large scale disturbances, particularly when anti-national elements join the fray, with or without involvements from across our frontiers. If the unity and integrity of our country is to be preserved it would be necessary to ensure security on all fronts and, besides, promote tolerance and communal harmony among our people.

Current and Expanding Threats

For appreciating the scale and complexity of our national security concerns it would be useful to keep in mind that India is a large country with land borders of over 15,000 kms, a coast line of over 7,500 kms, over 600 Island territories and an Exclusive Economic Zone of over 25 lakh sq kms. We also cannot afford to forget, even momentarily, that the internal situations obtaining in most of the countries in our immediate neighbourhood are generating serious threats to our national security.

While it may not be meaningful to recount the varied security threats which we have faced since Independence it could be said that, briefly, the more worrying internal security threats which our country is encountering today relate to the continuing proxy war in Jammu and Kashmir; Jehadi terrorism which has continued to grow both in its reach and spread; Left-Wing Extremism and the still active insurgencies in the North-East States.

After its successful foray in Punjab about three decades ago, in end 1989 Pakistan launched a proxy war in Jammu and Kashmir which is still continuing. In the past decades, Pakistan's Inter Services Intelligence (ISI) agency has continued to expand its terrorist activities across the length and breadth of the country. Besides, Pakistan terrorist cells have also been operating from bases in the Middle East and from the soil of at least two of our neighbours.

The activities of Pakistan based Jihadi groups have resulted in the security environment in the vast hinterland of our country continuing to remain threatened for the past many years now. A relatively more recent phenomenon, which is no less worrying than the importation of terrorism, is the birth of a number of radical counter groups which have been aggressively organising to retaliate against terrorist violence unleashed by the Jihadi networks. The emergence of such radical groups carries the grave danger of promoting hate politics and divisive ideologies which could lead to large scale communal violence and pose a most serious threat to our secular fabric, and even to our democratic framework.

The alarming activities of the Indian Mujahideen, which were first heard of in late 2007, have also been spreading. Investigation agencies have revealed that this group has been operating in India with the active support of an underworld network in Karachi, which works in collaboration with Pakistan-based Jihadi groups. The cadres of this outfit have the resources and capability of perpetrating serious violent incidents in various parts of the country.

ISI and Maoists

Besides providing ideological support, training, weapons, communication systems, funding and other required logistical support to the terror groups, the ISI, notwithstanding the foreign policy statements made by the Pakistan Government from time to time, has been continuing with its activities to enable cross-border infiltrations for intensifying violent activities in Jammu and Kashmir. Pakistan is continuing its proxy war in J&K.

According to certain recent reports, the ISI has also stepped up its activities to revive Sikh militancy in Punjab by providing financial and logistical support to establish terror modules from among militants in the Sikh Diaspora. It is also reported that the ISI has been pressurising various Sikh militant groups to arrive at operational understandings with each other and, besides, to join up with the Kashmir-centric militant outfits. The armed struggle being carried out by the Left Wing extremist groups, aimed at capturing political power, has emerged as perhaps the foremost internal security challenge to the country.

Of the various elements which subscribe to violence, the CPI (Maoist) is the largest group which has been responsible for the rather significant increase in incidents of violence since 2007. The year 2010 witnessed a sharp increase in violence caused by the Maoists in Chhattisgarh and West Bengal and a visible enhancement in the activities of this group in Bihar, Andhra Pradesh and Maharashtra. The incident at Dantewada, which resulted in the killing of 76 CRPF personnel, was the largest-ever Maoist strike against the security forces. There are reports that the ISI is striving to establish a linkage with the CPI (Maoist) group and the latter are trying to establish a nexus with the insurgent groups in the North-East region.

In so far as the activities of the various insurgent groups active in the North-East region are concerned, recent reports suggest that the number of incidents and the levels of violence have somewhat declined in the recent past, consequent to the Centre's initiatives to engage the warring groups in peace talks, some of which have been progressing well.

Serious public disorders have also been caused by varied other developments and the past year witnessed highly disruptive agitations in several parts of the country. Among these were the pro-Telengana agitation in Andhra Pradesh, the United Naga Council economic blockade in Manipur and the pro-Gujjar agitation in Rajasthan. All these agitations adversely affected the maintenance of peace and public order.

PRAKASH SINGH

India has been battling against terrorism of one hue or the other ever since the mid-fifties, when Phizo raised the banner of revolt in the Naga Hills. The battle has unfortunately been fought in an ad hoc manner. The attack on Mumbai on 26/11 eventually shook off the inertia of the country and marked the beginning of a new phase, characterised by a comprehensive response to the challenge of terrorism.

The Union Home Minister P. Chidambaram, with all the controversies he finds himself surrounded with, deserves full credit for trying to raise the counter-terrorism architecture. The National Investigation Agency (NIA) was set up. NSG hubs were established in Hyderabad, Kolkata, Mumbai and Chennai. Anti-terrorism and Counter-insurgency Schools were set up in some states. Coastal security was beefed up. The states were asked to strengthen their police infra-structure, etc.

In December 2009, while addressing a conference of the Intelligence Bureau, the Home Minister for the first time spelled out the need to have an over-arching National Counter Terrorism Centre. Its charter would include "preventing a terrorist attack, containing a terrorist attack should one take place, and responding to a terrorist attack by inflicting pain upon the perpetrators".

Power to Arrest, Search & Seizure

It was an ambitious scheme, which encountered opposition from other security related departments. After prolonged consultations, the outlines of the scheme were finally revealed through an executive order on February 3. The NCTC would function as a wing of the Intelligence Bureau and its functions would not be limited to collecting, coordinating and disseminating intelligence about the activities of terrorists but also include the powers of arrest, search and seizure under the Unlawful Activities (Prevention) Act. In other words, the Intelligence Bureau would be vested with police powers, albeit through the NCTC.

Chidambaram has drawn inspiration from the US National Counter Terrorism Centre which was established by a Presidential Executive Order in August 2004 and codified by the Intelligence Reform and Terrorism Prevention Act of 2004 (IRTPA). It was meant to lead the "nation's effort to combat terrorism at home and abroad by analysing the threat, sharing that information with our partners, and integrating all instruments of national power to ensure unity of effort". It was placed under the Director of National Intelligence but was not given any power of arrest, interrogation or investigation. The Indian version of the NCTC obviously goes beyond the US model.

Howsoever laudable Chidambaram's intentions may have been, he made three grievous mistakes in executing a much needed proposal. Firstly, the states were not consulted on such a sensitive issue affecting centre-state relations, which they should have been. The battle against terrorism can be fought successfully only with the combined efforts of the Centre and the states.

Secondly, the NCTC, both in USA and UK, are independent entities. Making NCTC part of the IB could be a disadvantage in the sense that objectivity would be at a discount and a mistake made by the IB was likely to be replicated by the NCTC. Thirdly, it was wrong in principle to have vested the Intelligence Bureau with powers of arrest and seizure. Intelligence organisations in democratic countries are not given such powers, which are normally associated with totalitarian regimes only. Besides, in the event of the central government getting derailed, as happened during the Emergency in India, these powers could always be misused to harass the political adversaries, branding them as terrorists or their collaborators.

States' Objection Untenable

The government has now called a meeting of the Chief Secretaries and Directors General of Police of all the states to sort out the thorny issues. Hopefully, there should be a meeting ground. There is absolutely no doubt that the country urgently needs a National Counter Terrorism Centre. It is also necessary that the NCTC should have a comprehensive reach across the length and breadth of the country and that its operations are not hamstrung by a narrow interpretation of the federal principle.

The objection of the states that the proposed NCTC impinges on the federal character of the constitution and that it is an encroachment on their turf is untenable. The ground reality today is that the states depend upon the Centre to discharge even their normal law and order responsibilities. Be it a caste conflict, a communal show down, festival arrangements, or any kind of bandh, the state's clamour for central forces to deal with the situation.

They forget then that under the Constitution it is their responsibility to deal with such situations. On the other hand, when the Centre takes an initiative to deal with the problem of terrorism which has inter-state or even trans-national ramifications, the states wake up to what they consider their constitutional rights and resent the Centre's alleged encroachment in their fiefdom. It has to be understood that dealing with terrorism would necessarily require Centre's help, involvement and guidance. The states, with their own resources, just cannot cope with the terrorist threat.

The country must have an NCTC and it must be a strong body with full authority over sharing, collation and dissemination of all intelligence relating to terrorism. However, the temptation to vest it with police powers must be resisted. Such powers would always arouse suspicion and the temptation to misuse them would always be there. The dialogue with the states should lead to a meaningful compromise. The proposed NCTC should neither be crippled nor made more powerful than is actually necessary for combating terrorism.

R K RAGHAVAN

The Central government and the non-UPA-led States are once again at war. This time it is about the legitimate role of the Centre in keeping a tab on terrorist activities in and around the country. A proposal of the Ministry of Home Affairs (MHA) to create a National Counter-Terrorism Centre (NCTC), which would coordinate the collection and dissemination of intelligence related to terrorism, and monitor appropriate follow-up action has run into trouble. It has been assailed by the non-UPA States as a brazen attempt to politicise the combat against terrorism, while at the same time diluting the States' role and authority.

The Home Minister Chidambaram's efforts to mollify the incensed States, led by Mamata Banerjee, saying that the exercise was one aimed at assisting the States rather than undermining their authority, have not cut much ice. The NCTC was to come into existence on March 1. Bowing to the desire of the States, the Centre has now suspended the proposal for a while. A meeting in New Delhi on March 12 with State Police Chiefs is proposed as part of a process of consultation with the States. To this extent, the MHA has demonstrated commendable sagacity and grace. Some may however look upon this as an act of making virtue out of a necessity, because policing of any kind in India is anyhow a collaborative exercise, and an estranged group of States is hardly conducive to promoting law and order.

Cooperation for Preventive Action

Why do we need a NCTC? I don't have to go far into the history of terrorism. Only last week did the HM announce the arrest of two Lashkar-e-Toiba (LeT) activists, who were planning to set off some explosives in a crowded locality in the capital. He also complimented the role of three unnamed States in catching the culprits before the attack.

What this instance would highlight is that preventive action- more than detection- calls for the pooling of information and its analysis before tipping off concerned agencies to move swiftly and nab the conspirators.

The essence here is one of unstinted willingness on the part of the agency that knows to share critical information with the one that needs to know. A turf war and one-upmanship are antithesis to a prompt and effective use of terrorist intelligence.

This is what happened in the case of 9/11 among U.S. organisations like the FBI, CIA, Pentagon and others, and what followed is history. Here, information was available in bits and pieces with several units engaged in the business of protecting the nation. They were either unwilling to share it with the others or did not know the significance of what they were holding. The result was calamitous.

The 9/11 Commission, that went into the whole episode, was appalled by this failure and the lack of appreciation by intelligence bodies of their complementary role. After thorough investigation, the Commission was convinced that the need of the hour was one single coordinating body at the centre. This was to be the NCTC, that was set up in 2004, and which reported to the newly created position of Director, National Intelligence (DNI) (not to be confused with the CIA Director), who was placed in the White House. Set up initially under an Executive Order of August 2004, it gained legal authority under the Intelligence Reform and Prevention of Terrorism Act (IRPTA) later in the year. This was in fulfillment of the 9/11 Commission recommendation: "Breaking the older mold of national government organisations, this NCTC should be a center for joint operational planning and joint intelligence, staffed by personnel from the various agencies."

Since its creation the NCTC in the US has given a reasonable account of itself, and there has been no major terror attack on the US Two incidents of 2009 however revealed the chinks. These were a US Army Major attack (November 5,2009) on a recruitment camp in Fort Hood resulting in the killing of 13 persons, and the aborted attempt (December 25, 2009) by a Nigerian national Abdul Muttalab (23) to set off an explosive device on board a Northwest- Delta Airlines aircraft flying from Amsterdam to Detroit.

An inquiry held in the matter was particularly critical of the latter incident, because, although information sharing was adequate, those at the analyst desk had failed "to connect the dots." The study concluded that the NCTC lacked in resources and a purposive organisation. This indictment alone would indicate that an NCTC was not a panacea for all current ills of the situation. A lot more was needed in terms of employee imagination and alertness.

Attacks despite MAC

This detailed reference to what has been the U.S. experience is because our NCTC was to be modeled after its U.S. counterpart. It was created soon after the Home Minister's visit to the U.S. following the 26/11 attack on Mumbai to study how the organisation had evolved in that country. It must however be brought on record that New Delhi did not have to re-invent the wheel.

This was because, under the NDA government, a Multi Agency Centre (MAC) had indeed been established on the recommendation of a Task Force set up in 2000 under the leadership of Gary Saxena, a former RAW chief. This MAC - in reality the current NCTC was to be within the Intelligence Bureau (IB) in a genuinely coordinating role. It was the result of an Executive Order, and MAC was not armed with any legal authority. It was entrusted with tasks of "joint analysis, joint assessment and joint identification of follow-up action." It was to get relevant tasks executed through other agencies, including the State Police.

While I am not aware of any critical evaluation of the MAC, the guess is that it was functioning unostentatiously and professionally. It is an entirely different matter that there were a number of terrorist incidents all over the country since 2000, including 26/11. Whether MAC could be assailed directly for this is a matter of dispute.

Anyhow, following the damage that 26/11 caused to India's image as a nation capable of taking care of the risks from terror- especially with a troubled neighbor such as Pakistan- with a hyperactive ISI with a notorious reputation for harbouring designs against India, the Home Minister Chidambaram could not rest without any proactive reorganisation of intelligence. This is the genesis of both the National Investigation Agency (NIA) and the more recent NCTC.

Reservations over NIA Too

There were initial reservations over the legal tenability of the NIA. The States were in course of time convinced that the NIA had its basis on the Constitutional mandate to the Union Government that it should safeguard the country's defence through an appropriate mechanism. The States were also satisfied that the NIA did not make any serious inroads into their authority.

This is however not the case with the NCTC set up under an executive order taking advantage of the provisions of the Unlawful Activities (Prevention) Act 1967.

In a letter to the States, Home Minister Chidambaram has explained the need for an NCTC. A note attached to the letter makes things even clearer. It says: "A body mandated to deal with counter terrorism must have, in certain circumstances, an operational capability. This is true of all counter terrorism bodies in the world. When engaged in counter terrorism operations, the officers must have the power to arrest and the power to search, which are the bare minimum powers that would be necessary. Besides, the powers conferred under section 43A must be read with the duty under section 43B to produce the person or article without unnecessary delay before the nearest police station (which will be under the State Government), and the SHO of the Police Station will take further action in accordance with the provisions of the CrPC."

The basic features of the contemplated NCTC are that it will be a separate body within the IB and report to the DIB. It will have powers of arrest and search. In this respect, it is very different from the NCTC of the US and its equivalent in many countries.

The Flip Side

It is the consensus among intelligence professionals the world over that, however powerful their organisations may be in an informal sense, never should they be burdened with legal authority that would make them more accountable to the law and judicial authority and also vulnerable to exposure through such overt actions as search and arrest.

This is why the proposal to arm the IB personnel with new powers has caused eyebrows to raise. I am not very sure whether the IB chief ever fell in line with the proposal wholeheartedly.

There are twin dangers here. First, arrests by IB officers will make them face judicial proceedings every other day. There is secondly the definite prospect of misuse of authority that would vitiate the ambience with an elitist organisation. The posting of IB personnel to man Immigration desks at ports way back in the 1970s brought its own problems that caused severe embarrassment to the higher echelons of the organisation.

What non-UPA Chief Ministers fear are questionable arrests that could be made by the IB on partisan grounds. A series of arrests in quick succession in a particular State would help to disseminate the impression that the State in question had become a haven for terrorists or suspects. Political propaganda on these lines also cannot be ruled out.

I do not think it is the case of any Chief Minister that the NCTC per se is a bad idea. They consider themselves as patriotic as anyone at the Centre promoting the new outfit. What they plead for is that the new creation should be just a coordinating body and nothing more. Their standpoint is that the exercise of police powers should remain the prerogative of the State Police as enshrined in the Constitution. Nothing should be done to disturb the equilibrium of this well conceived arrangement by the Fathers of the Constitution.

Fundamental to the debate however is the need to re-examine the distribution of powers under the Constitution.

There is a school of thought –whom is hard to wish away- that 'Police' and 'Public Order' should be brought under the Concurrent List. This takes into account the continuing decline in standards of policing all over the country and the abominable politicisation of forces.

It is an entirely different question whether giving a greater say to the Union Government in matters of policing will help to stem the rot. The management of the IPS Cadre by both the States and MHA has left a lot to be desired. Instances of individual officers defying State governments as well as the MHA at the instance of powerful politicians are a cause for concern.

When such undesirable and unprofessional activities are encouraged purely to serve narrow political ends, the apprehension that the proposed NCTC will not rise above politics in exercising its authority cannot be brushed aside. Ultimately, as in every other human activity, objectivity and integrity can alone take care of a situation sought to be protected by law, rules and regulations.

VED MARWAH

It is truly amazing that in a country, where terrorism poses the most serious threat to national security, setting up of a National Counter Terrorism Centre (NCTC) should become an issue of such fierce controversy.

India is afflicted with all types of terrorism: ideological, religious, and ethnic terrorism. The roots of 'Jehadi terrorism' are in our neighbourhood and the neighbour harbours deep animosity for our country since its birth. It has no hesitation in using terrorism as a tool to achieve its expansionist designs.

The break -up of the Indian Union and annexation of the state of Jammu and Kashmir have been part of its national agenda from the very beginning, irrespective of who ruled Pakistan. Insurgency in the Northeast and the challenge posed by left wing extremism by the Maoists are no less serious than jehadi terrorism even if their external dimensions are not as visible.

The situation could dramatically change with the Maoists in control in Nepal and China taking a more active interest in these groups.

And yet, even after more than three years since the daring 26/11 terrorist attack in Mumbai, which held the commercial capital of the country to ransom for two days, we cannot put in place an effective strategy to counter terrorism. Instead our rulers, both in the states and at the Centre, are shamelessly playing politics with this threat to gain electoral advantage.

Whether it is counter-terrorism, law or administrative mechanism for effectively dealing with this growing menace, we are stuck because of partisan politics. I am not aware of any other country in the world, where an issue of such importance for national security has become an issue for electoral battles.

We witness the strange spectacle of more than one cabinet minister publicly stating that the Batla House encounter in Delhi in 2008, in which a brave Inspector of the Delhi Police paid the supreme sacrifice, was fake. If senior ministers believe that the encounter was fake, what stops the government from holding an inquiry and taking action? Instead of making statements before the media, they should have taken up the matter with the Prime Minister and the Home Minister.

Need Not Disputed

It is in this background, therefore, that one can make sense of this new controversy about the NCTC. Do we need a National Counter Terrorism Centre, and if so, why? We need setting up of the NCTC for the simple reason that terrorism today has not just local and state-level dimensions, but also national and international dimensions. And the states in India have neither the resources nor the expertise to tackle this most serious national security challenge on their own. They require assistance and guidance from the central agencies. The need for very close and continuous cooperation to pre-empt, prevent and investigate incidents of terrorism cannot be over emphasised.

Moreover, terrorism is a multi-dimensional problem; security is only one dimension of the problem. Political, economic, social and external dimensions are as important and they are all interlinked. Only a balanced and flexible strategy that does not allow strategy to lean in any one direction, creating distortions in the other areas, can succeed.

A counter-terrorism strategy must monitor and coordinate things on all fronts. Even foreign policy initiatives can have direct and immediate internal repercussions on the ground in the affected areas. Similarly, internal security management can influence international opinion that no country can ignore in today's world. Moreover, there is a need for a centralised agency that can assess inputs from various agencies on continuous basis. Our counter terrorism strategy needs to be a step ahead of the terrorist groups and not behind them, if they are to pre-empt and prevent incidents of terrorism.

No Substitute for States

However, in a large and diverse country like India, it would be foolish to think that central agencies can be a substitute for the state agencies. NCTC or no NCTC, counter terrorism strategy cannot succeed without close and continuous coordination between the Centre and the states.

Close cooperation is also essential between the various central armed forces, investigating, intelligence and all other central agencies. This coordination is an absolute must and cannot be sacrificed for any reason whatsoever, if the country has to win this fight against terrorism.

It must be emphasised that the NCTC cannot replace other central or state agencies. Even if there was no constitutional provision, which places the police under state list, for practical reasons there is no way the central agency can win this battle on its own by excluding the state agencies. Any such attempt would be a non-starter.

We have been fighting terrorism since Independence in the Northeast, J&K and Punjab, but there has never been a problem of coordination between the centre and the states. It is only in the last few years that this problem has arisen, largely due to partisan politics. The solution to this problem has to be found at the political level.

The recent controversy about the setting of the NCTC is on two main grounds: one that it will function in the Intelligence Bureau, which is a secret organisation not under parliamentary oversight, and, therefore, is a retrograde step repugnant to democratic norms. And two, it encroaches on the powers which are under the constitution in the State List and, therefore, pose a threat to India's federal structure.

Ham-handed

The manner in which the NCTC was proposed to be set up through an executive order of the Union Home Ministry, without even pretence of taking the states on board, has only given rise to the suspicion that the Central government has a hidden agenda that has little to do with fighting terrorism. The net result has been to weaken and not strengthen the national resolve to fight terrorism. The trust deficit between the centre and the states has increased.

And again, what was the need for placing the NCTC under the IB? Giving it police powers like search and arrest would only further heighten the suspicion that the Central government wants to assume powers to target the states. It has already revived memories in some quarters of misuse of intelligence agencies during the Emergency years.

Instead of working together, as they have been doing till the issue of terrorism was politicised in the last few years, the turf battles between the central agencies and the states will only get worse.

It would be wrong to take only a legalistic view of the problem and argue that the legal basis for such powers of search, seizure, and arrest are already there under section 43A of the Unlawful Activities Prevention Act. It is also not true that its counterpart in the US has police powers. Nor is there much substance in the argument that it is essential to confer police powers to eliminate delay in operationalising intelligence reports. The biggest hurdle is mistrust between the state and the central governments that can frustrate all major initiatives of the NCTC. This mistrust will increase.

It is a classic case of good intentions but bad implementation. Ham-handed attempts to set up the NCTC by the central government have only weakened the fight against terrorism. All these controversies would only please the terrorist groups who are plotting against the very survival of our country, within and outside the country. While there is scope for different views on such an important subject, one hopes that the differences would be sorted out in an environment of mutual trust. An attitude of one-upmanship would not help. Let better sense prevail and broad political consensus reached both on the laws and the administrative framework required for combating terrorism.

B RAMAN

India has been facing the evil of terrorism since 1971 when two members of the Jammu & Kashmir Liberation Front (JKLF) hijacked an Indian Airlines plane to Lahore and set it on fire after asking the passengers and crew to leave the plane.

Except in J&K and the North-East, where the Army had to be asked to take over the leadership of counter-terrorism and counter-insurgency operations, in the rest of the country, the responsibility for dealing with terrorism vested with the State Police. In Punjab, it was the Police under the leadership of K.P.S.Gill, the Director-General of Police, that effectively brought the so-called Khalistani terrorism under control.

In Tamil Nadu, it was again the Police that brought the activities of the so-called Al Umma, a local terrorist organisation, under control. The police also dealt with the activities of the Liberation Tigers of Tamil Eelam (LTTE).

In Mumbai, the successful investigation of the 1993 serial blasts was carried out by the police. Thus between 1971 and 1993, the police forces in different States were able to deal effectively with terrorism with the help of intelligence inputs and guidance, where necessary, from the central intelligence agencies.

The infiltration of the Lashkar-e-Toiba (LET) and other Pakistani terrorist organisations into India — first into J&K and subsequently into other States of India — from 1993 onwards gave a new pan-Indian dimension to the evil of terrorism and made Indian counter-terrorism experts realise that the police alone, however capable, would not be able to deal with the jihadi octopus of Pakistani origin. The problem was aggravated by the emergence of the so-called Indian Mujahideen in 2007.

New Architecture

The need for a pan-Indian counter-terrorism doctrine and architecture was increasingly felt in the post-1993 years, but unfortunately no action has been taken to evolve such a doctrine and architecture. Despite terrorism of the jihadi kind, originating from Pakistan, assuming a pan-Indian and global dimension, we continued to deal with it in an ad hoc manner with the help of the police in different States.

The Task Force for the Revamping of the Intelligence Apparatus, headed by G.C. Saxena, former chief of the R&AW, which was set up by the Atal Behari Vajpayee Government in 2000, drew attention to our failure to address the problem of pan-Indian terrorism in a professional manner and suggested the creation of a Counter-Terrorism Centre (CTC) in the Intelligence Bureau to deal with terrorism in a coordinated manner.

The CTC suggested by it was patterned after the CTC of the USA's Central Intelligence Agency (CIA), which was then responsible for counter-terrorism in the US, since the terrorist threats to the US before 9/11 mainly emanated from abroad and were largely directed at US nationals and interests abroad. Since terrorism in India — whether regional or pan-Indian-was largely directed at homeland targets, the Saxena Task Force, of which I was a member, suggested that the proposed CTC should be part of the Intelligence Bureau and should work under the direction of the Director, Intelligence Bureau (DIB).

The CTC, as proposed by the Saxena Task Force, was essentially a preventive architecture responsible for introducing the principle of jointness in preventing terrorism. Jointness meant counter-terrorism experts from different agencies of the Government of India working together under the leadership of the DIB for analysing and assessing the intelligence collected by different agencies and the Police and giving directions for follow-up action.

The idea was that the follow-up action would still be taken by the State Police, but on the guidance and directions of the CTC, which was not given any executive powers of its own. The Vajpayee Government set up the CTC in the IB, but named it the Multi-Agency Centre (MAC). Since it was not given any executive powers to act independently on its own in the jurisdiction of the State Police, there was no objection to its creation from the States.

National & Internal Security

Before his death in January 2002, R N Kao, the founding father of the R&AW, met Vajpayee and told him that without the co-operation of the State Police, the Government of India would not be able to deal with terrorism effectively. He also expressed the view that the National Security Adviser, being an officer of the Indian Foreign Service, with no exposure to the State Police, would not be able to command the required co-operation from the State Police. He, therefore, suggested the creation of a post of Deputy NSA to be manned by a senior officer of the Indian Police Service either from the States or the IB.

Kao told me that Vajpayee reacted positively to his advice and said that he would initiate action for the creation of a post of Dy NSA to be manned by a police officer, who was an expert in internal security and who commanded the confidence of the State Police. By the time this post came into being, Kao passed away. When this post was created, it was filled up by another IFS officer, who was an unknown quantity in the States and who had very little expertise in internal security matters.

The 9/11 terrorist strikes in the US Homeland brought out inadequacies in the functioning of the CTC of the CIA. It was decided by the George Bush Administration in 2004 to set up an independent organisation called the National Counter-Terrorism Centre (NCTC) for ensuring jointmanship in dealing with terrorism and place it under the Director, National Intelligence. It also modified the counter-terrorism architecture in the US by creating a Homeland Security Council, which was distinct from the NSC, and placing it under a Homeland Security Adviser, distinct from the NSA.

When the Dr.Manmohan Singh Government came to office in 2004, it created a separate post of Internal Security Adviser on the pattern of the USA's Homeland Security Adviser and made him exercise leadership in all internal security matters, including counter-terrorism. M.K.Narayanan, former DIB, was appointed to this post.

In 2005, after the death of J N Dixit, the then National Security Adviser, Narayanan was designated as the NSA and asked to perform both the tasks of co-ordinating external and internal security duties. He was not able to devote adequate attention to internal security matters because of his preoccupation with the negotiation with the US on civil nuclear co-operation.

Internal Security Management in the Centre consequently suffered. The progress in the implementation of the Saxena Task Force's recommendation on counter-terrorism was slow and no attempt was made to draw up a co-ordinated Counter-Terrorism Doctrine and revamp our counter-terrorism architecture.

The result: The 26/11 terrorist strikes, which dramatically exposed the poor state of our preventive architecture. There was no co-ordinated follow-up action even on the limited intelligence that reportedly came from the US through the R&AW regarding the plans of the LET to launch sea-borne terrorist strikes in Mumbai.

Chidambaram's Plan

After taking over as the Home Minister post-26/11, Chidambaram, who has assumed total responsibility for counter-terrorism management, has sought to revamp the counter-terrorism architecture. He initiated in particular four steps.

Firstly, he decentralised the deployment of the National Security Guards and created the National Investigation Agency (NIA) to improve our investigation capabilities. Secondly, he instituted a system of daily meetings of the intelligence chiefs under his chairmanship to discuss the available intelligence and assess the evolving threats. Thirdly, he speeded up the implementation of the Saxena Task Force recommendation for the Multi-Agency Centre, which had gone into doldrums under ShivRaj Patil, his predecessor. And fourthly, after a visit to the US, he decided to set up an NCTC partly not totally on the pattern of the USA's counterpart.

While his first three steps did not meet with any opposition from the States, his attempt to create the NCTC has met with serious opposition because of his decision to keep it as part of the IB and give it independent executive powers of arrest and searches without the prior knowledge of the

State Police.

His idea probably was that to meet situations where a State Police dragged its feet for making an arrest, the NCTC should have its own powers of arrest so that it could make an arrest, produce the suspect before the Police and direct it to act against him.

This was a major encroachment on the powers of the State Police and without the prior concurrence of the States.

In his NCTC architecture, Chidambaram has made two significant departures from existing practices in countries such as the US. Instead of making the NCTC an independent institution, he has made it a part of the IB. By giving the NCTC independent powers of arrest, he has violated the widely held principle in other democracies that a clandestine intelligence agency should not have police powers of arrest, which could be misused for political purposes. His failure to consult the States beforehand and his attempt to confront the States with a fait accompli, which would have definitely infringed on their rights, have created so much opposition that the very principle of jointmanship in preventing terrorism through a body like the NCTC, now stands suspected as a politicised measure to circumvent the States.

Apparently, there were inadequate consultations even at the Centre as one could see from the opposition expressed by an increasing number of ex-R&AW officers to the move to make the NCTC a part of the IB. The controversy has not only become a Centre vs State issue, but is also threatening to become an IB vs R&AW issue.

At a time when there is an urgent need for unity of action against terrorism, creation of a preventive architecture against terrorism has become a highly contentious and politicised issue. While one has to welcome Chidambaram's decision to postpone the implementation till belated consultations are held with the States, it is doubtful whether the opposition-ruled States, whose suspicions have been aroused, will now agree to the creation of the NCTC at all even if it is not given executive powers. The whole concept, which is necessary, has become suspect in their eyes. It is very unfortunate.

There is no hurry to create the NCTC now. The MAC could continue to handle the tasks of follow-up action on the intelligence collected and prevention. The States have not objected to the MAC and have got used to it. Instead, Chidambaram should focus on revamping the counter-terrorism architecture by making the NCTC an independent institution, without executive powers working under the direction of the DIB, who could wear two hats as the head of the IB and of the NCTC.

The NCTC could work under the DIB but without becoming a part of the IB. It would be similar to the R&AW and the Directorate-General of Security, which are independent institutions working under Secretary (R), who wears two hats.

In his address to IB officers in 2010, Chidambaram had suggested the creation of a Ministry of Internal Security to focus exclusively on the operational aspects of Internal Security Management. There has been no follow-up on this since then.

The time has come to consider this proposal as part of the over-all revamping. None of these ideas would work unless he manages to reach a political consensus with other political parties and the States. Prior consultations with the States should be sincere and serious and not just a gimmick.[3]

AJIT DOVAL

Will the long-awaited National Counter Terrorism Centre (NCTC), which will come into existence on March 1, make a difference? Most commentators feel it won't. They say it is nothing more than affixing a fanciful American label that had fascinated home minister P Chidambaram on the decade-old Multi-Agency Centre (MAC). They also wonder why it took him three years to set it up.

It is true that the NCTC will not be what the minister declared it would be when he addressed Intelligence Bureau (IB) officers on December 23, 2009. At that meeting, he had described it as an outfit capable of "preventing a terrorist attack, containing a terrorist attack should one take place, and responding to a terrorist attack by inflicting pain upon the perpetrators". It is also true that in terms of its charter, authority, empowerment and resources, it cannot match its American namesake. However, it is certainly an improvement over what exists now. While the Indian centre has little in common with its US counterpart, their underlying doctrines have much in common. Of course, on matters of detail we have grossly missed out and the devil lies in the detail.

The MAC was created following the recommendations of the Group of Ministers, which was set up by the NDA in 2001 to suggest comprehensive reforms in India's national security apparatus. The outfit, headed by a part-time additional director in the IB, maintained a databank of terrorists and their collaborators, terrorist organisations, details of terrorist violence including their modus operandi, tactics, communication links, weapons and equipment used etc. The outfit had representatives from all central intelligence agencies, defence forces and central police organisations who were both contributors and beneficiaries of the all-source databank.

They met regularly to exchange and evaluate intelligence inputs, assess impending threats and worked out possible responses. The sharing of intelligence with MAC was, however, informal and unstructured, often leaving gaping holes. MAC did not collect intelligence or carry out intelligence operations. The NCTC, however, will be an integrated platform that will collect, evaluate and analyse intelligence, maintain a databank and coordinate counter-terrorist operations. Headed by a full time director, the NCTC will make sharing of intelligence and follow up operations efficient, faster and better coordinated.

The IB, despite being the nodal agency for counter terrorism, as a secret organisation was handicapped in several ways and had to play the role of an invisible hand ensuring that it did not cross the red lines. Their support in terms of providing intelligence, working out plans for physical action, covert operational and technical support etc was all informal. Often, operational intelligence and follow up plans, painstakingly developed at grave personal risks, were lost due to lack of professional expertise, sense of urgency, training, equipment, and even motivation of the local police. The IB could not intervene beyond a point. The NCTC, with powers accruing to it under section 43A of the Unlawful Activities Prevention Act (UAPA),

1967, to arrest anybody having a 'design to commit' or 'having committed' any act of terror, will be able to take preventive and proactive actions in real time on its own. Importantly, the law makes reliable intelligence "from personal knowledge or information given by any person" as the basis for undertaking such operations. The empowerment under UAPA should enable the NCTC to search and seize any 'building', 'conveyance' or 'place' that is suspected to have terrorist links and this will further enhance its effectiveness. Further, the NCTC will have the powers to requisition the services of the NSG or any other special force for undertaking counter-terrorist operations. In effect, it means that should the NCTC have reliable intelligence, it can under its own empowerment, co-opt central forces to complement the local police and make up for their deficiencies in trained manpower, equipment, logistics etc.

Taking advantage of its nationwide jurisdiction, the information gathered by the NCTC during search operations or initial questioning of the suspects, can be used to mount supplementary operations in any part of the country taking help of the local police to meet legal requirements. It will set in motion the chain of counter-terrorist actions in real time. This is distinct from situations in the past when many opportunities were lost due to legal-jurisdictional problems, hassles in priming up police forces which were out of the loop, delays in tying up logistics etc. The best operational intelligence is obtained within two to three hours of a successful operation when terrorists are questioned, documents are recovered and mobile phones are seized. However, the shelf-life of all these is just a few hours before the information is flashed by the media. The NCTC will be able to substantially cover this gap.

The fears expressed in some quarters that the head of NCTC, being a relatively junior officer, will be unable to deliver are unfounded. The NCTC will have all the clout that it needs because the IB chief, the senior-most police officer, under whom the NCTC head will work, will be able intervene whenever required. However, in order to maximise the advantages of having a counter-terrorism centre of this kind, the government must opt for a dynamic and relatively young additional director who is poised for higher future responsibilities.

Notwithstanding the gaps, the NCTC has much to offer. Over a period of time, it will be necessary to empower it more. It must acquire statutory status through an act of Parliament. The home ministry should look for officers with professional competence and motivation to man the organisation. The counter-terrorist units of the states should be re-organised on the pattern of the NCTC to bring about uniformity and seamless integration in national counter-terrorism efforts. Needless to say, the Centre must bear the costs. But eventually much will have to be done by the NCTC and this includes enhancing its intelligence capabilities, injecting speed and surprise in its operations and establishing an R&D unit and upgrading the use of technology.[4]

N MANOHARAN

The US has recently warned about the high possibility of a terror attack in India from groups like Lashkar-e-Toiba that "are looking for opportunities and countries through which they can infiltrate into India." India is one of the worst affected countries by terrorism and, in the recent period, it has witnessed more terrorist incidents than any other country in the world. India confronts varied forms of threats that range from militancy in Jammu & Kashmir, insurgency in the northeast of India, Left Wing Extremism in Central India, and jihadi terrorism threatening any part of the country. Then there are other threats, over and above the identified main forms, such as illegal migration, drug-trafficking, counterfeit currencies, small arms proliferation, and cyber warfare. All these determine the nature of terrorism confronted by India. Yet we lack a single overarching body dedicated to counter terrorism. Way back in 2009, the Union Home Minister P. Chidambaram outlined his vision for "the broad architecture of a new security system that will serve the country today and in the foreseeable future." His idea was to institute a National Counter Terrorism Centre (NCTC) on the lines of the American NCTC with control over intelligence, operations and investigation of all matters pertaining to terrorism. The NCTC's goals, according to Chidambaram, "will include preventing a terrorist attack, containing a terrorist attack should one take place, and responding to a terrorist attack by inflicting pain upon the perpetrators".

Although the time limit for constituting the NCTC was initially set as end-2010, it has now been revised to end-2011. Given the enormous bureaucratic hurdles and turf wars involved in setting up the new body, it will be a miracle if the NCTC comes up before the new deadline. The Home Minister, to avoid duplication, wants all related agencies (although they are part of different ministries) like Research and Analysis Wing (R&AW), Intelligence Bureau (IB), Joint Intelligence Committee (JIC), National Technical Research Organisation (NTRO), Directorate of Revenue Intelligence (DRI), Aviation Research Centre (ARC), Multi-Agency Centre (MAC), Defence Intelligence Agency (DIA), Central Bureau of Investigation (CBI), National Investigation Agency (NIA) to report to NCTC (under the Ministry of Home Affairs) on matters related to terrorism. However, there is intense resistance to this "submission". There is a pervasive fear that such an arrangement would lead to over-centralisation of powers in the Home Minister and the Ministry of Home Affairs emerging as "super ministry".

Although the above apprehension is farfetched, it is the responsibility of the MHA to convey in unambiguous terms NCTC's focus i.e. "terrorism only". It should be acknowledged that intelligence/investigation/security agencies have a far wider mandate than terrorism. Even on matters terrorism, the methodology of working would be cooperation and coordination and not subordination of one agency to the other. The final objective is to bring about synergy and cohesion in counter-terrorism efforts, by doing away with overlapping, duplications, bottlenecks and unnecessary hurdles. To achieve this objective, it is enough if NCTC functions as an umbrella organisation with representations from intelligence, investigation and security agencies. It should be in a position to integrate all instruments of national power, including diplomatic, economic, social, political, military, intelligence, and law enforcement to ensure unity of effort. It should happen at central, state and local levels. The tentacles of the NCTC should penetrate deep down upto district levels instead of being another top-heavy organisation. It need not follow any international model – US, UK or European – but that which suits India's capabilities and threats. It has to be innovative and proactive in its approach rather than defensive and reactive. 'Prevention' and 'protection' should be the main watch words. For this, the Centre should constantly monitor terror/militant groups, their support network, sponsors, sanctuaries, mode of operation, threat potential, and leadership and make periodic threat assessments for policy makers. In this regard, it can effectively use 'Crime and Criminal Tracking Network System (CCNTS), National Intelligence Grid (NATGRID), Central Monitoring System (CMS) and Unique Identification Authority of India (UIDAI). Personnel for NCTC could be pooled from relevant intelligence, investigation and security agencies headed by the senior most experienced officer on rotation basis with simple command structure. In this way, turf wars could be avoided, with the potential and efficacy of the agencies maximised.[5]

Notes

[1]   Accessed online at http://pib.nic.in/newsite/erelease.aspx?relid=56395 accessed on line on 13 Mar 1012

[2]   Ibid

[3]   'The Tribune Debate on 'NCTC' accessed online via http://www.tribuneindia.com on 19 Jan 2012

[4]   Working in real time, Hindustan Times, 12 Feb 2012

[5]   Dr. N Manoharan, NCTC: In Search of an Umbrella Body for Counter-terrorism, CLAWS web article accessed online via http://www.claws.in/ on 17 Dec2011

Appendix E

INTELLIGENCE AGENCIES

The Central Bureau of Investigation (CBI)

The Central Bureau of Investigation traces its origin to the Special Police Establishment (SPE) which was set up in 1941 by the Government of India. The functions of the SPE then were to investigate cases of bribery and corruption in transactions with the War & Supply Department of India during World War II. Superintendence of the SPE was vested with the War Department. [1]

Even after the end of the War, the need for a Central Government agency to investigate cases of bribery and corruption by Central Government employees was felt. The Delhi Special Police Establishment Act was therefore brought into force in 1946. This Act transferred the superintendence of the SPE to the Home Department and its functions were enlarged to cover all departments of the Government of India. The jurisdiction of the SPE extended to all the Union Territories and could be extended also to the States with the consent of the State Government concerned.

The DSPE acquired its popular current name, Central Bureau of Investigation (CBI) in 1963. Initially the offences that were notified by the Central Government related only to corruption by Central Government servants. In due course, with the setting up of a large number of public sector undertakings, the employees of these undertakings were also brought under the CBI purview. Similarly, with the nationalisation of the banks in 1969, the Public Sector Banks and their employees also came within the ambit of the CBI.[2]

From 1965 onwards, the CBI has also been entrusted with the investigation of Economic Offences and important conventional crimes such as murders, kidnapping, terrorist crimes on selective basis.

The SPE initially had two Wings. They were the General Offences Wing (GOW) and Economic Offences Wing (EOW). The GOW dealt with cases of bribery and corruption involving the employees of Central Government and Public Sector Undertakings. The EOW dealt with cases of violation of various economic/fiscal laws. Under this set-up, the GOW had at least one Branch in each State and the EOW in the four metropolitan cities, i.e, Delhi, Madras, Bombay and Calcutta. These EOW Branches dealt with offences reported from the Regions, i.e, each Branch had jurisdiction over several States.[3]

Over the years, demands were made on CBI to take up investigation of more cases of conventional crime such as murder, kidnapping, terrorist crime, etc. Apart from this, even the Supreme Court and the various High Courts of the country also started entrusting such cases for investigation to the CBI on petitions filed by aggrieved parties. Taking into account the fact that several cases falling under this category were being taken up for investigation by the CBI, it was found expedient to entrust such cases to the Branches having local jurisdiction.[4]

It was therefore decided in 1987 to constitute two investigation divisions in the CBI, namely, Anti-Corruption Division and Special Crimes Division, the latter dealing with cases of conventional crime, besides economic offences.[5]

Directorate of Revenue Intelligence (DRI)

The DRI in its present form is charged essentially with the collection of intelligence, its analysis, collation, interpretation and dissemination on matters relating to violations of customs laws, and to a lesser extent, anti-narcotics law.

The recognition of the need for a central organisation for gathering details of violations of economic laws in a continuous, organised manner was felt as early as 1953.This central organisation was essential to devise a strategy to deal with economic offenders and to alert the concerned customs formations. This resulted in the setting up of an organisation called the Central Revenue Intelligence Bureau in 1953.This organisation was charged with the responsibility of developing intelligence on matters connected with anti-smuggling and anti-corruption in the Customs and Central Excise formations all over the country. Now, the need for an exclusive organisation to deal with the menace of violation of fiscal laws was felt. The Directorate of Revenue Intelligence (DRI) was thus; formed in 1957.[6]

The original brief of DRI was extensive. There was no separate organisation to deal with either evasion of central excise duties or prevent narcotic drug trafficking. Thus, the charter of DRI, as it stood then, encompassed all aspects of work pertaining to customs, central excise and narcotics, which required control, direction and investigation from the Centre.

With the passage of time and the growth in the problems relating to effective control of violations of such diverse laws, the need for specialisation and expertise was felt. The result was the creation in 1978 of a separate Directorate of Anti-Evasion (now known as Directorate General of Central Excise Intelligence) to handle violations of Central Excise laws and creation of the Central Economic Intelligence Bureau in 1985 to co-ordinate activities amongst various enforcement agencies of the Department of Revenue. With the growing incidence of narcotics trafficking and in keeping with India's commitment to the international community under various conventions to tackle this problem, the Narcotics Control Bureau took shape in 1986, to co-ordinate the enforcement of anti-narcotics laws.

In order to ensure effective discharge of its responsibilities, DRI maintains close liaison with all the important enforcement agencies in India like the Central Economic Intelligence Bureau, Income Tax department, Enforcement Directorate, Narcotics Control Bureau, Directorate General of Foreign Trade, Border Security Force, Central Bureau of Investigation, Coast Guard, the State Police authorities and also with all the Customs and Central Excise Commissionerates. It also maintains close liaison with the World Customs Organisation, Brussels, and the Regional Intelligence Liaison Office at Tokyo, INTERPOL and foreign Customs Administrations.[7]

Directorate of Revenue Intelligence functions under the Central Board of Excise and Customs in the Ministry of Finance, Department of Revenue. Headed by Director General in New Delhi, it is presently divided into seven zones, each under the charge of an Additional Director General, and further sub-divided into Regional Units, Sub-Regional Units and Intelligence Cells with a complement of Additional Directors, Joint Directors, Deputy Directors, Assistant Directors, Senior Intelligence Officers and Intelligence Officers.[8]

The charter of duties of DRI is as under: ---

- Collection of intelligence about smuggling of contraband goods, narcotics, under-invoicing etc through sources of India and abroad, including secret sources.

- Analysis and dissemination of such intelligence to the field formations for action.

- Working out of intelligence by the Directorate officers themselves to a successful conclusion, where necessary.

- Keeping watch over important seizures and investigation cases.

- Associating or taking over the investigations which warrant specialised handling by the Directorate.

- Guiding important investigation/prosecution cases.

- Functioning as the liaison authority for exchange or information among the United Nations Economic and Social Commission for Asia and the Pacific (ESCAP) countries for combating international smuggling and customs frauds in terms of the recommendation of the ESCAP conference.

- Keeping liaison with foreign countries, Indian Missions and Enforcement agencies abroad on anti-smuggling matters.

- To keep liaison with CBI and through them with the INTERPOL.

- To co-ordinate, direct and control anti-smuggling operations on the Indo-Nepal border.

- To refer cases registered under the Customs Act to the Income Tax Department for action under the Income Tax Act.

- To keep statistics of seizures and prices/rates etc. for watching trends of smuggling and supply required material to the ministry of Finance and other Ministries.

- To study and suggest remedies for loopholes in law and procedures to combat smuggling.

Economic Intelligence Council

In order to facilitate coordination amongst the Enforcement Agencies dealing with economic offences and ensure operational coordination amongst them, a two tier system has been established by the Government of India with an Economic Intelligence Council at the Centre under the Chairmanship of Union Finance Minister, and 18 Regional Economic Intelligence Committees at different places in India.[9]

Central Economic Intelligence Bureau

It is well recognised that the evasion of one tax usually entails evasion of other taxes as well. For the purpose of effective information gathering, collation and dissemination, a close co-ordination between the Agencies enforcing different tax laws is essential.[10]

Hence, the Central Economic Intelligence Bureau was set up with the intention of creating a body which would coordinate and strengthen the intelligence gathering activities as well as investigative efforts of all the Agencies which enforce economic laws.[11] The Central Economic Intelligence Bureau is the apex intelligence & co-coordinating body for economic intelligence. Accordingly, the following functions have been entrusted to the Central Economic Intelligence Bureau:-

- To collect intelligence and information regarding aspects of the black economy which require close watch and investigation. Also, keeping in view the scene of economic offences, the Bureau is required to collect information and provide periodical and special reports to the concerned authorities;

- To keep a watch on different aspects of economic offences and the emergence of new types of such offences. The Bureau was made responsible for evolving counter -measures required for effectively dealing with existing and new types of economic offences;

- To act as the nodal agency for cooperation and coordination at the international level with other customs, drugs, law enforcement and other agencies in the area of economic offences.

- To implementation of the COFEPOSA (i.e. Conservation of Foreign Exchange & Prevention of Smuggling Activities Act, 1971 which provides for preventive detention of persons involved in smuggling and foreign exchange rackets under certain specified circumstances)

- To act as a Secretariat of the Economic Intelligence Council which acts as the apex body to ensure full co-ordination among the various Agencies including Central Bureau of Investigation, Reserve Bank of India, Intelligence Bureau etc.[12]

Narcotics Control Bureau (NCB)

The Narcotics Control Bureau was constituted with Headquarters at Delhi with effect from 17th March, 1986. The Bureau, subject to the supervision and control of the Central Government, is to exercise the powers and functions of the Central Government for taking measures with respect to:

- Co-ordination of actions by various offices, State Governments and other authorities under the NDPS Act, Customs Act, Drugs and Cosmetics Act and any other law for the time being in force in connection with the enforcement provisions of the NDPS Act, 1985.

- Implementation of the obligation in respect of counter measures against illicit traffic under the various international conventions and protocols that are in force at present or which may be ratified or acceded to by India in future.

- Assistance to concerned authorities in foreign countries and concerned international organisations to facilitate coordination and universal action for prevention and suppression of illicit traffic in these drugs and substances.

- Coordination of actions taken by the other concerned Ministries, Departments and Organisations in respect of matters relating to drug abuse.[13]

The Narcotics control Bureau is the apex coordinating agency. It also functions as an enforcement agency through its field units located at Bombay, Delhi, Calcutta, Madras, Varanasi, Jodhpur, chandigarh, Jammu, Ahmedabad, Imphal and Tiruvananthapuram. The Zonal Units collect and analyses data related to seizures of narcotic drugs and psychotropic substance, study of trends, modus operandi, collection and dissemination of intelligence and work in close cooperation with the Customs, State Police and other law enforcement agencies. The assistance provided by the Bureau has been acknowledged by other Governments and many international bodies.[14]

Joint Cipher Bureau (JCB)

The Joint Cipher Bureau is the agency responsible for cryptanalysis. It works under Department of Defence (R&D), Ministry of Defence. The inter-services Joint Cipher Bureau have primary responsibility for cryptology and SIGINT, providing coordination and direction to the other military service organisations with similar mission. It uses modern technology for code breaking or coding sensitive and secret information for protection.[15] The Joint Cipher Bureau is also responsible for issues relating to public and private key management. The agency holds specialised direction finding and monitoring equipment.[16]

The agency specialises in research, design and development in cryptology. It achieves the above aim by application of mathematical, statistical and other scientific techniques, pertaining to cryptology. The agency is involved in computer based programming-writing and establishing programme segments and modules on given cryptological problems.[17] The Joint Cipher Bureau is also responsible for issues relating to public and private key management.[18]

All India Radio Monitoring Service (AIRMS)

The Central Monitoring Service of All India Radio monitors all radio broadcasts in India as well as all foreign radio broadcasts which can be received in India.

Central Monitoring Services based in New Delhi, Jammu and Kolkata is taken over by NTRO, National Technical Research Organisation in 2005 and now working as open source intelligence unit.[19]

The Aviation Research Centre (ARC)

Post 1962 War, the need was felt to create new capability for collecting ELINT and imagery from aerial based platform over our territory in our air space .Hence ARC was created under Directorate General of Security (DGS) and placed under the overall control of Director Intelligence Bureau (DIB) .The IB and R&AW got separated in 1968, hence DGS and ARC now comes under R&AW.[20]

ARC is responsible for airborne SIGINT operations. It holds aircrafts whose PHOTOINT flights are flown across the borders. These aircrafts are also fitted with advanced signal monitoring equipments. ARC is part of the Research and Analysis Wing (R&AW) of the Cabinet Secretariat, India. The first head of the ARC was R N Kao, the founding chief of R&AW.[21]

Another important branch under the operational control of the RAW is the Directorate General of Security (DGS). This agency has oversight over organisations like the Special Frontier Force (SFF), the Special Services Bureau (SSB) etc... Liaison with the military is maintained through the Military Intelligence Advisory Group and the Military Advisor to the Director RAW.[22]

Directorate General of Military Intelligence (DGMI)

India's military intelligence traces its origins to the appointment in 1885 of Maj Gen Sir Charles Metcalfe MacGregor as head of the Intelligence Department of the British Indian Army. Headquartered in Shimla, the Department was primarily tasked collection and analysis of intelligence relating to Russian troop dispositions in Central Asia. The departure of the British in 1947 marked the low point, as the British left behind very little in the way of assets or infrastructure for the Intelligence Corps of the newly independent India.[23]

Through the 1960s, Military Intelligence was largely focused on field security services rather than external intelligence collection. Responsibilities primarily consisted of policing the army, rooting out corruption and misuse of facilities and equipment by Army personnel. Subsequently, the increasing deployment of Army units in support of civil authorities has led Military Intelligence to focus on counter-insurgency operations.[24]Post 1990, the

DGMI has been given additional responsibility to collect tactical intelligence on defence related developments in Pakistan besides R&AW.[25]

The DGMI's capability for intelligence collection is limited. It is essentially restricted to the collection of tactical military intelligence and some amount of signal intelligence and its main role is to make strategic and tactical military assessments and disseminate them within the Army.[26]

Special Security Bureau

The Special Security Bureau is unique, as it is both an intelligence agency and also a specialised commando organisation for behind enemy line operations. Its strength is currently about two battalions.[27]

Directorate of Air Intelligence

Air Force intelligence responsibilities include imagery intelligence collection MiG-25R and Jaguar reconnaissance aircraft. During the 1971 war with Pakistan, Russian satellite imagery provided India with information on Chinese force deployments. And with advances in the Indian space program, the Indian Air Force will be acquiring independent space-based imagery intelligence capabilities.[28]

Naval Intelligence

The Navy Directorate of Signal Intelligence can intercept signals by means of communication equipment. Intercepts are routed through the Director of Naval Operations/Director of Naval Signals as part of operational tasking.[29]

Notes

[1] This section draws in parts from official website of CBI at http://www.cbi.gov.in accessed online on 13 Mar 12.

[2] Ibid

[3] The 24 th Report of Parliamentary Standing Committee on the working of CBI,2008

[4] CBI, Annual Reports 2009, 2010 and 2011.

[5] Ibid

[6] The brief has been prepared based on inputs from official website of DRI http://www.dri.nic.in

[7] Ibid

[8] Ibid

[9] India: Foreign Policy & Government Guide, Volume 1 , Intelligence and Security Units pp.109-115

[10] Ibid

[11] India: Foreign Policy & Government Guide, Volume 1 , Intelligence and Security Units p.111

[12] http://www.ceib.nic.in/toc_1.htm accessed online on 12 Dec2011

[13] Ibid

[14] Official website of NCB http://www.ceib.nic.in/ncb.htm accessed online on 11 Dec 2011

[15] Dr Indira Chowdhury , Mid Day Bangalore, 11 February 2008

[16] Ibid

[17] http://www.upsc.gov.in/recruitment/advt/2008/advt0508.htm#2

[18] India: Foreign Policy & Government Guide, Volume 1 ,Ministry of Defence Intelligence units p.117 http://www.globalsecurity.org/intell/world/india/jcb.htm on 13 Mar 2012

[19] India: Foreign Policy & Government Guide, Volume 1 , Intelligence and Security Units p.101

[20] B. Raman, Intelligence: Past, Present, and Future (New Delhi, India: Lancer Publishers & Distributors, 2002), p.58-59

[21] Spies in the Himalayas: Secret Missions and Perilous Climbs by M.S. Kohli and Kenneth Conboy, 2002, pp.54-56

[22] http://www.fas.org/irp/world/india/raw/

[23] India: Foreign Policy & Government Guide, Volume 1 ,Ministry of Defence Intelligence units p.120

[24] India: Foreign Policy & Government Guide, Volume 1 ,Ministry of Defence Intelligence units p.120

[25] B. Raman, Intelligence: Past, Present, and Future (New Delhi, India: Lancer Publishers & Distributors, 2002), p.63

[26] Executive Summary of the Kargil Review Committee Report as presented in Rajya Sabha, 25 February, 2000, accessed on line at http://rajyasabha.nic.in/25indi1.htm#8

[27] Ibid

[28] Ibid

[29] Ibid and http://polityinindia.wordpress.com/2010/08/12/indias-intelligence-agencies/ accessed online on 12 Jan 2012

THE HISTORICAL INTELLIGENCE LAPSES

It is prudent to consider a few well known historical intelligence lapses both in India and abroad to drive home the point of intelligence vulnerability and inadequacy even with the developed nations. Japanese attack on the US naval fleet at Pearl Harbour in 1941, the Arnehm Bridge massacre of British troops by German Resistance forces in World War II and 9/11 attack on Twin Towers are classical examples of incidents which probably could have been averted if available intelligence was not ignored. The US/CIA's inability to detect India's nuclear explosions in 1974 and 1998 brought US intelligence community under direct line of fire of the nation. The tribal invasion of J&K in 1947, the Chinese build-up in Aksai Chin in 1962 and Mumbai 26/11 terror strike definitely fall in this category in our country. The views of strategic community on role of intelligence vary in above mentioned incidents. This is a debatable point as to who should take the blame. However, these incidents definitely throw light on importance of intelligence as an organ of the statecraft. These cases also highlight that ignorance of intelligence warnings, for what so ever been the reason, have always catastrophic and detrimental to national interests.

The cases more relevant to content of this book have been included by me in the Chapter IV of this book as case studies. The 1962 and the Kargil War, along with Mumbai terrorist strikes have been analysed as case studies to drive home the point of lack of assessment and coordination at the national level. The other incidents have been included in this appendix .This appendix has been included to drive home a point that intelligence coverage is required 24x7 and being surprised is always on the cards and thus systemic failures must not be clubbed as intelligence failures. There is ample information available in the open domain about these operations but the scholars may find it difficult to locate them at one place. With this as aim, a few well known historical intelligence lapses both in India and abroad have been compiled below.

PEARL HARBOUR: VARIOUS VIEW POINTS

There are not two tragic dates in the last century that reside in the collective American psyche, which are December 7, 1941, the Japanese attack on Pearl Harbour, and September 11, 2001. On December 7, 1941, the Japan attacked the US naval fleet at Pearl Harbour, Hawaii. On 11 September, 2001 a series of four suicide attacks were committed in the United States to strike the areas of New York City and Washington, D.C. Although, nearly 70 years apart, both tragedies were failures by the intelligence community in their collective ability to unearth secretive operations that had devastating impact on national security.[1]The views of strategic community on role of intelligence in preventing these incidents vary. The both view points are enumerated in succeeding paragraphs.

Despite the efforts of no less than nine in depth investigations, however, the circumstances surrounding the attack on Pearl Harbour remain controversial. References continue to surface in official and public writings that do not accurately address the underlying causes for the defeat, ranging from new interpretations of the existing data to revisionist conspiracy theories. "One of the most prevalent assertions is that Pearl Harbour resulted from a "failure of intelligence."[2]

There is no doubting the fact that there was an American intelligence failure in December 1941, as the Japanese Pacific Fleet managed to cross the Pacific and attack the American Fleet based at Pearl Harbour without being intercepted or even detected. "The success of the Japanese attack on Pearl Harbour represents an excellent case study on national preparedness that has influenced each generation of American military leaders since December 1941.The story of Pearl Harbor is one of national unpreparedness and failure of intelligence".[3]

"Despite the claims of its critics, the United States intelligence community provided adequate warning that the Japanese would probably initiate hostilities on or about December 7, 1941. The root of the problem lay with the traditional attitude towards intelligence held by national and military decision makers. The United States, prior to Pearl Harbour was never comfortable with the establishment and maintenance of a professional intelligence community. The nature of intelligence work did not correspond with the country's democratic ideals, and the use of intelligence was seen as a necessary evil for use only in times of war. This prevented the establishment of an appreciation for the role of intelligence in supporting government and military requirements. It also limited development of an intelligence profession and doctrine.[4]

The question remains as to whether the American failure was one of collection or analysis and this is a point in which American strategic analysts David Kahn and Roberta Wohlstetter come to very different conclusions about. Whilst Kahn advocates the view that the American failure was due to a lack of available intelligence to be collected, Wohlstetter, in 1962 stated her belief that there was enough relevant intelligence to point to the fact that the Japanese Fleet was on its way to attack Pearl Harbour and that the error was in analysis, which overlooked this relevant intelligence, due to 'background noise'.[5]

Christopher Andrews refers to disorganised and under resourced US intelligence community in 1941 and like Kahn, comes to the conclusion that with MAGIC (the Japanese diplomatic code broken in September 1940) and traffic analysis, there was not enough intelligence available to successfully detect the Japanese fleet or its intentions. Kahn states that only one form of intelligence appeared to offer relatively solid information about Japanese naval matters: traffic analysis. Kahn continues by stating that there was no significant HUMINT (Human Intelligence) as the United States had no spies anywhere in the world or SIGINT (Signals Intelligence) other than traffic analysis and MAGIC, which still, were not going to yield any relevant information concerning top secret Japanese Naval plans. Altogether, America could have had no idea that the Japanese Fleet was about to attack Pearl Harbour, due to the lack of intelligence. Kahn refers to the insufficiency of cryptanalysts as America's greatest blunder at Pearl Harbor, as there was a severe lack of interest, investment and co-ordination in the intelligence service. [6]

Indeed in 1929 the Secretary of State, Henry L Stimpson closed the cryptanalysis agency as he believed gentlemen do not read each other's mail which left only the underfunded Naval and Army cryptanalysis units that worked on a competitive and definitely in-efficient manner by adopting a odd and even day system between the Army and Navy units. There was little ability to collect intelligence on Japan as the means were not available, Kahn argues convincingly. What Kahn is saying is that Roberta Wohlstetter is wrong in saying that analysis was the fault, because there was nothing to analyse! Christopher Andrews in his book "For The Presidents Eyes Only", reinforces Kahns argument by stating that Americans simply didn't expect an attack on Pearl Harbour, because it was thought technically impossible, and also because America was blinded by a racism that led the Americans to underrate Japanese abilities and will Americas military and political leaders thought Japan incapable of successfully executing a precise plan aimed at tactical surprise against the United States of America.[7] This racial element coupled with the misguided assumption that Pearl Harbour was safe from attack, left America unsuspecting and limited as far as military intelligence on Japan was concerned. Whilst Kahn states that you rarely find what you are not looking for Andrew points to the fact that Roosevelt was; and although looking, was not necessarily expecting in the right place. Kahn ends his article by talking about the legacy of Pearl Harbor, and concludes that Pearl Harbor has taught the United States to gather more information and to evaluate it better.[8]

Above all, Kahns argument is much more water tight than that of Wohlstetter and very well argued allying the relevant facts with his argument. The conspiracy theories do not counter his argument, but offer various reasons for his conclusion; that there w as no intelligence available to indicate that a Japanese attack was coming, let alone where, but on close analysis they can be seen as The facts as we can see them certainly seem to advocate Kahn's thesis as little intelligence was available to Washington, which was because intelligence service was under rated and therefore underfunded. However, Christopher Andrew does highlight the fact that the Americans were severely disadvantaged by their racial prejudices which blinded them, leading to a fatal underestimating of Japanese capabilities. The failure was indeed one of collection as America's lack of investment and faith in intelligence led to a lack of information on Japanese Naval matters and the failure of the United States to detect the Japanese attack on Pearl Harbor. The simple answer is that the intelligence, good although it was in certain areas, was not good enough.[9]

THE BATTLE OF ARNHEM

Background

The Battle of Arnhem was fought in and around the Dutch towns of Arnhem, Oosterbeek, Wolfheze, Driel and the surrounding countryside from 17–26 September 1944. It is a famous Second World War military engagement.[10]

After sweeping through France and Belgium in the summer of 1944, the Allies were poised to enter the Netherlands. Field Marshal Bernard Montgomery favoured a single thrust north, over the branches of the Lower Rhine river, allowing the British 2nd Army to bypass the German Siegfried Line and attack the Ruhr. To this end, the Allies launched '**Operation Market Garden**' on 17 September. Paratroopers were dropped in the Netherlands to secure key bridges and towns along the Allied axis of advance. Farthest north, the British 1st Airborne Division, supported by men of the Glider Pilot Regiment and the Polish 1st Independent Parachute Brigade, landed at Arnhem to secure bridges across the Nederrijn. Initially expecting a walkover, British XXX Corps planned to reach the British airborne forces within two to three days.[11]

The British forces landed some distance from their objectives and were quickly hampered by unexpected resistance especially from elements of the 9th SS and 10th SS Panzer Divisions. Only a small force was able to reach the Arnhem road bridge while the main body of the division was halted on the outskirts of the city. Meanwhile, XXX Corps was unable to advance north as quickly as anticipated and failed to relieve the airborne troops according to schedule. After four days, the small British force at the bridge was overwhelmed and the rest of the division became trapped in a small pocket north of the river, where they could not be sufficiently reinforced by the Poles or XXX Corps when they arrived on the southern bank, nor by the RAF's resupply flights. After nine days of fighting, the shattered remains of the airborne forces were withdrawn in 'Operation Berlin'.[12]

With no secure bridges over the Nederrijn, the Allies were unable to advance further and the front line stabilised south of Arnhem. The 1st

Airborne Division had lost nearly ¾ of its strength and did not see combat again.[13]

Intelligence

Many military commentators and historians believe that the failure to secure Arnhem was not the fault of the airborne forces (who had held out for far longer than planned), but of the operation as a whole.[14] Due to poor intelligence, the British were told to expect only limited resistance from German reserve forces. A serious challenge to their operation was not expected and many men believed that their work would lead to the ending of the war. Some men, anticipating a period of occupation in Germany, packed leisure equipment in their kit or in the sea tail. The optimistic mood prior to the operation would have tragic consequences .However, Browning's intelligence officer, Major Brian Urquhart, obtained information from the 21st Army Group in Belgium and Dutch resistance that German armour was present around Arnhem.[15] This was backed up with aerial reconnaissance that he ordered to be flown. Browning, however, was dismissive and ordered his chief medical officer to have Urquhart sent on sick leave. In fact, SHAEF was aware that there were almost certainly two Panzer divisions at Arnhem but with the operation looming, chose to ignore them. Such information would have been gleaned from Ultra intercepts that the Allied Airborne Army was not privy to and therefore could not act upon them.[16] The view points of strategic analysts again vary but it is clear that reasonable amount of warnings were given by intelligence agencies but they were not explicit in their assessment of quantum of threat.

9/11 TERRORIST STRIKES ON TWIN TOWERS: A CHRONOLOGICAL ANALYSIS

It has been unearthed later that as 2001 began, counterterrorism officials in US were receiving frequent but fragmentary reports about threats. Indeed, there appeared to be possible threats almost everywhere the United States had interests including at home. However, the agencies shouldn't have lowered their guard.

During 2001, Director of Central Intelligence (DCI), George Tenet, was briefed regularly regarding threats and other operational information relating to Osama Bin Laden. He in turn met daily with President Bush, who was briefed by the CIA through what is known as the President's Daily Brief (PDB). The PDB is considered highly sensitive and is distributed to only a handful of high-level officials. There were more than 40 intelligence articles in the PDBs from January 20 to September 10, 2001, that related to Bin Laden.

In the spring of 2001, the level of reporting on terrorist threats and planned attacks increased dramatically to its highest level since the millennium alert. At the end of March, the intelligence community disseminated a terrorist threat advisory, indicating a heightened threat of Sunni extremist terrorist attacks against US facilities, personnel, and other interests.

"On March 23, in connection with discussions about possibly reopening Pennsylvania Avenue in front of the White House, the National Security Advisor Condoleezza Rice was warned that domestic or foreign terrorists might use a truck bomb, their "weapon of choice" on Pennsylvania Avenue. She was warned that this attack would result in the destruction of the West Wing and parts of the residence. She was also told that he thought there were terrorist cells within the United States, including Al Qaeda. "

In response to these threats, the FBI sent a message to all its field offices on April 13, summarising reporting to date. It asked the offices to task all resources, including human sources and electronic databases, for any information pertaining to "current operational activities relating to Sunni extremism." It did not suggest that there was a domestic threat.

In late May, reports indicated possibility of a hostage plot against Americans abroad to force the release of prisoners. The reports included the name of Sheikh Omar Abdel Rahman, the "Blind Sheikh," who was serving a life sentence for his role in the 1993 plot to blow up sites in New York City. The reporting noted that operatives might opt to hijack an aircraft or storm a US embassy. This report led to Federal Aviation Administration (FAA) information circular to airlines noting the potential for "an airline hijacking to free terrorists incarcered in the United States." Other reporting mentioned that Abu Zubaydah was planning an attack, possibly against Israel, and expected to carry out several more if things went well. On May 24 alone, counterterrorism officials grappled with reports alleging plots in Yemen and Italy, as well as a report about a cell in Canada that an anonymous caller had claimed might be planning an attack against the United States.

Reports similar to many of these above were made available to President Bush in morning intelligence briefings with DCI, Tenet, usually attended by the Vice President, Dick Cheney and the National Security Advisor, Condoleezza Rice. While these briefings discussed general threats to attack America and American interests, the specific threats mentioned in these briefings were all overseas.

Threat reports surged in June and July, reaching an even higher peak of urgency. The summer threats seemed to be focused on Saudi Arabia, Israel, Bahrain, Kuwait, Yemen, and possibly Rome. The danger could have been anywhere including a possible attack on the G-8 summit in Genoa. A June 12, CIA report passed along biographical background information on several terrorists. It commented that one Khalid Sheikh Mohammed was recruiting people to travel to the United States to meet with colleagues already there. The report indicated that the recruitment was being done so that they might conduct terrorist attacks on Bin Laden's behalf. On June 22, the CIA notified all its station chiefs about intelligence suggesting a possible Al Qaeda suicide attack on a US target over the next few days. DCI, Tenet asked that all US ambassadors be briefed.

That same day, the State Department notified all embassies of the terrorist threat and updated its worldwide public warning. In June, the State Department initiated the Visa Express program in Saudi Arabia as a security measure, in order to keep long lines of foreigners away from vulnerable embassy spaces. The programme permitted visa applications to be made through travel agencies, instead of directly at the embassy or consulate.

A terrorist threat advisory distributed in late June indicated a high probability of near-term "spectacular" terrorist attacks resulting in numerous casualties. Other reports were very clear in their warnings. The title of reports were self explanatory which said, "Bin Laden Attacks May be Imminent" and "Bin Laden and Associates Making Near-Term Threats." The latter reported multiple attacks planned over the coming days, including a "severe blow" against US and Israeli "interests" in coming days.

On June 21, near the height of the threat reporting, US Central Command raised the force protection condition level for US troops in six countries to the highest possible level, 'Delta'. The US Fifth Fleet moved out of its port in Bahrain, and a US Marine Corps exercise in Jordan was halted. US embassies in the Persian Gulf conducted an emergency security review, and the embassy in Yemen was closed. The Carrier Strike Group (CSG) had foreign emergency response teams, known as Foreign Emergency Support Team (FESTs), ready to move on four hours' notice and kept up the terrorism alert posture on a "rolling 24 hour basis."

On June 25, six separate intelligence reports showed Al Qaeda personnel warning of a pending attack. An Arabic television station reported Bin Laden's pleasure with Al Qaeda leaders who were saying that the next weeks "will witness important surprises" and that US and Israeli interests will be targeted. Al Qaeda also released a new recruitment and fund-raising tape. The intelligence reporting consistently described the upcoming attacks as occurring on a calamitous level, indicating that they would cause the world to be in turmoil and that they would consist of possible multiple but not necessarily simultaneous attacks.

On July 2, the FBI Counterterrorism Division sent a message to federal agencies and state and local law enforcement agencies summarising information regarding threats from Bin Laden. It warned that there was an increased volume of threat reporting, indicating a potential for attacks against US targets abroad from groups "aligned with or sympathetic to Osama Bin Laden."

Disruption operations against al Qaeda-affiliated cells were launched involving 20 countries. Several terrorist operatives were detained by foreign governments, possibly disrupting operations in the Gulf and Italy and perhaps averting attacks against two or three US embassies. In mid July, reporting started to indicate that Bin Laden's plans had been delayed, maybe for as long as two months, but not abandoned. On July 23, the lead item for CSG discussion was still the al Qaeda threat, and it included mention of suspected terrorist travel to the United States. [17]

On July 31, a Federal Aviation Administration (FAA) circular appeared alerting the aviation community to "reports of possible near-term terrorist operations ... particularly on the Arabian Peninsula and/or Israel." It stated that the FAA had no credible evidence of specific plans to attack US civil aviation, though it noted that some of the "currently active" terrorist groups were known to "plan and train for hijackings" and were able to build and conceal sophisticated explosive devices in luggage and consumer products.[18]

On August 1, the FBI issued an advisory that in light of the increased volume of threat reporting and the upcoming anniversary of the East Africa embassy bombings, increased attention should be paid to security planning. It noted that although most of the reporting indicated a potential for attacks on US interests abroad, the possibility of an attack in the United States could not be discounted.[19]

On August 3, the intelligence community issued an advisory concluding that the threat of impending al Qaeda attacks would likely continue indefinitely. Citing threats in the Arabian Peninsula, Jordan, Israel, and Europe, the advisory suggested that Al Qaeda was lying in wait and searching for gaps in security before moving forward with the planned attacks.[20]

Analysis

The 9/11 Commission found that the intelligence community suffered from a lack of institutional imagination before the September 11 attacks.[21] This made it impossible for most analysts and policymakers to accurately gauge the terrorist threat. Had they better understood the danger of Al Qaeda they could have taken steps to improve warning intelligence. More imagination also might have helped analysts reveal the crucial network of terrorists that planned and executed the attacks. In other words, the intelligence community could not "connect the dots" because it was not sufficiently imaginative.

The Intelligence Community came under severe criticism after 9/11 but they were equally appreciated for their role in Operation "Naptune Spear". The intelligence agencies should take their crtisism in positive sense. The above chronological analysis fully establishes that the indicators of impending terrorist strike were available but the assessment making of intelligence agencies was not of desired standards to make a cohesive assessment. The agencies couldn't provide specific warning which could have been acted upon by security agencies.

Notes

[1] Darin Swan ,Opana and Intelligence Failures, accessed on line via http://umuc.academia.edu/ DarinSwan/Papers/1464661/Opana_and_Intelligence_Failures on 26 Feb 2011

[2] Ibid

[3] This section draws on "Pearl Harbour: Failure of Intelligence? By Robert F. Piacine, Lt Col, USAF accessed online via http://www.blackvault.com/documents/ADA397295.pdf on 26 May 2012

[4] Ibid

[5] Roberts Commission ± Attack upon Pearl Harbor by Japanese Armed Forces.´Ibibilio.org. 28 Jan. 1942 accessed online via http://www.ibiblio.org/pha/pha/roberts/roberts.html, on 14 Apr. 2011

[6] Ibid

[7] Christopher Andrew , 'For the President's Eyes Only: Secret Intelligence and the American Presidency from Washington to Bush' accessed online via

[8] Ibid

[9] This section draws mainly on David Kahn, The Intelligence Failure of Pearl Harbour, Foreign Affairs (Fall 1991) Page 148 accessed online via http://www.oxbridgewriters.com/ essays/military/the-intelligence-failure-at-pearl-harbor.php

[10] Middlebrook, Martin (1994). Arnhem 1944: The Airborne Battle. Viking,p.67

[11] http://www.market-garden.info/ accessed online on 16 Sept 2011

[12] Ibid

[13] http://www.defendingarnhem.com/index.htm accessed online on 16 Sept 2011

[14] Badsey, Stephen (1993). Arnhem 1944, Operation Market Garden. Osprey Publishing Ltd,pp.167-190

[15] Ibid

[16] Evans, Martin (1998), The Battle for Arnhem. Pitkin, pp.57-105

[17] The Evolution of the U.S. Intelligence Community- An Historical Overview.´ U.S.Government Printing Office. March 1, 1996. ³Preparing for the 21st Century: An Appraisal of U.S. Intelligence; Appendix A.´ March 6, 2008.http://www.access.gpo.gov/ intelligence/int/int022.html, accessed 24 Apr. 2011

[18] Ibid

[19] " National Commission on terrorist attacks upon the United States, " The System Was Blinking Red" accessed online via http://govinfo.library.unt.edu/911/report/ 911Report_Ch8.htm on 13 Feb 2011

[20] Joshua Rovner and Austin Long , Intelligence Failure and Reform: Evaluating the 9/11 Commission Report 5. Breakthroughs, Vol. 14, No. 1 (Spring 2005), pp. 10-21. 1September 11

[21] This section draws mainly on 9/11 Commission Report accessed online via http:// govinfo.library.unt.edu/911/report/911Report.pdf on 15 Feb 2011

Appendix G

SUCCESSFUL INTELLIGENCE OPERATIONS

The success of intelligence agencies remains a secret since numerous threats or incidents have been prevented in the past. However, their inability to prevent some incidents is widely reported. 'Operation Moses', raid on Entebbe Airport, 'Operation Neptune Spear' and 'Operation Shakti' are hardly known to general public but 9/11 and 26/11 do not need any elaboration. The contribution of the intelligence community to the victory over Pakistan in 1971, successful counter intelligence programme before 1974 and 1998 nuclear tests, restoration of normalcy in Mizoram and Punjab has been scantly attributed to intelligence agencies but the 1962 War or Kargil Intrusion or Mumbai Terrorist Strikes have been widely reported as 'intelligence failures'.[1] The role of the Indian intelligence agencies in providing inputs that act as a proof to the international community of Pakistan Army's involvement in Kargil intrusion has hardly been reported or remembered by the country.[2]

It is recommended that few events or incidents where the intelligence played a role in their successful conduct should always be mentioned by analysts while examining the performance of our intelligence agencies. The analysis of the incidents where the intelligence played a role in their successful conduct would add to the requisite balance of the analysis. It is, then, left to the readers to assess the performance of intelligence agencies when both successes and so called 'failures' are placed before them. There is ample information available in the open domain about these operations but scholars may find it difficult to locate them in one place. With this as a backdrop, a few cases of successful intelligence operations have been compiled below.

'OPERATION MOSES'

'Operation Moses' refers to the covert evacuation of Ethiopian Jews (known as the "Beta Israel" community or "Falashas") from Sudan during a famine in 1984. Ethiopian Jewish refugees wanted to immigrate to their national ancestral homeland, Israel. Thousands of Beta Israel had fled Ethiopia on foot for refugee camps in Sudan. They wanted to shift to Israel via Sudan, as this was their only hope. Beginning November 21, 1984, 'Operation Mosses' involved the air transport of some 8,000 Ethiopian Jews from Sudan directly to Israel, ending January 5, 1985. The operation, named after the biblical figure Moses, was a cooperative effort between the Israel Defense Forces, the Central Intelligence Agency, the United States embassy in Khartoum, mercenaries, and Sudanese state security forces.[3]

Israeli officials apparently approached the United States and asked for help in rescuing the Ethiopian Jews from Sudan. The United States provided Sudan with large amounts of aid and consequently enjoyed a great deal of leverage over Numeiry, the President of Sudan. In 1984, the Sudanese President was in urgent need of further US aid because of his country's failing economy, civil unrest, and the need to take care of nearly half million refugees living there. The problem was that, as a member of the Arab League, Numeiry could not afford to be seen as helping the "Zionists." The US officials were well aware of the instability in Sudan and were hesitant to do anything that might further endanger Numeiry's regime.[4]

It was in this context that a representative of Sudan came to the United States in June 1984 to ask for additional economic aid. The US promised aid if Sudan could help by allowing the United States to take the Ethiopian Jews out of the refugee camps. Mossad and the Sudanese secret police then devised the secret operation.

'Operation Moses' began on November 21, 1984, and continued until January 5, 1985. Every night during that period, except the Sabbath, buses would pick up groups of about fifty-five Ethiopian Jews from the refugee camps and take them to Khartoum where they would board Boeing 707s. The planes belonged to Trans European Airlines, a Belgian company owned by an Orthodox Jew. The airline was routinely employed as charter planes to carry Muslim pilgrims to Mecca. Altogether, thirty-six flights carrying approximately 220 passengers flew first to Brussels and then on to Tel Aviv. A total of 7,800 Ethiopian Jews was rescued by this method.

News of the airlift eventually leaked out. When the Israeli government confirmed the stories, the Sudanese ordered the operation stopped. Sources say that all of the Jews in the Sudanese refugee camps would have reached Israel if the airlift had continued for only two more days. Instead, the officials believed that as many as two thousand Jews were left behind in the camps. Once the story broke in the media, the Arab countries pressurised Sudan to stop the airlift. Some 1,000 Ethiopian Jews were left behind. Many were evacuated later in the US-led Operation Joshua.[5]

The US officials had considered resuming 'Operation Moses', but Numeiry , the President of Sudan, .did not want a repeat of the earlier fiasco. Instead, he agreed to a quick, one-shot operation. Numeiry insisted, however, that the planned operation be carried out secretly by the Americans and not the Israelis and that the flights not go directly to Israel. Within the next week, $15 million of the $200 million in aid for Sudan that had been withheld was released. The remainder was sent later to Sudan.[6]

To avoid a possibility of disclosure, the President Reagan wanted the operation carried out within three to four days. Weaver took an embassy plane to check out the runway of a remote airstrip near Gedaref, midway between the camps where most of the Ethiopian Jews were living, and found that it would be acceptable for the operation.[7]

On March 28, 1985, the operation, codenamed "Sheba," began with Ethiopian Jews from Israel working for the Mossad identifying the Ethiopian Jews in the camps and taking them by truck to the airstrip. The airstrip itself was eight miles outside of Gedaref, just far enough so that it would be difficult to spot the planes from the town.

Planes designed to hold ninety passengers each were prepared at the American base near Frankfurt, West Germany. Planes filled with food, water, and medical supplies were flown from an Israeli military base near Eilat to the airstrip in Sudan. These camouflaged US Hercules transports landed at twenty-minute intervals to pick up their passengers. Sudanese security officers cordoned off the area and by 9:00 a.m., all the Ethiopian Jews were evacuated. Instead of going to an intermediate destination, the planes flew directly to an Israeli air force base outside Eilat where the passengers were greeted by Prime Minister Shimon Peres. The organisers had prepared to airlift as many as two thousand Ethiopian Jews from the camps, but they found only 494, so three planes returned from Sudan empty.

At the end of 'Operation Sheba', Israeli officials believed that all of the Ethiopian Jews had been evacuated from the refugee camps in Sudan. In fact, a handful was left in the camps and anywhere from seven thousand to fifteen thousand are estimated to be still living in Ethiopia today. Those remaining behind were mainly the very old, the sick, the very young, and the women who, for one reason or another, could not make the arduous journey to Sudan.[8]

The secrecy, with which these operations were planned and executed, is a lesson for intelligence operatives. It was an operation of large magnitude involving intelligence agencies and security forces of different countries with diplomatic ramification. However, full credit should be given to the intelligence agencies and security forces for planning and executing such an operation.

RAID ON ENTEBBE AIRPORT

'Operation Entebbe ' was a counter-terrorist hostage-rescue mission carried out by the Special Forces of the Israel Defense Forces (IDF) at Entebbe Airport in Uganda on 4 July 1976. A week earlier, on 27 June, an Air France plane with 248 passengers was hijacked, by members of the Popular Front for the Liberation of Palestine and the German Revolutionary Cells, and was flown to Entebbe, near Kampala, the capital of Uganda. Shortly after landing, all non-Israeli passengers, except one French citizen, were released.[9]

The IDF acted on intelligence provided by the Israeli intelligence agency Mossad. In the wake of the hijacking and hijackers threatening to kill the hostages if their demand to release their prisoner was not met. A rescue operation was planned and the plans included preparation in case of armed resistance from Ugandan military troops. [10]

The operation took place at night, as Israeli transport planes carried 100 commandos over 2,500 miles (4,000 km) to Uganda for the rescue operation. The operation, which took a week of planning, lasted 90 minutes and 102 hostages were rescued. The IDF members had to fly seven hours, land safely, drive to the terminal area where the hostages were being held, get inside, and eliminate all the terrorists before any of them could fire. The element of surprise was probably the biggest edge that Israel held .The fact that no one expected the Israelis to take such risks was precisely the reason that they took it. Five Israeli commandos were wounded and one was killed. All the hijackers, three hostages and 45 Ugandan soldiers were killed, and thirty Soviet's built MIG-17s and MIG-21s of Uganda's air force were destroyed. The rescue operation named 'Operation Thunderbolt' is sometimes referred to retroactively as Operation Jonathan in memory of the unit's leader, Yonatan Netanyahu. He was the older brother of Benjamin Netanyahu, who served as the two-time Prime Minister of Israel from 1996 to 1999 and from 2009-present. [11]

The 'Operation Thunderbolt' struck a blow at international terrorism. It resonated far and wide. It showed that we could counter terrorism, and that it was worth cooperating to do so. The credit for instilling such confidence in the international community must go to intelligence community of Israel which provided valuable intelligence to IDF. It is unfortunate that such successful intelligence operations are rarely reported by the world media while reporting 'intelligence failures'.

'OPERATION SHAKTI'

It was a matter of great pride for India's intelligence community that US intelligence could not fathom their counter intelligence efforts before nuclear tests in 1974 and 1998. The extracts of various US reports have been included below to bring out the outrage in the US against their intelligence community which could not assess Indian intentions in spite of their best efforts over prolonged durations. This brings out the successful actions taken by Indian intelligence community to conceal the intentions of our Government.

India's first nuclear explosion took place in the Rajasthan desert at Pokhran, on May 18, 1974. On May 11, 1998 India again "surprised" the world with five nuclear tests, and joined the US, Russia, Britain, France and China in the nuclear club. Israel remained the sole undeclared member. The documents show that US intelligence failed to warn of India's nuclear tests despite tracking nuclear weapons potential since the 1950s.[12] Long before India detonated a nuclear device in May 1974, the US Intelligence Community was monitoring and analysing Indian civilian and military nuclear energy activities.[13]

Over the last five decades, the United States has gathered intelligence on Indian nuclear activities, civilian and military, through all the means at its disposal which included human intelligence, open source collection, communications intelligence, and overhead reconnaissance. Those activities, as demonstrated by the documents, allowed American intelligence analysts to provide decision makers with far more detailed assessments of Indian nuclear activities than would be available from public sources. At the same time, other documents show that the collective efforts of the organisations gathering intelligence on Indian nuclear activities including the Central Intelligence Agency, National Security Agency, National Reconnaissance Office, Defence Intelligence Agency, and State Department did not result in the US intelligence analysts warning the government officials of India's nuclear tests that were carried out in May 1974 and May 1998.[14] One of the pledges of the Bharatiya Janata Party (BJP) in its 1998 election campaign was to induct nuclear weapons into India's arsenal. It carried out that promise with two sets of tests on May 11 and 13 to the surprise of the US Intelligence Community.[15] The global response was initially one of shock, because the Indian government's decision to test, and all preparations leading up to the test, had been kept completely secret.[16]

The second reaction of outrage in the United States was directed, not at the Indians, but at the US intelligence agencies that had failed to detect the imminent test.[17] The primary locus of this outrage was in the Congress, where Senator Richard Shelby, Chairman of the Senate Intelligence Committee, called it "a colossal failure of our intelligence-gathering, possibly the greatest failure for more than a decade." Shelby announced Congressional hearings and the CIA immediately announced that its own high level panel would look into the matter. A "senior State Department official" was quoted saying the intelligence failure "ranks right up there with missing the collapse of the Soviet Union."[18]

The successful counter intelligence operation before both nuclear tests by the Indian intelligence agencies made US intelligence community grope in the dark about their intentions. The operations of such magnitude require high degree of coordination besides backing of the government. The Indian intelligence agencies deserve full kudos for keeping the intention of the government a secret till last minute thereby surprising the whole world.

TECHNICAL INTELLIGENCE DURING KARGIL WAR

The technical intelligence capabilities of R&AW helped establish the direct involvement of Pakistan Army in Kargil War in May, 1999. We could provide a proof to the international community that then Pakistan Army Chief, General Pervez Musharraf, was in daily telephonic contact with Lt Gen Mohammad Aziz, the Chief of General Staff (CGS), in Rawalpindi from his hotel room in Beijing. All these conversations were intercepted by the R&AW, when Indian intelligence agencies were under fire after 26/11[19] . The tapes showed that it was the Pakistani Army which had occupied the Kargil heights violating the Line of Control (LOC) and not the Kashmiri Mujahideen as claimed by Musharraf. It established that it was the Pakistan Army which shot down an Indian Air Force (IAF) plane and asked the Hizbul Mujahideen to claim the responsibility for it. The tapes showed that Musharraf had launched his operation without the knowledge of Nawaz, many of his Corps Commanders, the ISI, the chiefs of the Air Force and Navy and his Foreign Office. He got nervous after the IAF went into action and there were reports of the Indian naval ships moving from the East to the West coast.

The success of technical intelligence capabilities of our intelligence agencies needs to be well documented. With their help, we could provide a proof to the international community of what Pakistan had been denying for long. China's low-key reactions to Pakistani allegations against India could also be attributed to their knowledge of the Pakistani Army's hand in Kargil.[20]

'OPERATION NEPTUNE SPEAR'

An effective response to any unforeseen security challenge necessitates three prongs namely intelligence, decision makers and reaction elements who respond to the produced intelligence to remain in the same grid and work as a team to read the situation continuously and react within the shortest possible time. The intelligence gathering and assessment making infrastructure, decision makers and reaction elements are recommended to be meshed into one single point contact which would reduce the reaction time of our response to such attacks.[21]

The 'Operation Neptune Spear' is the ultimate example of synergy and inter-meshing of all three organs of state craft as mentioned above. The US intelligence community had a major role in the success of the operation. The details related only to the collection and processing of intelligence are appended below.

Osama bin Laden, the founder of the al-Qaeda organization responsible for the September 11 attacks in the United States, was killed by gunshot wounds to his head and chest on May 2, 2011, in a 40-minute raid by United States special operations forces. The raid, code named 'Operation Neptune Spear' also known as the Abbotabad Operation, took place at his house in Bilal Town, Abbottabad, Pakistan. At the conclusion of the raid, the US forces took Bin Laden's body to Afghanistan for identification before burying it at sea within 24 hours of his death. The declaration that Osama's body was buried in the sea is contested as it was eventually leaked that his body was perhaps not buried in the sea.

The operation was authorised by President Barack Obama and carried out by members of the United States Navy SEALs from the Naval Special Warfare Development Group (DEVGRU), informally referred to by its former name, SEAL Team Six, under the command of the Joint Special Operations Command, in conjunction with the US Central Intelligence Agency (CIA) operatives. The team was sent across the Afghan to launch the attack.[22]

Derivation of intelligence

American intelligence officials discovered the whereabouts of Osama bin Laden by tracking one of his couriers, as bin Laden was believed to have concealed his whereabouts from al-Qaeda foot soldiers or top commanders. Identification of al-Qaeda couriers was an early priority for interrogators at CIA black sites and Guantanamo Bay detention camp.[23]

In 2004, an al-Qaeda prisoner named Hassan Ghul told interrogators that Al-Kuwaiti was close to Bin Laden as well as Khalid Sheik Mohammed and Mohammed's successor Abu Faraj al-Libi. Ghul further revealed that al-Kuwaiti had not been seen for a long period, a fact which led the US officials to suspect he was travelling with Bin Laden. When confronted with Ghul's account, Khalid Sheik Mohammed stuck to his original story. Abu Faraj al-Libi was captured in 2005 and told CIA interrogators that Laden's courier was a man named Maulawi Abd al-Khaliq Jan. Al-Libi was transferred to Guantánamo in September 2006. He denied knowing Al-Kuwaiti. Because both Mohammed and al-Libi had minimised al-Kuwaiti's importance, officials speculated that he was part of Bin Laden's inner circle.[24]

In 2007, officials learned Al-Kuwait's real name, though they will not disclose the name nor how they knew it. The CIA never found anyone named Maulawi Jan and believed al-Libi made it up. In 2010, a wiretap of another suspect picked up a conversation with al-Kuwaiti. CIA officials located al-Kuwaiti and followed him back to Bin Laden's compound. Al-Kuwaiti and his brother were killed along with Bin Laden in the May 2, 2011 raid.

A telephone conversation between al-Kuwaiti and another operative monitored by the CIA led the agency in August 2010 to track al-Kuwaiti to the compound in Abbottabad. Using satellite photos and intelligence reports, the CIA determined the identities of the inhabitants of the mansion to which the courier was traveling. In September, the CIA concluded that the compound was "custom-built to hide someone of significance", and there was a likelihood that it was Osama Bin Laden's residence. Officials surmised that he was living there with his youngest wife.[25]

The US National Counterterrorism Center, using drone-derived intelligence, developed "what amounted to a detailed four-dimensional 'map' of the bin Laden compound and its occupants and their patterns of living and working." This map was used to create a model of the compound for practice runs.[26]

CIA director Leon Panetta issued a memo that also credited the National Security Agency and National Geospatial-Intelligence Agency for contributing to the intelligence-gathering that made the raid possible. After an intelligence-gathering effort on the courier's Pakistan compound that began September 2010, Obama met with his national security advisers on March 14 to create an action plan. They met four more times (March 29, April 12, April 19 and April 28) in the six weeks before the raid, including once on March 29, 2011 when Obama personally discussed the plan with Vice Admiral William H. McRaven, the commander of the U.S. Joint Special Operations Command. On April 29, at 8:20 am, Obama convened with Brennan, Thomas E. Donilon, and other national security advisers in the Diplomatic Reception Room and gave the final order to raid the Abbottâbad compound. A senior administration official told reporters after the operation was completed that the government of Pakistan had not been informed of the operation in advance. The raid planned for that day was postponed until the following day due to cloudy weather. After President Obama authorised the mission to kill or capture Osama bin Laden, CIA Director Leon Panetta gave the go-ahead at midday on May 1. [27]

The above case study highlights the painstaking efforts which go into successful intelligence operations. It also brings out the high degree of coordination required amongst various agencies before any operation. It requires great deal of patience on part of intelligence agencies that are constantly under pressure to deliver. Even the decision makers and security forces are under constant pressure to deliver. But, the intelligence operations require patience under such situation of growing pressure from expectations of general public. Such operations also demand support and confidence of policy makers, which may not always be forthcoming. The intelligence agencies, the decision makers and security forces have to remain in the same grid and support each other. If all such gradients are available, the recipe is more likely to be good. It was clearly demonstrated in the 'Operation Neptune Spear' discussed above.

Notes

[1]   Prem Mahadevan , "The Politics of Counter-Terrorism in India — Strategic Intelligence and National Security in South Asia"; I.B. Tauris & Co, London,2012 p.13

[2]   B.Raman, " Did Musharraf Tell Nawaz About Kargil Plans?, Global Geopolitics Net , June 06, 2008 accessed online through http://ramanstrategicanalysis.blogspot.com/ on 17 Dec2011

[3] Mitchell Bard and Howard Lenhoff ,'America's Role in the Rescue of Ethiopian Jewry' accessed online through http://www.jewishvirtuallibrary.org/jsource/Judaism/ejus.html on 16 Mar 2011

[4] Ibid

[5] http://www.israelmilitary.com/israeli-mossad--1104.aspx accessed online on 16 Dec2011

[6] Ibid

[7] http://www.israelmilitary.com/israeli-mossad--1104.aspx accessed online on 16 Dec2011

[8] TV Movie 'Raid on Entebbe (1976)'

[9] http://www.israelmilitary.com/israeli-mossad--1104.aspx accessed online on 16 Dec2011

[10] Ibid

[11] The Entebbe Rescue Mission, Israel Defense Forces accessed online via http://www.jewishvirtuallibrary.org/jsource/Terrorism/entebbe.html on 13 Mar 2011

[12] Jeffrey Richelson, *U.S. Intelligence and the Indian Bomb, accessed online through* http://www.gwu.edu/~nsarchiv/NSAEBB/NSAEBB187/index.htm on 11 Jan 2012

[13] National Security Archive Electronic Briefing Book: *India and Pakistan - On the Nuclear Threshold*, accessed online through http://www.gwu.edu/~nsarchiv/nukevault/ebb367/ on 21 Dec2011

[14] Jeffrey T. Richelson *Spying on the Bomb: American Nuclear Intelligence from Nazi Germany to Iran and North Korea* (W.W. Norton, 2006)

[15] Document 37: Office of Near Eastern, South Asian, and African Analysis, Central Intelligence Agency, *India: BJP Flexing Muscles, But How Far Will It Go?*, May 29, 1998. Secret Source: Freedom of Information Act Request

[16] George N. Sibley The Indian Nuclear Test: A Case Study in Political Hindsight Bias accessed online through http://wws.princeton.edu/research/cases/nucleartest.pdf on 21 Dec2011

[17] Daniel Morrow and Michael Carriere, "The Economic Impacts of the 1998 Sanctions on India And Pakistan" accessed online through http://cns.miis.edu/npr/pdfs/morrow64.pdf on11 Jan 2012

[18] Thomas, Evan; Barry, John and Liu, Melinda. "Ground Zero," Newsweek, U.S. Edition, 25 May 1998, pp. 28-32

[19] B.Raman, " Did Musharraf Tell Nawaz About Kargil Plans?, Global Geopolitics Net ,

June 06, 2008 accessed online through http://ramanstrategicanalysis.blogspot.com/ on 17 Dec2011

[20] " B Raman, "Pak Army Chief Caught Yapping" accessed online via http://www.southasiaanalysis.org/notes/note21.html

[21] "Obama Announces Killing of Osama bin Laden", The *New York Times*. Retrieved 20 Dec, 2011

[22] Richard Lardner , "US tells court bin Laden photos must stay secret" , Associated Press dated Sept 27, 2011

[23] Yousaf Raza Gilani (May 9, 2011). "Pakistan PM's speech on Osama Bin Laden situation". *International Business Times*. Retrieved on 25 Aug, 2011.

[24] "Tracking use of bin Laden's satellite phone"., *The Wall Street Journal.*, May 28, 2008. Retrieved May 8, 2011

[25] http://www.washingtonpost.com accessed online on 05 May 2012

[26] Dean Nelson; Rob Crilly (May 8, 2011). "Osama bin Laden killed: Hidden in plain sight", *The Daily Telegraph* (London). Retrieved on 21 Dec 2011.

[27] http://shadowspear.com/special-operations/93475-operation-neptune-spear-bin-laden.html accessed online on 23 Dec 2011

Bibliography

Books

India's External Intelligence –Secrets of Research and Analysis Wing (RAW), Maj Gen VK Singh, Manas Publications ,2007

Inside IB and RAW, The Rolling Stone that Gathered Moss, K. Sankaran Nair, Manas Publications,2008

Ashok Raina, Inside R&AW: The Story of India's Secret Service (Vikas,New Delhi, 1980)

Intelligence and Statecraft – The Use and Limits of Intelligence in International society – Peter Jackson and Jenifer Siegel- Praeger Publishers – 2005

Security and Intelligence in a changing world – New perspectives for the 1990,s- A Stuart Farson, David Stanford and Wesley K Wark. Frank Cass and co ltd

Strategic Intelligence –Don McDowel- The Scare crow Press, Inc UK, 2009

Intelligence services- Analysis, Organisation and Function – Dr Bhashyam Kasturi- Lancer Publication-1995

War, Strategy and Intelligence – Micheal T Handel (London 1990)

India and the China Crisis- Steve Hoffman (California 1991)

Inside RAW: the story of India's secret service. Raina, Asok New Delhi: Vikas Publications, 1981

Krishna Dhar, Maloy. *Fulcrum of evil: ISI, CIA, Qaeda nexus*. Manas Publications

B. Raman, *Intelligence: Past, Present, and Future* (New Delhi, India: Lancer Publishers & Distributors, 2002)

B. Raman, The Kaoboys of R&AW: Down Memory Lane (New Delhi: Lancer Publishers, 2007)

Maloy Krishna Dhar, Open Secrets: India's Intelligence Unveiled, New Dehli, Manas Publications, 2005)

Michael Herman, Intelligence power in peace and war, Amazon.co.uk, Oct 1996

Israel's Secret Wars: A History of Israel's Intelligence Services" by Ian Black and Benny Morris 1992

From surprise to reckoning: the Kargil Review Committee report, Sage Publications, New Delhi, 2000

The Politics of Counter-Terrorism in India — Strategic Intelligence and National Security in South Asia, Prem Mahadevan; I.B. Tauris & Co, London, 2012

Praveen Swami, 'India, Pakistan and the secret jihad: the covert war in Kashmir, 1947-2004', Taylor & Francis, 2007

Nicola Perugini, 'Anthropologists at War: Ethnographic Intelligence and Counter-Insurgency in Iraq and Afghanistan', International Political Anthropology, Vol.1, No. 2 (2008)

SS Trivedi, Secret Services in Ancient India, Allied Publication, 1984

India: Foreign Policy & Government Guide, Volume 1

Abram N. Shulsky and Gary J. Schmitt, Silent Warfare: Understanding the World of Intelligence (Dulles, Virginia: Brassey's, 2002)

Richard K. Betts, Enemies of Intelligence: Knowledge and Power in American National Security, (Columbia University Press, New York, 2007)

Richards J. Heuer, Psychology of Intelligence Analysis, Center For The Study of Intelligence, Central Intelligence Agency, 1999

Dr. Rob Johnston, "Analytical Culture in the US Intelligence Community, An Ethnographic Study", (Washington DC, 2005)

Jeffrey T Richelson, 'The U.S. Intelligence Community, Fourth Edition, (Westview Press, 1999

Ian Black and Benny Morris, "Israel's Secret Wars: A History of Israel's Intelligence Services

Samuel M. Katz, "Soldier Spies: Israeli Military Intelligence" (Presidio Pr, May 1994)

Jerome Clauser, 'An introduction to Intelligence research and Analysis, revised and edited by Jan Goldman, (Pentagon Press, 2010)

Jeff Bardin, Cyber Counterintelligence Doctrine - Offensive CI, 02 Jun 11

Intelligence Officer's Bookshelf — Central Intelligence Agency

Gale Encyclopedia of Espionage & Intelligence:China, Intelligence and Security

Nicholas Eftimiades, Chinese Intelligence Operations, 1994

Jeffrey T. Richelson Spying on the Bomb: American Nuclear Intelligence from Nazi Germany to Iran and North Korea (W.W. Norton, 2006)

G Chatterjee, Effective Interrogation-Naxalsm- Police-Intelligence, Manas Publication , 2011

Journals

Agni: Forum For Strategic And Security Studies Vol X,No 4

CLAWS Journal Summer Edition 2011

USI Journal, Apr-Jun 2009

Strategic Analysis Volume, 36, number 2, March2012

Articles

Rahul Bedi, "Indian intelligence gathering undermined by budget cuts," *Jane's Intelligence Review* (1July 2004): 2.

Srinath Raghavan , Intelligence Failures and Reforms

The Perils of Prediction: Indian Intelligence and the Kargil Crisis by
    Mahadevan Prem

PVR Rao . Defence without Drift (Bombay 1970) pp307-08

Praveen Swami, "For a paradigm shift", Frontline Volume 18 - Issue 07,
    Mar. 31 - Apr. 13, 2001. New Delhi

Ajmer Singh 'Turf war in intel units hampers war on terror'-, Mail Today
    July 16, 2011

Saikat Datta ," Creating a successful Intelligence and Counter –Terrorism
    Matrix: Lessons from 26/11" The CLAWS Journal summer 2011 edition

After Mumbai: Points for Action - International Terrorism Monitor—Paper
    No. 474 ,South Asia Analysis Group ,01 Dec 2008 ,accessed on line at
    http;//www.southasiaanalysis org/paper 30/paper 2949.html on 30 Dec
    2010

 Anil Bhat "Information and Security, Where Truth Lies?" Manas
    Publications'2008

Mitchell Bard and Howard Lenhoff,'America's Role in the Rescue of
    Ethiopian Jewry'

Lieutenant General Kamal Davar, "Drum-beating has no place in the business
    of intelligence" Rediff mail, April 15, 2003

Reports

The Kargil Review Committee Report. published by Sage

Ministry of Home Affairs, *Annual Report 2006-07* (Government of India:
    2007), 28, 31-32.

Official 1962 War History,prepared by the Ministry of Defence accessed
    on line at http:/www.bharat rakshak .com/ARMY/History/1962 war /
    pdf/1962,chapter 10.pdf on 26 Feb 2011

Official 1965 War History, prepared by the Ministry of Defence accessed
    on line at http:/www.bharat rakshak .com/ARMY/History/1965 war/

pdf/1965, chapter 09.pdf on 20 Jun 2011

Official 1971 War History, prepared by the Ministry of Defence accessed on line at http:/www.bharat rakshak .com/ARMY/History/191971 war/ pdf/1971, chapter 19.pdf on 09 Sept 2011

The NIA Bill 2008 accessed online at http://nia.gov.in/acts/ The_National_Investigation_Agency_Act_2008.pdf on 10 Dec 2010

Unpublished IDSA Task Force Draft Report on Intelligence Reforms

ORF Report on Intelligence Bill for Coordination, Control and Oversight of Intelligence agencies

The Second Edition of the Interagency Threat Assessment and Coordination Group's Intelligence Guide for First Responders

Headquarters Army Training Command, Intelligence Application In Information Age: The Need to Sharpen the Gaze" May 2010: Seminar Report

http://www.nctc.gov/docs/ITACG_Guide_for_First_Responders_2011

Interviews

Lt Gen R K Sawhney (Retd), former Director General Military Intelligence, New Delhi, 24 Nov 2010

Ambassador Satish Chandra, former Deputy NSA and Secretary, National Security Council Secretariat (NSCS)

Mr DC Nath, former Special Director, Intelligence Bureau, New Delhi, 24 Nov 2010

Dr Bhasham Kasturi, New Delhi, 15 Jun 2011

Rana Banerji, former Special Secretary R&AW and head of Task Force on intelligence reforms at Institute of Defence Studies and Analysis (IDSA),New Delhi, 10 Nov 2011

Lt Gen DS Chauhan, Director General, Defence Intelligence Agency, New Delhi, 10 Jan 1011

Col RSN Singh, former R&AW officer on 19 Jan 2011

Professor Arun S. Dalvi, Head of Department, Defence and Strategic Studies, Pune University on 26 Oct 2011

Professor Vijay Khare , National centre of International Security and Defence Analysis (NISDA), Pune on 26 Oct 2011

Nitin Pai, editor of 'Pragati', on 07 Feb 2012

Amb Kanwal Sibal, Former Foreign Secretary, on 16 Aug 2011

Lt Gen BS Powar, PVSM, AVSM   on 20 May 2011

Sushant Shareen, Senior Fellow, Vivekananda International Foundation

Dr Mohan Guruswamy, Economic Advisor

Mr Iftikhar Gilani, Journalist

Note: A large number of serving officers of civil and military intelligence agencies have been interviewed in the course of this research. However, majority of them expressed a desire to remain anonymous. Their names have deliberately not been included in this list.

Index

V

www.ingramcontent.com/pod-product-compliance
Lightning Source LLC
Chambersburg PA
CBHW031416270326
41929CB00010BA/1474